WALKER ROYCE

**DISCOVER AND ENJOY THE HIDDEN POWER
OF THE ENGLISH LANGUAGE**

eureka!

MORGAN JAMES PUBLISHING • NEW YORK

eureka!

ISBN: 978-1-60037-944-4 (Paperback)
      978-1-60037-945-1 (eBook)
Library of Congress Control Number: 2011922094

Published by: Cover/Interior Design by:
MORGAN JAMES PUBLISHING   Rachel Lopez
1225 Franklin Ave Ste 32   rachel@r2cdesign.com
Garden City, NY 11530-1693
Toll Free 800-485-4943
www.MorganJamesPublishing.com

DEDICATION

Dedicated to an angelic conifer.
Or is she a coniferous angel?

TABLE OF CONTENTS

PREFACE

English is a wonderfully diverse language. If you ask fifty different people to describe an object, an event, or an idea, you will get fifty different perspectives, each articulated with distinct words and style. There are no absolutes—no best writer, best speaker, best style—and no best words. However, there are patterns and principles of English usage that are generally persuasive and misusage patterns that are generally ineffective.

Diversity of thought and communications is critical to teamwork, to achievement in the workplace, to teaching, learning, and parenting, and to growing our networks of friends and family. The perspective from which you attack a problem, tell a story, listen to someone else's position, or write a message is important to understanding the solution, the moral, or the point. If you are capable of looking, reasoning, and hearing different perspectives, you can be far more effective at communicating and achieving progress in most endeavors.

I have gained this insight after 50 years on earth—learning, working, partnering, parenting, supervising, and surviving tough circumstances. I don't remember anyone coaching me to look outside my norms, to examine problems from different points of view, or to communicate differently based on the situation or the audience. Yet over my lifetime, this sort of thinking has struck me as one of the key lessons that should be taught earlier and reinforced throughout our educational years. Finding the right perspective is when breakthroughs occur.

One of my retirement dreams is to build an adolescent leadership camp where kids can learn some of the things they don't learn in school. Key elements will include working out personal values, practicing teamwork, and problem solving through a variety of puzzles, games, and workshops. After fleshing out a blueprint for this camp and discussing it with friends, I realized that many of the camp elements relate to lessons learned in communicating more effectively.

This book captures material that represents one step en route to my camp vision. It synthesizes some provocative perspectives on the English language into a loosely connected set of lessons on communicating effectively and observing your communications and those of others.

Communications are the foundation for humans to live together in harmony. Most of us would benefit from improving our communications skills. This should come as no surprise: Millions of teachers, parents, and supervisors emphasize this every day. Yet it seems like our communications skills are not improving. School-age children and young adults, aspiring workers, and even mature professionals seem disinterested in their communications skills. Plenty of good stuff is available to teach people who are motivated to learn. Therein lies the problem: lack of motivation. My contention is that people who really **enjoy** the English language are much more motivated to improve.

How do we motivate more people to enjoy English? With carrots and sticks. The carrots are the attractive elements, styles, and usage patterns that this book will dangle in front of you to improve your effectiveness and enjoyment in listening, reading, speaking, and writing. Our language can be surprisingly entertaining, and the amusement possible (and probable) with English is a big, juicy carrot. The sticks are the repulsive, ugly complexities and misusage patterns that some readers need to be beaten over the head with until they realize just how ineffective and annoying some communications styles can be.

Observing the diverse ways in which other people use our language is a critical prerequisite for observing and judging our own communications effectiveness. This can be both eye-opening and painful. Observe the breadth and depth of English usage. Notice successful usage, misusage, and amusing usage. Reflect on why a communication was effective or ineffective. The time you spend can result in significant personal returns.

Now get ready for a strange collection of topics, puzzles, lists, anecdotes, and practical lessons. What they don't teach you in school is how to enjoy English! If you enjoy it more, you will pay more attention.

INTRODUCTION

Have you ever thought about the breadth and depth of the English language? First there are basic elements: letters, phonics, words, punctuation, sentences, and paragraphs. Then there are deeper elements: anagrams, homonyms, heteronyms, homophones, synonyms, antonyms, jargon, palindromes, dialects, acronyms, oxymorons, pleonasms, puns, slang, and many others. It is these deeper elements that provide an almost infinite spectrum of possibilities for communications and miscommunications, as well as for fun and games.

English is a complex human creation, and it is as quirky as those of us who speak it. We expect certain structural attributes: symmetry, regularity, consistency, and logical construction of words and phrases. In general, our language delivers well on these features, but occasionally, or even frequently, quirks surface. A whirlwind tour through some counterintuitive usages illustrates this point.

A *slim chance* and a *fat chance* mean the same thing. A *wise man* and a *wise guy* are very different. One must *do* something to *undo* what has already been done. *Unto* means the same as *to* in most usages. *Quite a few* means *quite many*. *Pineapples* have nothing to do with *pines* or *apples*. A house can *burn up* or *burn down* with the same outcome. *Filling in* forms and *filling out* forms produce the same results. We have noses that *run* and feet that *smell*. Many women get a *permanent* wave about every six weeks. We fire employees who *hardly work* and praise them if they *work hard*. We make *amends* but cannot make one *amend*. *Folk* and *folks* are both plural and mean the same thing.

Being a word pervert, I have spent entirely too much time thinking about the following curiosities. *Nonword* is a word. We can dis*cuss* something and still *cuss*. *Furious* means full of fury and *joyous* means full of joy, but *gorgeous* does not mean full of gorge. A man *with hair* sounds much hairier than one *with hairs*. Why can't we be *chalant, plussed, combobulated,* or *gruntled*? Why can't we use *oderants* and *perspirants*? Why can we *remember* things when we never *membered* them to begin with? Of all the *odds* and *ends* in your drawer, is the largest one an *odd* or an *end*? And finally, observe that *stifle* is an anagram of *itself*.

These peculiarities might confuse some people, but to me they represent the spectrum of opportunities for surprise and wonder that make English so powerful, puzzling, humorous, and entertaining. It is a remarkably beautiful language.

Are we not drawn onward, we few, drawn onward to new era? Although this contrived question takes a little poetic license, it is an admirable creation. Try reading it backward. Such mirror-imaged letter sequences are called palindromes. Individual words can be palindromes: *refer, tenet, kayak, rotator.* So can contrived phrases. Here's another: *some men interpret nine memos.* That is even odder!

Even odder is a strange word couplet that introduces another aberration. English contains seemingly contradictory words that, used together, can make sense in certain contexts. For example, "These jumbo shrimp are delicious," or "Just act naturally." *Jumbo* is the opposite of *shrimp*, and someone who *acts* is clearly not being *natural*. These phrases are called oxymorons. (For some spellcheckers and copy editors—but not mine—the preferred plural would be *oxymora*.) There is not much practical use for oxymorons except to elicit a smile.

Imagine how confusing English must be to people who are learning it as a second language. A Japanese colleague wrote me an email saying that he wants to "clothes the deal as soon as possible." He also wrote, "My team'll get the work done and the competition'll have no chance of winning if my boss'll approve my proposal." It is easy to see how such mistakes seem logical to some writers but laughable to some readers. English is rich with such opportunities.

English speakers understand that English is a rat's nest of inconsistent rules. Most people who learn it as a second language find it extremely challenging compared to their native tongue. Although English may seem overly complex, from a different perspective it is a breathtakingly beautiful beast. Within its grammar rules, exceptions to rules, word forms, and styles dwells alluring beauty. Inherent in the complexities of English are tremendous opportunities for simple mistakes or plays on words that can result in both intentional and coincidental entertainment.

Everyone has experienced hilarious typographical errors. In a presentation I gave to some U.S. Air Force generals, the word *uninformed* was mistakenly spelled *uniformed*. These uniformed officers laughed when I commented that they wouldn't have noticed this typo because uninformed and uniformed were synonyms within the conference room where we were meeting. (The purpose of the seminar was to inform uninformed uniformed officers.)

This anecdote is a *facetious* example of how a one-letter difference can alter the meaning of a word, a sentence, or a whole topic. Words that look the same or sound the same can *actually* have wildly different meanings. To communicate effectively, readers, writers, speakers, and listeners need to be careful about word selection, punctuation, spelling, and context.

Of the two italicized words in the preceding paragraph, *facetious* is one of my favorites. (It has all five vowels in alphabetical order.) *Actually* is actually one of the ugliest words in our language. I can't resist ridiculing such impotent adverbs. Actually, I hope that you actually understand how overused the word actually actually is.

Words count. One secret to good communications is to use the right words to say things as clearly as possible. Instead of choosing the simple word, or the precise word, too many people opt for the unusual word. (Notice that *unusual* is self-defining. What other seven-letter words in the English language contain three *u*s?) There are good times to use unusual words, and the best communicators make use of them when they are trying to make a point that requires a precise word. In most instances, however, the simple word results in the most clarity.

Many people have a tendency to speak or write without being direct. They choose a mushy word with a fuzzy meaning, or they use excessive verbiage. (*Verbiage* sounds like two words that, crammed together, have just the right connotation: verbal garbage.) A more extreme word for roundabout communications would be *circumlocution*, a beautifully self-defining and unusual word. It has powerful sounds —a soft *c*, two hard *c*s, a short *u*, a long *u*, and an *ml* phonetic sound, all wrapped into one word. It is hard to parse the five syllables in your brain and reason through what the word means.

(Therein lies the self-definition.) It is a long-winded and somewhat snobby way to say *unclear, evasive,* or *beating around the bush.* Despite being unusual, *circumlocution* is a precise and useful word. In the proper context, it has teeth. When you hear it, it sinks in and sits with you; it has an impact that you will remember.

Synonyms are a powerful language element with wondrous usage and misusage patterns. Most synonyms mean roughly the same thing. You choose one over another because it more precisely captures the subtle detail you need for your context.

Precise words used thoughtfully help you communicate more clearly. Consider three words that most people use interchangeably: moron, imbecile, and idiot. Most everyday usage suggests these three words are just synonyms for *stupid*. A little research reveals that *moron, imbecile,* and *idiot* are clinical definitions of intelligence, or the lack thereof. These definitions are considered obsolete; the words are now used mostly with derogatory connotations. Being a stupidity aficionado, I exercise these words frequently, mostly to describe my own actions. I use them not as synonyms but rather to focus my thoughts on just how stupid I was. Here are their precise definitions:

Moron: A person with a mental age of from eight to twelve years. Generally has communications and social skills enabling some degree of academic education or vocational training.

Imbecile: A person with a mental age of from three to seven years. Generally is capable of some degree of communications and can perform simple tasks under supervision.

Idiot: A person with a mental age of less than three years. Generally is unable to learn connected speech or guard against common dangers.

With this understanding, wouldn't you use these words differently? Isn't it moronic just how many non-morons in the world misuse the word *moron*?

Then there are homonyms. Here is an example of homonyms at work to create a smile (or a groan):

A man goes to his psychiatrist. "Doc, I keep having these alternating recurring dreams. First I'm a teepee, and then I'm a wigwam, then a teepee, then a wigwam. It's driving me crazy. What's wrong with me?"

The doctor replies, "It's simple. You are too tense."

Such humor is known as a pun, and puns are one of the most beautiful dimensions of our language. As I was writing this book, I read a letter to the *New York Times* editors that aligned well with my purpose for the book.

To the Editor:

"Pun for the Ages," by Joseph Tartakovsky (OP-Ed, March 28), is an entertaining and informative review of the positive and negative aspects of wordplay, and well timed in its proximity to April Fool's Day.

But he doesn't mention one relevant and important point. America is facing a crisis of escalating illiteracy. In 2007, a report by the National Endowment for the Arts concluded that students' reading skills are stagnating or falling, and that employers routinely complain that new hires are unable to write clearly or even to comprehend what they read.

How can this problem be addressed? Humor is a powerful motivator. Word play can encourage reading and language learning at all levels. Young children love puns, and playing with words helps them expand their vocabulary and master language skills.

Adults from other parts of the world who study English delight in the multiple meanings of many words.

As for the contention that puns are sometimes greeted with groaning and scorn instead of laughter, remember what diamond cutters say: "They can't all be gems!"

Don Hauptman
New York, March 28, 2009
The writer is the author of *Cruel and Unusual Puns*, a celebration of spoonerisms.

Humor is one entertaining usage of English. The creative writing possibilities provide another channel of diversion and mental exercise. Many of the puzzles contained in this book will force you to think outside your normal frame of reference. Here is a preview of the word gymnastics to follow.

PUZZLE 1. OBSERVATIONS OF AN ORTHOPEDIC SURGEON

Ankle bones can degrade easily from getting hit. Inside joints, key ligaments meet nerves. Ordinary photographs quickly reveal swollenness. The usual visualizing with X-rays yields zilch.

What is unique about these observations of an orthopedic surgeon? Can you see the obvious pattern of word selection? It cannot be coincidental.

Puzzle 1 demonstrates creative contortions that are possible with English. If you need a hint, count the words. (Hyphenated words count as one.) That number will give you an obvious clue for solving the puzzle. Try to create a similarly formed paragraph that makes sense. It is surprisingly hard to do, and a great exercise for an English class teaching creative writing. Such an exercise requires you to think explicitly about word selection, sentence style, syntax, and semantics in a totally different way.

This book contains a uniquely crafted set of puzzles that are mostly tests of observation skills. Some of them are frivolous, some challenging, and most contort our language in entertaining ways that should leave readers saying, "This author is nuts." That's the reaction I hope for and what my daughters and friends have said to me for years. They have also learned some new ways to look at words, to find humor in language, to evaluate problems from different perspectives, to engage in battles of wits, and to enjoy English. The puzzles provide memorable lessons about diversity of perspective.

Many people's lives are enriched by the puzzles and games they play at work, at home, and at leisure. These pastimes provide opportunities to extract enjoyment, accomplishment, and entertainment from the everyday situations we all encounter. These one-of-a-kind puzzles are sprinkled here and there to reinforce some of the topics treated in the text. Although you can tackle these puzzles alone, they are much more fun to reason through with a group. A variety of perspectives will help provide the clues and breakthroughs you need to reach a solution.

The puzzles are intended to help people experience the power of teamwork and diversity of thought, and to improve observational and out-of-the-box problem solving skills. They are simple to explain and require relatively basic knowledge. Solving them mostly requires an ability to observe from a new perspective and reason in non-obvious ways.

The answers to most of the puzzles are not provided. Why not? This is partly because I am a sadistic ogre, but also because discipline is a part of meaningful exercise. Putting a puzzle aside for awhile allows you to take a fresh look and examine it from a different perspective. If the solutions were provided, too many people would look them up and spoil the workout. This would be like cutting short your run or skipping out of yoga class early. In most cases, the puzzles have an obvious answer. Once you find a solution, you will know it is right. Readers who want a push in the right direction can find some hints in Appendix C.

Navigating This Book

This book is targeted at a diverse audience, including adolescents, mature adults, professionals, English teachers, and people learning English as a second language. One of my writing challenges was to integrate loosely connected topics and materials that appeal to a broad spectrum of interests and intellectual levels. One consequence of writing for such a broad audience is that the chapters will not always be part of an obvious sequential thread. Although occasionally there is content in a later chapter that assumes the reader has completed an earlier chapter, most chapters can be read as standalone topics.

The first half of the book briefly covers the basics of English. Most of this material explores the more fascinating elements of our language that give it such depth, breadth, and intrigue. It is meant to be more entertaining and diversionary than instructive and process-oriented. Some elements of English that you don't think much about are discussed, with numerous judgments on attractive and repulsive usage.

The second half of the book presents some serious observations, lessons learned, and guidance for improving your ability to communicate. By exploring communications styles and a few high-stakes types of communications (professional presentations, selling ideas, interviews, and romantic offerings), some key aspects of communicating with purpose are illuminated.

Applying the English language effectively in school, at home, at work, at play, and in interpersonal relationships is a powerful skill. As with any power tool, you can make progress or do harm, depending on your skill and knowledge. You can accomplish much more with a chain saw than you can with a scout knife, but you can also do substantially more damage. Similarly, good ideas can be obfuscated, good relationships can be ruined, and good humor can bomb if you misuse the language or deliver it in a sloppy way.

There is always tension when people communicate. When two people use the same style of communicating, there is less tension and more comfort. With opposing styles, there is typically more tension and less comfort. Is tension always bad? Not necessarily. However, too much comfort or too much tension leads to less productive communications, while a balanced tension leads to more effective communications.

In the many roles we play in our lives—parents, colleagues, supervisors, subordinates, spouses, friends, neighbors, teachers, coaches, trusted advisors, strangers—we use a broad spectrum of behavioral and communications styles. Our behavior, whether it is actions, words, facial expressions, or emotions, is perceived by others and communicates our intentions, feelings, and judgments.

Our oral and written communications are a significant aspect of how we form relationships with other people. Communications are the exchange of information between transmitters and receivers, and the key to effective communications is that transmitters and receivers must be in synch. The serious parts of this book lay the groundwork for understanding how to get in synch with others.

ACKNOWLEDGEMENTS

Many people and sources deserve acknowledgment for the material compiled into this book. My wife and puzzle partner Jennifer helped me reason through many of the organizational dilemmas and content decisions. She also inspired me to write all this stuff down as a tangible step toward my vision for a leadership camp. My daughters Cameron and Emily were the primary puzzle testers over many years, and they helped me hone the puzzles. One of my dreams is to get their children into a camp and teach them to be word perverts like me. Many of the New England Geocachers also deserve some credit for testing these puzzles in mystery Geocaches. My editor, Karen Ailor, improved the organization, content, and presentation considerably with her editing skills and English savvy. If you think this book reads well, blame her. In the spots where it reads a little rough (like most of the puzzles), blame me. I probably wore her down battling for poetic license.

The chapter art is a product of *www.wordle.net*. This great little website has many uses, and it was perfect for providing an overview of the dominant words in each chapter.

Many web sources were researched to collect some of the trivia and word lists in the first few chapters. The more helpful sites are referenced in the bibliography.

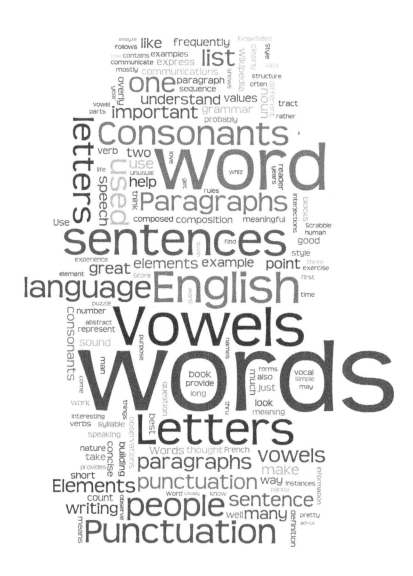

CHAPTER 1

The ABCs of English

As the English language has evolved over the past few hundred years, we have created some interesting elements. No one designed the language we use today; its architecture was created more or less after the fact. We can describe English construction pretty accurately and fairly concisely. But if we try to represent it completely and precisely, the result is very, very messy. Most of us learned English by trying to understand all the messy parts. It was no fun.

Many people would think it ridiculous even to attempt to introduce the English language in a few short pages. I disagree. It is a challenging exercise in communications. Start with a complex concept that takes a lifetime to master and boil it down into its basic elements. This thinking has led to most of the world's scientific breakthroughs, and it is one of the skills possessed by good coaches and teachers. Simplify. This section provides my solution to this challenge. For an excellent and concise treatment of English, read *Write Right! A Desktop Digest of Punctuation, Grammar, and Style*, by Jan Venolia.

Parts of Speech

The basics of English can be captured in just nine classes of words traditionally called parts of speech. Here they are in (my) priority order:

1.	verb	expresses an action, occurrence, existence
2.	adjective	modifies a noun
3.	noun	names a person, animal, thing, place, idea, quality, act
4.	interjection	exclaims
5.	adverb	modifies a verb, adjective, adverb
6.	preposition	relates one noun to another
7.	pronoun	stands in for a noun
8.	conjunction	connects words
9.	article	precedes a noun

Why this priority? The order reflects my opinion as to which words count the most when writing or speaking. And some words do count more than others. Actions speak louder than the other parts of speech; consequently, verbs are at the top of the list. Many people would place nouns at the top, but most nouns are usually obvious, and they become interesting only when they are specialized (through adjectives) or when they do something (through verbs). Interjections are one of the more underused parts of speech.

The introduction of emoticons (such as smiley faces) in online communications has increased the popularity of communicating with interjections. Emoticons are simply modern-day substitutes for interjections. I have never used a smiley face, preferring the challenge of building "tone" into my style with interjections and careful word choices.

Prepositions, pronouns, conjunctions, and articles are lower priority because they are mostly mundane necessities. Adverbs, on the other hand, are intentionally low on the list. I think adverbs are the most abused part of speech in today's everyday language. They clutter prose with redundancy, exaggeration, and unnecessary complexity. Learn what adverbs are best used for so that you can be more selective about their use.

PUNCTUATION

Be wary when something is defined by expressing what it is not. This is usually a sign that the definer cannot articulate the meaning clearly or doesn't understand the subject clearly. Nevertheless, this is the best way to define punctuation: all the stuff that is not letters or numbers. The primary elements of punctuation are shown in Table 1-1.

TABLE 1-1. *Punctuation Primer*

Punctuation	Symbol	Primary Usage
Period	.	Ends a sentence or abbreviation
Exclamation mark	!	Ends a sentence with emphasis
Question mark	?	Ends a sentence that asks a question
Comma	,	Separates ideas or elements in a sentence
Semicolon	;	Joins related but independent clauses
Colon	:	Introduces enumerated lists and consequences
Hyphen	-	Joins words and separate syllables
Dash	—	Connects compound words or names, separates syllables, shows a range in words or numbers
Brackets	( ) [ ] { } < >	Frame words considered a group or used for explanation
Apostrophe	'	Indicates omitted letters or shows possession
Quotation marks	" "	Indicate quoted speech or unusual word usage
Ellipses	...	Indicate omissions of words or letters

Punctuation marks are symbols that serve two primary purposes. First, they help clarify the syntax (structure) and semantics (meaning) of the words that are strung into sentences, paragraphs, and pages. Second, they help the reader understand the pauses and tones intended by the author.

The role of punctuation is best described in Lynne Truss's classic work, *Eats, Shoots & Leaves.* How important is punctuation? It is much more important than it appears on the surface. Here are some simple demonstrations.

Punctuate the following sequence of words to form a complete sentence.

A woman without her man is nothing

If you are male, you probably punctuated this sentence by putting a period at the end.

A woman without her man is nothing.

If you are female, you may have punctuated this sentence differently.

A woman: Without her, man is nothing.

A change in punctuation turns the meaning of the sentence upside down. Here is another example.

Don't stop.   This means keep going.

Don't! Stop!   This means the opposite of "Don't stop."

Here is a longer paragraph. This is a little more tortured, but it is still easy to see the power of punctuation. The words are exactly the same in both paragraphs; only the punctuation changes the entire meaning.

Dear Jack,

I want a man who knows what love is all about. You are generous, kind, thoughtful. People who are not like you admit to being useless and inferior. You have ruined me for other men. I yearn for you. I have no feelings whatsoever when we're apart. I can be forever happy—will you let me be yours?

Jill

Dear Jack,

I want a man who knows what love is. All about you are generous, kind, thoughtful people, who are not like you. Admit to being useless and inferior. You have ruined me. For other men, I yearn! For you, I have no feelings whatsoever. When we're apart I can be forever happy. Will you let me be?

Yours, Jill

These examples illustrate the primary purpose of punctuation: to help you express your intent. The secondary purpose is to help the reader with the flow and rhythm of the words, sentences, and paragraphs. Whereas punctuation was originally invented so that written words could be read aloud, it has evolved into a much more important element of communicating with the proper intent.

The book jacket of *Eats, Shoots & Leaves* provides a nice example of the beauty of the English language and why there are so many jokes and plays on words that we get to enjoy.

> A panda walks into a café. He orders a sandwich, eats it, then draws a gun and fires two shots in the air.
>
> "Why?" asks the confused waiter, as the panda makes toward the exit. The panda produces a badly punctuated wildlife manual and tosses it over his shoulder. "I'm a panda," he says, at the door. "Look it up."
>
> The waiter turns to the relevant entry and, sure enough, finds an explanation.
>
> "Panda. Large black-and-white bear-like mammal, native to China. Eats, shoots and leaves."

That last misplaced comma is consequential. It demonstrates that punctuation is a powerful means for enhancing clarity.

WORDS

The word is the most basic element of our language, the atomic unit of language that has some meaning. Words are composed of only two sub-elements: vowels and consonants.

What are vowels? The simple definition is a, e, i, o, and u. Here is a more precise definition from *Wikipedia.org*:

> A vowel is a sound in spoken language, pronounced with an open vocal tract so that there is no build-up of air pressure at any point above the glottis. This contrasts with consonants, where there is a constriction or closure at some point along the vocal tract.

Vowels are the key building blocks of most English words. There are only 127 words in *The Official SCRABBLE® Players Dictionary* that have no vowels; 107 of these include *y*. Conversely, there are only five words that are all vowels (aa, ae, ai, oe, and eau).

What are consonants? The simple definition is all the non-vowels. The more technical definition is a speech sound produced by occluding, with or without releasing (p, b, t, d, k, g), diverting (m, n), or obstructing (f, v, s, z, etc.), the flow of air from the lungs. Here is *Wikipedia*'s definition of *consonants*:

> In articulatory phonetics, a consonant is a speech sound that is articulated with complete or partial closure of the upper vocal tract, the upper vocal tract being defined as that part of the vocal tract that lies above the larynx. Consonants contrast with vowels.

Good grief! Can you imagine the geniuses way back when coming up with those definitions and selling them to academic authorities who blessed them as the standards?

What are the most popular letters in the English language? Although the answer varies depending on the context of the analysis, the result will come out something like the distribution-of-letter frequency shown in Figure 1-1.

FIGURE 1-1. *Letter Frequency in English (Source: Wikipedia.org)*

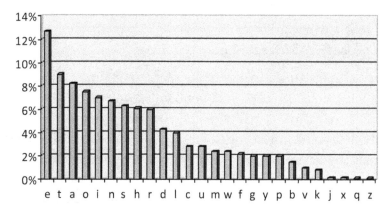

It is important to know this information if you work crossword puzzles, solve cryptograms, play Scrabble®, or watch Wheel of Fortune. It is also worth knowing for the everyday enjoyment of English. It is easier to remember if you group the letters into five sets:

Very frequent	E T A
Frequent	R H I N O S
Average	C L U D
Infrequent	M W F G Y P B V K
Very infrequent	J X Q Z

PUZZLE 2. VOWEL BLENDS

The object of this puzzle is to find the shortest English words that contain each of the possible 25 vowel digraphs (two-letter blends of vowels). Each word must be three letters or more. Score 1 point for each letter used. Score 10 points for each digraph that you can't find a word for.

aa _____ ae _____

ai _____ ao _____

au _____ ea _____

ee _____ ei _____

eo _____ eu _____

ia _____ ie _____

ii _____ io _____

iu _____ oa _____

oe _____ oi _____

co _____ ou _____

ua _____ ue _____

ui _____ uo _____

uu _____

90 letters or fewer	Scrabble® whiz
91-95 letters	Crossword puzzle whiz
96-105 letters	Average Joe
106 letters or more	Try again

PUZZLE 3. CONSONANT BLENDS

The object here is to find the shortest English words that contain the following 25 consonant digraphs (two-letter blends of consonants). Each word must be three letters or more. Score 1 point for each letter used. Score 10 points for each digraph that you can't find a word for.

bb _____   bt _____

cc _____   cn _____

dd _____   df _____

ff _____   gg _____

gp _____   hh _____

jj _____   kk _____

ll _____   mm _____

nm _____   nn _____

pp _____   rr _____

sd _____   ss _____

tt _____   vv _____

ww _____   yb _____

yg _____

115 letters or less   Scrabble® whiz
116-125 letters   Crossword puzzle whiz
126-140 letters   Average Joe
141 letters or more   Try again

PUZZLE 4. LETTER SEQUENCES

Ten different three-letter alphabetical sequences can be found in legitimate English words. For example, the word *first* contains the sequence rst, and the word *define* contains the sequence def. Can you identify the other eight? Here are all the combinations.

abc	bcd	cde	def	efg	fgh	ghi	hij	jkl	klm	lmn
nop	opq	pqr	qrs	rst	stu	tuv	uvw	vwx	wxy	xyz

Five of the three-letter sequences in Puzzle 4 can begin words. Only one three-letter sequence is a word all by itself.

The four silly sentences in Puzzle 5 were contrived from a set of words that have a subtle similarity. Try to figure out the common characteristic that each word exhibits and put the words in the correct order. When you figure out the common characteristic, the order should be obvious. An elementary school student can solve this puzzle. It just takes a keen sense of observation outside your normal frame of reference.

PUZZLE 5. FIRST IMPRESSIONS

1. Opaque jade cubes befuddled emerald experts.
2. Double-use jeep vehicle teams seemingly evaded enemy efforts.
3. Decent eight-cheese pizzas are ideal.
4. Wise, aged zebras usually escape cagey elephants.

If you need a hint to solve this puzzle, see Appendix C.

The combination of consonants and vowels into a spoken sound is called a syllable. These are the building blocks of words. *Wikipedia* defines *syllable* as follows:

> A syllable is a unit of organization for a sequence of speech sounds. For example, the word *water* is composed of two syllables: *wa* and *ter*. A syllable is typically made up of a syllable nucleus (most often a vowel) with optional initial and final margins (typically, consonants). Syllables are often considered the phonological building blocks of words. They can influence the rhythm of a language, its prosody, its poetic meter, its stress patterns, and so forth.

Prosody is another word for tone. For example, you can say the words *what is that* so that your tone implies a question, a surprise, excitement, or sarcasm. This is the prosody element of the sound.

English vowels and consonants are particularly attractive for putting together words that have teeth—in other words, for creating memorable, meaningful word usage in a specific context. While I can't prove that English has more toothy words than other languages, I believe that people prefer to express their emotions in English rather than French. Here's why.

Canada recognizes both English and French as official languages, and all traffic signs, menus, and public literature are exhibited in both languages. I studied French for many years in school, and while I cannot speak it well, I can understand 60% of what I read or hear. During a year I spent in Montreal, I attended a couple of professional hockey games where the crowd was largely French Canadians. Their clear preference for speaking, with one obvious and notable exception, was French. Sitting in the stands and enjoying some great hockey, I had to strain to understand the people around me **except** when they used profanity.

It struck me as trés odd that when they cursed, they used English expletives exclusively. I think this was because the folks who invented the King's English took great care to create profanity with consonant and vowel sequences that people love to say. Start with a hard opening constriction; follow with a soft middle sound; and close with a hard constriction. All of our fun-to-say profanity follows this common pattern. (Consider the old George Carlin routine about the seven words you can't say on television.) The French (and everyone else) love to swear in English. I didn't hear anyone say *merde*, which sounds too subtle and soft and romantic. You just can't match the joy of expressing emotions with English expletives.

Words count. The difference between good writing and good speaking is mostly in word selection and sentence structure. English has evolved over hundreds of years so that we can communicate more clearly and use a single meaningful word to describe the same thing that previously required several words. Yet most people recognize only a small percentage of the words in the English language. Most of the words are obscure and rarely needed. However, the larger your vocabulary, the more concise you can be. A poor choice of words may obscure a great thought. Good ideas are not worth much if they are not communicated effectively. Communicating an idea by writing it down is a great way to organize thoughts, analyze alternatives, and reason through its strengths and weaknesses.

For most people, the key obstacle to communicating better is the tendency to be verbose. We use several words when we need only one meaningful word. We end up sounding *overly long-winded* (a self-defining example). *Long-winded*, a word that has teeth, is memorably self-descriptive. It means verbose or overly wordy in getting to the point. Overly long-winded therefore means overly, overly wordy. Why take the emphasis off a great word like *long-winded* by adding a redundant word like *overly*? Such annoyingly meaningless verbosity is covered really extensively and with overly long-winded and very redundant wordiness in a later chapter following this one. Ha!

Your choice of words in every communication is a key element of your style and effectiveness. Many of us evolve from children who say exactly what they mean to educated adults who feel compelled to demonstrate their advanced education by using strange words and complex structure to beat around the bush. Aristotle provided some great advice on this topic. Paraphrased:

> Think as wise men do, and speak as common people do, so that everyone may understand.

Here are some simple word selection principles that help achieve this goal.

1. Use a familiar word rather than an unusual one.
2. Use a concrete word rather than an abstract word or phrase.
3. Use a single word rather than a roundabout phrase.
4. Use a short word rather than a long one.

If you stray from these principles, as a writer or a speaker, it should be to serve a specific purpose or to make a more precise point. When you use unusual, abstract, or long words, there should be a reason: The alternative word should communicate your intent more precisely. In most cases, people use unusual, abstract, or long words either to add diversity to their wording or to raise the level of perceived literacy expected by the reader. In either case, the alternative word inhibits reading and understanding. Here are some typical tradeoffs.

Familiar Word	Unusual Words
expect	presuppose, envisage
ruin	sabotage, obliterate
limit	ceiling, demarcation, utmost
honest	trustworthy, truthful, candid
enough	sufficient, adequate

make	render, constitute, fabricate, synthesize
home	residence, household, domicile

Concrete Word	**Abstract Words or Phrases**
feasible	attainable, reasonable, viable, of a feasible nature
compare	examine, observe, perform a comparison of
complex	involved, intricate, complex in nature
abstract	indefinite, deep, in an abstract way
analyze	consider, evaluate, perform an analysis of
explore	look into, investigate

Single Word	**Phrase or Circumlocution**
toward	in relation to
with	in relation to
in	with regard to
most	the majority of instances
some	in a number of cases
can	is prepared to

Short Word	**Longer Words**
total	totality, entirety
use (verb)	utilize, employ, exploit
start (noun)	initiation, inception, commencement
lack	deficiency, inadequacy, insufficiency
change	modification, transformation, metamorphosis
complex	complicated, convoluted
limit	limitation, delimit

The next chapter contains a concise discussion of wordiness.

One intriguing window into English word usage is a list of the 100 most commonly used words. There is no authoritative, mathematically provable list, but studies done by *Oxfordonline.com* and other organizations provide lists that are close enough to stimulate some interesting observations. The list shown in Table 1-2 was published on *Wikipedia*. Some of the words represent more than one word. For example, *be* represents many of the conjugated forms of the verb *to be*, such as *is, are, be,* and *was.*

TABLE 1-2. *The 100 Most Frequently Used Words in the English Language*

1 – 20	21 – 40	41 – 60	61 – 80	81 – 100
the	this	so	people	back
be	but	up	into	after
to	his	out	year	use
of	by	if	your	two
and	from	about	good	how
am	they	who	some	our
in	we	get	could	work
that	say	which	them	first
have	her	go	See	well
I	she	me	other	way
it	or	when	than	even
for	an	make	then	new
not	will	can	now	want
on	my	like	look	because
with	one	time	only	any
he	all	no	come	these
as	would	just	its	give
you	there	him	over	day
do	their	know	think	most
at	what	take	also	us

The most frequently used words are pretty boring as a group since they mostly represent the fundamental building blocks of the language: general pronouns, articles, conjunctions, prepositions, and so forth. However, a closer look at the relative frequencies of words resulted in some intriguing observations.

1. *I* is #10; *we* is #27. I think we can be pretty self-centered.
2. *To be* (existence) is the most popular verb, followed by *to have* (ownership). The only other verbs to make the list are *say, will, get, make, know, see, look, come, think, use, work, want,* and *give.* These popular verbs are primarily the things humans do that differentiate us from other life forms.
3. Our order of interest in asking questions is *what, who, which,* and *when. Why* and *where* don't even make the list. This does seem to reflect human nature. We care about outcomes more than the causes.
4. The word *take* (#60) is used much more frequently than the word *give* (#97). Again, this seems to be an accurate reflection of human nature.

5. The word *one* is used frequently. The number *two* is also on the list. This is significant because in many cases, *one* is used as a pronoun or article, not as a number.

6. The most frequently used noun is *time* (#55); the next is *people* (#61). People must be concerned about time.

7. *Year* is the most frequently used measure of time, followed by *day*. This is counterintuitive to me. It suggests that more people think long-term than short-term. I suspect that if you included all the instances of *yesterday, tomorrow,* and *Monday, Tuesday, Wednesday, Thursday, Friday, Saturday,* and *Sunday*, the use of *day* words would dominate the word *year*.

8. The word *he* shows up before *his*, and both are more frequently used than their feminine equivalents. The word *her* precedes *she*. Does this mean men are more often subjects and women are more often objects? This was certainly true in the past. I wonder how this is changing in today's writing.

9. The words *good* (#65), *well* (#89), and *new* (#92) are the only adjectives on the list. Who says we are all pessimists? *Well* is also used as an adverb, the only one on the list. I like that.

10. The word *first* (#88) shows up in the top 100. Coming in first and knowing what is first are clearly important to most people.

11. Why is there only one word with more than 6 letters? Just *because.*

These observations say much about humans. It would be interesting to compare all of your conversations and writings, to analyze them and come up with your list of most frequently used words. This would probably say a lot about who you are.

Sentences

Words are probably the most important building blocks of communications. They capture elementary concepts, things, names, actions, and characteristics. Some dogs can understand a vocabulary that includes a couple hundred words. Humans are far more capable intellectually. Depending on age, education, and environment, we have vocabularies that range from many hundreds to many thousands of words. What separates humans from other life forms—and it is a huge quantum leap—is that we can take these thousands of words and compose them into sentences to make observations and value judgments, express opinions, state facts, ask questions, and communicate other information to other people. A collection of sentences can then be composed to tell a story, discuss a quandary, describe an experience, or develop a more complete description of some topic.

Wikipedia defines *sentence* as follows:

> In linguistics, a sentence is an expression in natural language—a grammatical and lexical unit consisting of one or more words, representing distinct and differentiated concepts, and combined to form a meaningful statement, question, request, command, etc.

Sentences have numerous rules of grammar that govern how words can be composed into well-structured, meaningful expressions. There are many different ways to express a thought using the same words, and even more ways to express it using different words with similar meanings.

Some sentences roll right off the tongue; others torture us on the way out of our mouths. Well-constructed sentences help the reader and the listener understand your thoughts as you intend them. Poorly constructed sentences can strain or confuse your audience. The hardest sentence for most people to say is probably, "I was wrong," although not because of the mechanics of speech.

The most useful advice tends to be concise. Here are two examples that have struck nerves deep in my brain and etched themselves into my permanent memory.

From *The Four Agreements*, by Don Miguel Ruiz:

1. Be impeccable to your word.
2. Don't make assumptions.
3. Don't take things personally.
4. Do the best you can.

In fewer than 20 words and four short sentences, Ruiz provides four observations that would make profound differences in most people's perceived happiness. In my experience, people who appear to be happy deep inside as well as on the surface practice these Four Agreements as natural instincts.

Some short sentences in *Cowboy Ethics*, by Owen and Stoecklein, capture values that represent the culture of the American West and position these values as foundations that Wall Street could learn from.

1. Live each day with courage.
2. Take pride in your work.
3. Always finish what you start.
4. Do what has to be done.
5. Be tough, but fair.
6. When you make a promise, keep it.
7. Ride for the brand.
8. Talk less and say more.
9. Remember that some things aren't for sale.
10. Know where to draw the line.

I've spent more than 30 years in the business world of information technology, spanning defense contracting and commercial product development. In my experience, the guidance offered in *Cowboy Ethics* strikes me as sound, and not routinely practiced. The economic crisis of 2008-2009 clearly exposed the need for more cowboy ethics on Wall Street and in Washington. The most successful people I know—those who have made the biggest contributions to humankind, not to their bank accounts—have practiced most of these cowboy ethics as innate values in their everyday activities and long-term careers.

The two examples above are extraordinary. They demonstrate two common, recurring themes in great pieces of communication: They are concise and they have impact. Much of the material that follows builds on these themes.

Here is a list of my core values:

1. **Self-respect**. Personal health (mental, physical, spiritual) is a prerequisite to happiness.
2. **Sincerity**. Practice what you preach. Hypocrisy is always poisonous.
3. **Production**. Value what you produce more than what you consume.
4. **Teamwork**. Celebrate team results over individual accomplishments.
5. **Environmentalism.** Treat nature as a sanctuary of shared resources.
6. **Insight**. Diversity of thought and critical thinking are crucial components of progress in any field.
7. **Sharing**. Communicate with purpose. Stress accuracy over precision.
8. **Priorities**. Do what you should before you do what you want.
9. **Integrity**. Build trust in all relationships. Always take the high road.
10. **Balance**. Build usable broad skills. Avoid obsessions.

This list is the result of a mental exercise I undertook to craft a set of values that captures the lessons I've learned in life in as few words as possible. This is a great exercise for anyone. First, it is an insightful way to observe an important dimension of yourself, namely, your core values. Sharing it with others—your spouse, your children, your therapist, your parole officer—is a way to keep yourself honest and discuss your observations about what is truly important. Second, it is a great exercise for illuminating and practicing word selection and concise sentences. Writing down your values is deeply personal, and you will become acutely aware of how important each word is when you try to express your values in as few well-structured sentences as possible.

Paragraphs

This excerpt from *Wikipedia* defines *paragraph*:

> A paragraph is a self-contained unit of a discourse in writing dealing with a particular point or idea. A paragraph typically consists of a unifying main point, thought, or idea accompanied by supporting details. The nonfiction paragraph usually begins with the general and moves toward the more specific so as to advance an argument or point of view. Each paragraph builds on what came before and may consist of one or many sentences.

Paragraphs are governed mostly by the style of the speaker or author. There are no rules for composing paragraphs, but there are effective and ineffective styles. Consistently long paragraphs intimidate readers. Consistently short paragraphs distract them. Well-constructed mixtures of long and short paragraphs, headings, lists, figures, tables, and other elements of composition provide structure to help the reader navigate your communications style. They also help readers understand the varying depth and breadth of the storyline.

It is important to consider these three elements — words, sentences, and paragraphs — when writing, reviewing, speaking, listening to, and observing others. How you compose words into sentences and sentences into paragraphs are big differentiators in your ability to communicate.

Composition and Style

There are 200,000 to 300,000 words in the English language. There is no exact count since there are no rules about what constitutes a single word. For example, is *thought* one word, or do we count it once as a noun and once as a verb? Are singular and plural nouns counted once or twice? It is also ambiguous whether to count jargon (such as the baseball terms *homer, pitch-out, double-header*), proper names (*Paris, Jack, February*), or foreign words commonly used in English (*adios, burrito, habeas corpus, aloha, sushi, karate*).

According to *Askoxford.com*, the Second Edition of the *Oxford English Dictionary* contains more than 210,000 words (including 47,000 words that are obsolete). More than half of these words are nouns, about one-quarter are adjectives, and about one-seventh are verbs. The rest are interjections, conjunctions, prepositions, adverbs, and other forms. If distinct meanings of words were counted separately, the total number of words would probably approach three-quarters of a million. With hundreds of thousands of words that can be composed into jillions of sentences and an infinite number of different paragraphs, composition advice is pretty complicated. As with any other topic of infinite dimensionality, it is impossible to be very prescriptive. However, we can observe writing styles (patterns of grammar and composition) that represent more effective communications.

Grammar is well summarized in Write Right, by Jan Venolia, and many other English reference books such as The Chicago Manual of Style. One indication of the complexity of English grammar is the ineffectiveness of grammar checkers provided in modern word processors. While spell checkers work pretty well at finding spelling mistakes and recommending alternatives, grammar checkers are rarely used because they provide little help. The rules of grammar, their exceptions, and the complications of context still favor human reasoning over programmed assistance. English grammar is best learned by reading, writing, and observing.

When it comes to style, one book has stood out for three decades as the benchmark for English composition: *The Elements of Style*, by Strunk and White. This book, which has fewer than 100 pages, has sold more than 10 million copies and is a must-read for anyone keen on improving their writing skills.

Authors, whom many people revere as standout communicators, are not immune from poor communications techniques. Sometimes, we write drivel (defined as senseless composition). When we do, our audience turns off or, worse yet, finds humor in it. As an author, I constantly observe my own communications flaws and do my best to maintain a sense of humor so that I can laugh and learn from my own mistakes. Writing this book, which observes some good and bad patterns of writing and speaking, is like spitting into the wind. If you do uncover some odd usage, feel free to laugh. Trust me: My copy editor had me in stitches with some of the drivel I composed in early versions. Most of the remaining instances of drivel are intentional sarcasm on my part, meant to provide humorous examples. Any unintentional instances that remain are just examples of me being human.

CHAPTER 2

The Beauty of the Beast

English uses 26 letters: 21 consonants and 5 vowels. We can create jillions of words, such as the word jillion, which is a slang word that means some indefinitely large number. Some words have a single consistent meaning; some have numerous context-specific meanings. For example, the words brain, north, golf, automobile, jury, and woman have pretty consistent meanings wherever they are used. On the other hand, try to figure out the meanings of these words without knowing the context in which they're used: right, down, space, bridge, state, and branch.

English has some very special classes of words:

- Words that contain exactly the same letters as other words but in a different order are called *anagrams*. Examples: canoe and ocean.
- Words that are spelled with different letters and mean the same thing (in some context) are called *synonyms*. Examples: love and adore.
- Words that have opposite meanings are called *antonyms*. Examples: forward and reverse.

- Words that contain different letters and are pronounced the same are called *homonyms*. Examples: gnu and knew.
- Words that are spelled the same but have a different meaning are called *homographs*. Examples: lead (a heavy metallic element) and lead (to be out front).
- Words that sound the same but are spelled differently are called *homophones*. Examples: not, nought, and knot.

Then we have jargon (terminology and word usage that are meaningful only within a specific field of interest), slang (terminology and word usage that are meaningful only within a specific subculture), colloquialisms (regional slang), and much more. How confusing!

No, how beautiful! This opens up tremendous opportunities for creative writing, diverse styles, puzzles, and humor that are unparalleled in other languages. Except in English-speaking countries (India, New Zealand, Australia, the United Kingdom, and so forth), you rarely see puzzle books, crossword puzzles, or word games. And don't these same cultures have a virtual monopoly on comedy and comics? Where else do you see such a thriving community of comedians? I think this is largely due to our language, which facilitates such a diversity of plays on words, puns, and subtle misusages of words.

Here are a few trivial facts about English words:

1. The longest common word with all the letters in alphabetical order is *almost*. Isn't it strange that the longest word with this characteristic is only six letters?
2. The longest word you can make using only four different letters is *senselessness*.
3. The longest common word with no vowels is *rhythms*.
4. The longest consecutive alphabetical sequence that shows up in English words is only four letters long (RSTU, as in *overstuff* and *understudy*).
5. *Ough* can be pronounced in many different ways, as in Scarborough (uh), cough (off), dough (oh), hiccough (up), bough (ow), rough (uff), thought (aw), and through (oo).

6. The word *therein* contains 12 substrings that are also English words (the, there, he, her, here, herein, er, ere, re, rein, I, in).
7. The first number spelled out that contains an *a* is one thousand.
8. If you could make an infinite list of the whole numbers and arrange them alphabetically, the last number listed would be zero.

That last piece of trivia raises a strange question for philosophers and mathematicians: Can you define another infinite list that has a last element?

Puzzle 6 contains a diversion that consumed me for a few years in the late 1990s and became one of my obsessions. This was before there were online dictionaries and other useful tools for word perverts like me to use. The puzzle consists of a short essay. Read it and observe the various word choices and sentence flow. The prose may not be appealing at first; it will certainly seem strained and convoluted. Once you solve the puzzle, it should be more appealing for its bizarre characteristic. This sort of creative writing is challenging mental exercise. Try making up your version and *then* tell me how convoluted it is.

PUZZLE 6. A QUESTIONABLE PREOCCUPATION WITH VOCABULARIES

This unorganized, nefarious, and unforgivable documentation is my offering to those tenacious puzzle solvers and delusional word voluptuaries. I work at a mountainside oceanarium that serves alliaceous bouillabaisse with cauliflower for malnourished tourists. A mendacious mountaineer, I have bivouacked abstemiously among the tallest sequoias. I am also ambidextrous, mustachioed, and perspicacious, but not overanxious with speculation on the graciousness with which discouraged ideologues will facetiously appreciate this inconsequential regurgitation of language beautification.

This sacrilegious education is authorized by unsanctioned authorities who are unequivocal fountainheads of miscellaneous puzzle regulation. These unrecognizable, ultraconservative millionaires popularized this puzzle's groundbreaking equation. The solution's boundaries are not insurmountable, but any underestimation of the "strangeness" of this paragraph could result in pandemonium, undiagnosed exhaustion, and evacuation from one's subordinate sanity. This could lead to communicable pneumonia rather than the unavoidable neurological euphoria of uncomplicated stupefaction. The revolutionary title is simultaneously an ostentatious hint and a precarious permutation of encouraging words for those unaccomplished milquetoasts of the word-puzzle persuasion who need evolutionary rejuvenation and emasculation of their egos.

The unprofessional words *menstruation* and *ejaculation* also belong here, but why? Any denunciation or repudiation of the gregarious sentence structure would be uncomplimentary and result in attenuation of hallucinogenic brainwaves. One precaution: The word choices are not unintentional. I could provide an unapologetic evaluation of the auditioned dialogue to be caught on audiophile audiotape. No more prosecutorial recapitulation, or continuance. Most discombobulated solvers get it instantaneously, with an autogenesis of an uncoordinated desire to be institutionalized.

Solve this puzzle by answering three questions:

1. Can you quantify the strangeness of this essay with one numeric measure?
2. Can you identify two additional words that meet this strangeness standard?
3. Can you find the two most special words in the context of this puzzle?

Once you have solved this puzzle, you will likely say to yourself one of two things: "What kind of rubbish is this?" or "That is a trivial, yet breathtaking, example of the beauty of our language." I hope it will be the latter.

WORDS WITHIN WORDS AND WORDS AMONG WORDS

One beautiful aspect of English is the amount of overlap in letter sequences, word roots, prefixes, and suffixes. You won't see this unless you look for it. My brain is wired to observe and notice such things, and these next few puzzles explore this strange perspective of our language.

Traditional word search puzzles are not very challenging. They are too mechanical with no real reasoning behind them. The following pages present a few different versions of word searches that will expose you to the strange world of hidden words within normal text. Although the challenge is still to search for words, they have all been disguised within proper English prose. Here are a few general tips:

1. The hidden words may be in plain sight; namely, the word may stand alone in a sentence as a normal word.
2. The hidden word may be a substring (like the word *car* is a substring in the word *careful*) or a superstring (like the word *wish* is a superstring spanning three words in the phrase "...*now I should go*..."
3. Weird sentence structure and unnatural word choices are the clues to uncovering hidden words.
4. Sometimes an odd sentence structure or unnatural word choice is simply misdirection to confuse the solver. Sometimes the hidden words are present in a normal sentence structure and word choices.

Not only are these word searches fun to solve, they are fun (and challenging) to construct. As you read these puzzles, you may come to the conclusion that some of this is drivel. I confess: Some of it is. Please grant me poetic license and enjoy the puzzles. Then try constructing a sentence that sounds more natural. Asking a rookie to solve these unique, enjoyable puzzles in a taxicab is hopeless on a week night. If I have attracted you into my world of word perversion, I will have at least succeeded in opening your mind to a new set of mental exercises.

Here's a simple example. One of the sentences in the last paragraph contains all of the pieces of a well-known board game hidden within the words. Can you find them? You may or may not have noticed that as*king* a *rook*ie to solve these uni*que,* en*j*oyable puzzles in a taxica*b is hop*eless on a wee*k night*. And you thought that was the perfect example of drivel!

The contrived paragraphs in Puzzle 7 contain at least 124 different letter sequences for animals. The wording is strange and sometimes forced, but therein you find the clues. There are also a few bluff words and decoys just to keep you guessing. With a few exceptions, every three-letter word that represents a different animal is included. There are also animals of 4, 5, 6, 7, and 8 letters. The sequences can be found in different hiding places.

1. Some are in plain sight, as a normal word such as *Jay*.
2. Some are substrings within a single word, such as *ant* in the word *antique.*

3. Some span multiple words, such as *fox* in ...stif*f Ox*yContin.
4. Punctuation is used as camouflage in this puzzle and should be ignored in identifying letter sequences.

As one hint, here are the numbers of hidden animals for each word length: 47 three-letters, 34 four-letters, 21 five-letters, 12 six-letters, 8 seven-letters, and two eight-letters. See how many different animals you find buried in the puzzle.

PUZZLE 7. WORD SAFARI

My mother Jill amazes me. Her only vehicle is a grubby <u>antique</u> police car I bought for her on a lark with my millions. She epitomizes a flamboyant woman on the go. Attempting to pique her desire, I smartened up and met her at a pleasant eatery in the main section to share some guacamole and Crown Royal. I regret that we have been avoiding our kids for a year, so we decided to fly them up and away from Iceland with their sealed, new travel kits. Our son Jay had lost rich sums in a sticky glob steroid sham. Steroids are not terrible murderous drugs, but we abhor seeing our son crave new vices to rely upon. Yesterday, Jay caught a bad germ. He was feeling undermined by a nasal monotone. Fortunately, he went to a doctor for a medical cure and was put routinely on stif<u>f Oxy</u>Contin. Our boy sternly resisted swallowing the pill for a second or two. Then musk oil was sponged on his naked body and he became leery when he heard eerie noises. The attending nurse monitoring Jay was a half-inch taller than him. In khaki winter pants, a bronze braid, and frumpy thongs, her job assignment was wandering the corridors and acting tough as nails. She ate a sugar cube, moaned, howled like a dog, started disco dancing, slugged an intern, and asked why nurses can't elope in a spacesuit. It was surreal to see a pediatric attendant lose it on the job. At least <u>Jay</u>, a keen and shrewd observer, does not rock the boat. It bugs me to see someone stagger, trip up, or slip. I get sad when big egos prey on others. Many of those who gloat are selfish cowards and the rest of them are board-certified loons. I want to live a gleeful life of learning, be a very good role model, and have a long natural lifespan. There is no prestige realized from work, but a good job is one key long-term item for calmly making it through life.

Hidden in the contrived paragraphs of Puzzle 8 are 100 different letter sequences for major American cities. The wording is strange and sometimes forced, but therein you find the clues. There are two cities from each state. Each city is either over 50,000 in population or is one of the top 10 most populated cities in its state. Some city names could come from multiple states, but to solve this puzzle and get just two from each state, you will need to pick the right city-state pair.

The first 50 cities are relatively easy, the next 40 are more difficult, and the last 10 will require most people to spend some serious time on the internet to solve the puzzle correctly. The sequences can be found in different hiding places. Some are in plain sight, as a normal word such as *Lincoln*. Some are substrings within a single word, such as *Mobile* in the word *automobile*. Some span multiple words such as *Brooklyn* in the words …*brook. Lynn* …

Note that in this puzzle, punctuation is used as camouflage and should be ignored.

PUZZLE 8. WORD GEOGRAPHY

Paul, Lynn, Jack, Alan, Charles, Tony, Norm, and Louise drove their auto*mobile*s to Helen's cabin on the lake. Charles arrived in a <u>Lincoln</u> first; Paul was second in a Plymouth, and Norm showed up last. Louise had auburn hair and was Jack's only daughter. Helen is from a happy home, very chic, a go-getter, and a freewheeling globetrotter. I entered the cabin that some say is just pleasant. A few others might call it provocative or plush. I loved the gazebo, stone walls, and garden veranda with little rocking chairs next to a meandering <u>brook. Lyn</u>n donated the boorish art for display. There was a statue of a pueblo Indian, a polished marble bust of Fred Flintstone, and a bronze statue of old man Chester Arthur near the pine bluff on the high point of the property. The gazebo is elevated over water, looking out on a barren corral, eight pig pens, and rock hills that looked all askew.

Happier, relaxed and thirsty, we drank sugary tea, scones with butter, Columbian coffee, and cola. Then I ate a taco made of mahi-mahi and a sandwich. I tasted the salmon roe but it had an odd odor of fennel, ginger and rotting pineapple. Tony and Paul played their harmonicas perfectly with Alan. Singing old Dionne Warwick tunes about providence and frank fortitude, our voices carried afar. "Good Night," Tony said with a perplexing tone as he sat up. Eloquently, he recited a poem with frank lines about independence.

First and foremost, we wanted a real ranch or a genuine cabin. We found one last August. After months, we looked for land on a lake with a long beachfront. There were no cabins for sale matching the modest options we desired: a mineral spring, fields for an easy dock entry, and running water. Townspeople were busy unsnarling tons of traffic on cordoned-off streets. We knew Arkansas roads need more rule of law to neutralize the chaos. We wanted to help a sorry set of traffic cops park some cars out of danger. "Man, townspeople should take time out for a cinema with a nice holiday tone," Jack remarked.

We found a rich Monday real estate report. Land rentals required significant one-year leases, but rent on the available lots was very irregular. "Am I even reading this right?" Helen asked, as she skimmed for details. Most folks we knew haven't been hunting. Tony had a lifetime game stamp and he was a full-time MP. His pal Norm, a confirmed buffalo hunter and also a first-rate MP, elected to hunt bear with him, I noticed. Dressed in khaki, he is scary. I was ill-advised by an old Vietnam pal that hunting urban gorillas would make us heros. Well, that makes about as much sense as this puzzle.

Synonyms

Synonyms are different words that have similar meanings for a specific usage. Saying the same thing another way, synonyms can be substituted for all the words in that sentence:

Synonyms: Distinct lexemes with comparable connotations in a given context.

The word *synonym* is also one of the few words in the English language for which there are NO synonyms! Look it up. *Askoxford.com* claims that there are four other words with no synonyms: millionaire, fish, fruit, and toothbrush. We can find synonyms or some of the secondary meanings of those words, but for their main meaning, there are none.

Which word has the most synonyms? According to *Askoxford.com*, that honor goes to the word *good*, with 380 synonyms. Who says we humans are pessimists? We have invented 380 words that mean good and only 324 that mean bad!

Synonyms have evolved over time. Most of the base words were created arbitrarily and represented unique names at some time. Then new words (synonyms) evolved to refine the original word in some way so that it better suited a specific context.

Peter Roget's *Thesaurus of English Words and Phrases*, first published in 1852, was considered a necessity for students and wordsmiths born before the computer age. Today, with online dictionaries, thesauruses, and *Wikipedia*, we all take such references for granted. Imagine the incredible effort required to compile a thesaurus and keep it up to date without these online tools. With all the various usages of words in different contexts, as well as the continuing evolution of slang, jargon, and technical terminology, this would be an incredibly complex undertaking. Roget revolutionized the quality of writing across the English-speaking world, and I think he was an underappreciated workhorse of the 19th Century. He has always been one of my heroes for inventing such a powerful tool.

The diversity of the English language and our never-ending struggle with accuracy and the precision of word meanings have resulted in an incredibly rich collection of synonyms. The following example demonstrates the breadth and depth of describing a state so loved by humans that they invented a ridiculous number of words for the same condition. You won't find this in a thesaurus.

My research suggests that the word with the record number of synonyms that mean precisely the same thing is *drunk*. Although *good* may have 380 synonyms, many, many of these have different meanings across multiple contexts. *Drunk* means drunk: under the influence of alcohol to the point that you have lost your sensible decision-making capability. Here are 120 words that are synonyms for drunk. There are many more than I have listed here; this is just a solid sampling of the most popular.

befuddled	belligerent	bent	besotted
blacked-out	blasted	blind	blitzed
blocked	blotto	boiled	bombed
bunkered	bricked	buttered	buzzed
caned	canned	clobbered	cockneyed
cranked	crapulous	crocked	cut
destroyed	dipso	dragged	drunk
embalmed	euphoric	fermented	floating
fried	giddy	gone	groggy

hammered	hammerlocked	happy	high
hooched	impaired	in rare form	inebriated
intoxicated	juiced	legless	liquored-up
lit	loaded	looped	lubed
lushed	marinated	mellow	merry
messed up	obliterated	obliviated	out of it
overloaded	pasted	pickled	pie-eyed
pissed	plastered	plotzed	plowed
polluted	pounded	ramboed	ripped
roaring	rocked	sauced	sculpted
shellacked	shickered	shitfaced	slammed
slopped up	sloshed	smashed	snockered
snookered	sodden	soused	sizzled
spaced	stewed	stiff	stinking
stinko	stocious	stoned	swacked
tanked	3 sheets to the wind	tied one on	tight
tipsy	toasted	tomahawked	torque
trashed	trolleyed	tweaked	twisted
under the influence	under the table	under the weather	unsober
wallpapered	wasted	whipped	wiped
woozy	wrecked	zoned	zonked

I think it is safe to conclude that words with many synonyms are popular interests of humans.

ANTONYMS

Antonym is a synonym for *opposite*. Antonyms are much more complex and restricted than synonyms. Many words have no antonym. For example, what is the opposite of candle? If you try to get precise about antonyms, you quickly get into descriptions of binary opposites (like positive and negative), gradable opposites (like high and low), directional opposites, complements, and other interesting minutia. The term *antonym* was created in the 19th Century and has become a well-accepted element of our language.

Auto-antonym and *contranym* are terms used to describe words that, used in two different contexts, have opposite meanings. These sorts of words are one of the special features of our language. Here are some everyday auto-antonyms.

Anxious	looking forward to or dreading
Argue	to be for or against
Buckle	to fasten together or fall apart
Cleave	to split apart or cling together
Continue	to proceed or postpone
Downhill	an easier approach or a worse approach
Dust	to remove dust or add dust
Exceptional	outstanding or problematic
Fast	high speed or stationary
Fight with	to fight against or fight alongside
Fix	a predicament or a solution
Go off	to start or stop
Handicap	a disadvantage or an advantage
Hardly	roughly or lightly
Hold	to conduct or postpone
Lease	to lend or borrow
Left	remains or departs
Overlook	to watch over or fail to see
Oversight	avoiding a mistake or a mistake
Replace	to restore or remove
Resign	to quit or renew
Sanction	to endorse or ban
Screen	to show or hide
Seed	to remove seeds or add seeds
Spare	extra or meager
Table	to postpone or address now
Trim	to remove excess or add decorations
Weather	to erode away or withstand
Windup	start or finish

Homonyms, Homophones, and Heteronyms

Homonyms and homophones are etymological coincidences with no real rhyme or reason as to how they came about. Technically, homonyms are words that are spelled the same and pronounced the same, yet have different meanings, such as left (a direction) and left (the past tense of leave). Homophones are words that are pronounced the same but have different spellings (such as to, too, and two).

Finally, heteronyms have the same spelling but different pronunciation (such as close [to shut] and close [nearby].)

- Same pronunciation, same spelling: homonyms
- Same pronunciation, different spelling: homophones
- Different pronunciation, same spelling: heteronyms
- Different pronunciation, different spelling: everything else

Most references treat homonyms and homophones as one thing: words that sound alike but have different meanings. What word pronunciation has the most homophones? I found one that has six different homophones: air (breathable gas), are (one hundredth of a hectare), e'er (poetic contraction of ever), ere (eventually), err (to act human, according to the old proverb), and heir (object of inheritance).

There are many lists of homonyms and homophones on the web. Here is a list with three or more sound-alike words.

air	are	e'er	ere	err	heir
boar		Boer		boor	bore
sew		so		sol	sow
carat		caret		carrot	karat
cere		sear		seer	sere
adds		ads		adze	
ade		aid		aide	
aisle		I'll		isle	
aye		eye		I	
bases		basis		basses	
buy		by		bye	
cay		key		quay	
cents		scents		sense	
Chile		chili		chilly	
chord		cord		cored	
cite		sight		site	
dew		do		due	
do		doe		dough	
ewe		yew		you	
flew		flu		flue	
for		fore		four	

gnu	knew	new
hoard	horde	whored
holey	holy	wholly
idle	idol	idyl
knot	naught	not
lays	laze	leis
lea	lee	li
lochs	locks	lox
mall	maul	moll
meat	meet	mete
oar	or	ore
pair	pare	pear
peak	peek	pique
Pole	pole	poll
poor	pore	pour
praise	prays	preys
precedence	precedents	presidents
rain	reign	rein
raise	rays	raze
rapped	rapt	wrapped
rho	roe	row
right	rite	write
road	rode	rowed
seas	sees	seize
slew	slough	slue
tea	tee	ti
teas	tease	tees
their	there	they're
to	too	two
toad	toed	towed
vain	vane	vein
wail	wale	whale
ware	wear	where
way	weigh	whey
weald	wheeled	wield
whined	wind	wined
yore	you're	your

Heteronyms are words that are spelled the same but have subtle differences in pronunciation when used in different contexts or as different parts of speech. For example, it takes only a minute to explain the minute pronunciation differences in heteronyms. You will naturally pronounce the first instance *min-it* and the second instance *my-noot*. Imagine someone learning English as a second language trying to parse all these subtle inflections. In the common heteronyms listed below, many of the pronunciations are different only in the accent, or emphasis on syllables, with which the word is pronounced.

Abstract	Abuse	Advocate	Affect
Aggregate	Alternate	Approximate	Arithmetic
Associate	Attribute	August	Axes
Bass	Bow	Bowed	Buffet
Close	Combine	Compound	Conduct
Conflict	Console	Consummate	Content
Contest	Contract	Convert	Converse
Convict	Crooked	Defect	Defense
Deliberate	Desert	Designate	Digest
Do	Does	Dove	Drawer
Duplicate	Estimate	Excuse	Graduate
House	Incense	Incline	Insert
Insult	Intern	Intimate	Invalid
Invite	Laminate	Lather	Laminate
Lead	Live	Minute	Moderate
Mow	Multiply	Number	Object
Offense	Perfect	Permit	Pervert
Polish	Precipitate	Predicate	Present
Primer	Process	Produce	Project
Pussy	Read	Rebel	Rebel
Recall	Recollect	Record	Recount
Recreation	Refuse	Regress	Relapse
Relay	Reject	Remake	Repeat
Reprint	Resent	Reside	Resign
Resume	Retouch	Reuse	Rewrite
Row	Sake	Secreted	Separate
Sewer	Slough	Sow	Subject
Suspect	Syndicate	Tear	Use
Wind	Wound		

The confusion with these words, and hence their beauty, is that it is easy to construct sentences using the same word twice but in contexts where they are pronounced differently in each instance. Here are a few creations.

- Our company did not lead the market in lead-based paint sales.
- If we produce more produce, it will promote better health.
- The city dump had to refuse more refuse.
- She wanted to polish off the Polish sausage before drinking her soda.
- I object to this object being included.
- The dove dove to avoid the hawk.
- The cameras will record several world records at the Olympics.
- The invalid had an invalid license.
- My eyes were tearing as they were tearing up my contract.
- A bandage was wound around the wound on his finger.
- We can't desert our forces in the desert.
- The bass player loved to go bass fishing.
- What does the buck do when the does return?
- We will intimate this idea to our most intimate friends and family.
- We will subject the subject to stressful circumstances.
- He should sow his seeds after he milks his sow.
- I can present the present to her.
- Wind up the game before the wind gets any stronger.
- They will close the road when the river gets close to overflowing.

Puzzle 9 is a fun word search puzzle that challenges your knowledge of all the standard keyboard symbols and their names. Today, we communicate mostly through computers and keyboards. Just how much do you know about all the symbols on your keyboard? The entire set of symbols and names is indeterminate, and I suspect everyone will do some web searching on "keyboard symbols" to research some of the different names that represent the various keystrokes.

Hidden in the three (incredibly articulate) paragraphs of Puzzle 9 are 145 different letter sequences that represent symbols for keys on standard computer keyboards. The sequences can be found in different hiding places. Some are in plain sight, as with a normal word such as *six* representing the symbol 6 on a keyboard. Some are substrings within a single word, such as the word *bee* in <u>bee</u>ts or the word *be* in *al<u>be</u>it*, both representing the symbol B. In this puzzle, homophones—like *be* and *bee* —count as different words. Some span multiple words, such as *three* in the words *Both re-elected* representing the symbol 3. Note that in this puzzle, punctuation is used as camouflage and should be ignored in identifying letter sequences.

The letter sequences must be at least two letters long and must be made up of acceptable English words, with one exception (*paren*, which is given as an example). Most of the symbols are represented with one word, but there are 15 symbols that require two words (like *open paren* and *close paren*). The symbol words you are looking for are usually the accepted identifier (like *plus* for +), but occasionally there are well-accepted aliases (like *add*). A few are rather sneaky like *effor* (representing function key 4 or F4) in effort. Note that both *ef* and *for* are acceptable English words. Reference *The Official SCRABBLE® Players Dictionary* if you aren't familiar with the various two- and three-letter words for the letters of the alphabet. There are 18 different two-letter words in the solution to this puzzle.

Many symbols are represented more than once but use different letter sequences representing the same symbol. *Period* and *full stop* are examples of such synonyms for the symbol "."on the keyboard. *Be* and *bee* are examples of different homophones for the letter B. Multiple occurrences of the same letter sequence do not count. Each letter sequence must use non-overlapping letters. For example, the letter sequence *bee* in *beets* counts as one hidden symbol, but those same letters cannot be used for the letter sequence *be*. You would need to find a different letter sequence, such as *be* in *albeit*, to count each as a different instance of a symbol. All these examples are underlined in the following text to get you started. How many different letter sequences can you find?

PUZZLE 9. SYMBOL HUNT

We returned and entered the semi-colonial lodge. F*or* approximately five dollars, I ate a pound of leftover hash (with su*per-iod*ized salt), *bee*ts, peas, carrots and vanilla layer cake *six* inches wide. "Let elders queue up first," the Deejay piped over the intercom. Mad and baring its teeth, a dog sat by its homely, overweight master. I skied back, spaced-out in a daze. Rocky at times, I paused and came to a *full stop*. I was seeing double! You may have thought I had a stroke, al*be*it a brief one.

Both *re-*elected teachers eventually won equal seats that were *open.*

<u>Paren</u>ts lashed out left and right. The polling spaces were too <u>close.</u> <u>Paren</u>tal mob anger has taught our youth to have less than positive energy. They break down at a young age, especially when inertia is greater than ever. Until demanding caretakers decipher and underscore this grave control issue, we need a shift in protocol. Only doting, exotic movie stars question the negative trends. These scapegoats ignite ire. We yearn to rescue all of our best. Won't this slippage down result in less rampage? Upper central Midwest kids function okay. Why not seize each one and put them in useful *eff*orts?

Here are a few prime quotes for a number of the Humvee's solid, useful selling points: enough trunk space, barium hubcaps, locking rims, sharp vertical lines, p<u>add</u>ed seatbacks lashed with hemp, stick shift, power foot brakes, platinum heat dampers, and <u>*plus*</u>h carpet inserts that last forever.

One fun way to solve this puzzle is to provide it to a group and see who can find the most symbols in a given time, or see who can find the most symbols that no one else discovered.

In my solution, 679 out of the 1,164 total letters in these passages are used in 145 different hidden symbols—that is 58% of the letters.

ANAGRAMS

An anagram is a rearrangement of the letters in a word or phrase to form a different word or phrase. *Cameron*, my daughter's name, is an anagram of *romance*. *Corey*, my dog's name, is an anagram of *Royce*. And *stifle* is an anagram of itself! That last sentence is one of my favorite lines in this book. Anagramming is great mental exercise and the basic skill required to master the game of Scrabble®.

There are many anagram servers on the internet that can help you assess and analyze anagrams. Some anagrams are pretty ironic. Here is a list of some of the better ones.

Dormitory	= Dirty room
Elvis	= Lives
Listen	= Silent
Clint Eastwood	= Old West action

Madame Curie	= Radium came
The countryside	= No city dust here
Astronomers	= Moon starers
Postmaster	= Stamp store
The eyes	= They see
The Morse code	= Here come dots
Slot machines	= Cash lost in'em
Conversation	= Voices rant on
Mother-in-law	= Woman Hitler
A gentleman	= Elegant man
A decimal point	= I'm a dot in place
Eleven plus two	= Twelve plus one
Debit card	= Bad credit
The IRS	= Theirs
Spandex	= Expands
abcdefghijklmnopqrstuvwxyz	= Cwm fjord bank glyphs vext quiz
abcdefghijklmnopqrstuvwxyz	= Mr. Jock, TV quiz PhD, bags few lynx

You get the idea.

Puzzle 10 contains a few anagrams of some of my favorite speakers, writers, and commentators. (Even the heading "Great Pundits" has some good anagrams: drug patients, ratting dupes, purged titans.) See if you can figure them out.

PUZZLE 10. ANAGRAM TRIVIA

GREAT PUNDITS	THIN HINT
1. Tall ferocity hero	An exceptional communicator
2. Ruined blather	A must for international travelers
3. Stroll whiz	The king of mental exercise
4. Most sad act	High-tech hero
5. Ferric handyman	Great teacher of complex stuff
6. Foggier well	Reasoned, graceful writer
7. Monkeys write	*The* benchmark for news
8. El mild sinner	Most articulate funnyman
9. Mean brothel kin	Gifted speaker but overly biased

There are more than 1000 three-letter words in *The Official SCRABBLE®
Players Dictionary*. There is one set of three letters that can be anagrammed
into five different three-letter words. There are only six possible ways
to rearrange three letters, and in this case five out of six of them are
acceptable words.

Can you identify these five words?

Finally, there are two different sets of three letters that can be anagrammed
into four different three-letter words. Can you identify both of these sets
of four words?

MNEMONICS

Some things are hard to remember, especially when they are ordered sets. For
example, if you wanted to remember the first four men on the moon, you could
memorize the names Neil Armstrong, Buzz Aldrin, Pete Conrad, and Alan Bean. If
your brain works like most other brains do, that set of unassociated names is hard
to remember. A mnemonic device is an associated phrase or poem or visual that
can be more easily remembered and related back to the original data. In the men-
on-the-moon case, I have constructed a simple mnemonic: Nab-a-P-cab. When I
remember that, it is easy to reconstruct the order and the names from the initials of
the four astronauts.

Our brains are well suited for remembering complex things like pictures,
structures, songs, smells, tastes, spatial relationships, emotions, and faces. We
use these to make sophisticated models of the world we live in. Our memory
banks store such complex things very effectively. Most people have trouble
remembering a poem or an essay word for word, but when those words are put
to music, it is amazing how easy it is to remember them, with the tune acting as
the mnemonic.

Much of the information we want to remember is presented as long strings
of words on a printed page. Although writing is great for conveying complex
logic and arguments, our brains do not easily store and remember written
information. Mnemonics are particularly useful to students who need to
memorize certain lists of stuff. They are also useful to anyone trying to remember

trivia or knowledge needed for everyday purposes. In 9ᵗʰ grade biology class, I struggled to remember the proper order of the taxonomic classification of living organisms.

1. Kingdom
2. Phyla
3. Class
4. Order
5. Family
6. Genus
7. Species

My classmate and I came up with a simple mnemonic as a memory aid: *Kings Play Chess On Fine Green Sand*. I have never forgotten that silly phase—partly because it is silly, but mostly because the associated words combine into an image that my brain is good at recalling.

Another example is the order of the planets in terms of their distance from the sun.

1. Mercury
2. Venus
3. Earth
4. Mars
5. Jupiter
6. Saturn
7. Uranus
8. Neptune
9. Pluto (Although Pluto has been stripped of its planet status, I still use it for my mnemonic.)

My Very Excellent Mnemonic Just Speeds Up Naming Planets. This phrase is easier to remember than the list and gives you confidence in determining the correct order. Here are a few other examples of mnemonics.

- I before E except after C. A simple rhyme to help us in spelling.
- Every good boy deserves favor. The treble clef stave notes. And you thought it was just the name of a Moody Blues album!
- Roy G. Biv. The sequence of colors in the visible spectrum: red, orange, yellow, green, blue, indigo, violet.

- Please excuse my dear Aunt Sally. Used by programmers and mathematicians to define the order of operation for mathematical expressions: parentheses, exponentiation, multiplication, division, addition, subtraction.
- HOMES. The five great lakes: Huron, Ontario, Michigan, Erie, Superior.
- Spring forward and fall back. An easy way to remember how to reset clocks when daylight savings time comes and goes.
- A simple poem to remember how many days there are in each month:
  Thirty days hath September,
  April, June, and November.
  All the rest have thirty-one,
  Excepting February alone,
  Which hath but twenty-eight, in fine,
  Till leap year gives it twenty-nine.

The last rhyme doesn't work for me; I still have trouble remembering which months have 31 days and which don't. I prefer a nice visual mnemonic that is easily created by putting your fists together, thumb to thumb, and counting the months across the high points and low points of your knuckles (see Figure 2-1). Each high point (knuckle) is a month that has 31 days; each low point is a month that has 30 days (or 28/29 for February).

FIGURE 2-1. *Using Your Fists to Remember the Days in Each Month*

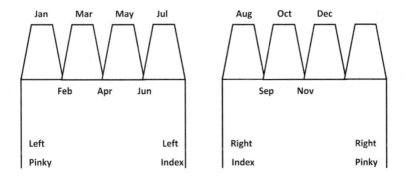

JARGON

Jargon is one of the joys of our language. Lawyers have their own jargon; so do doctors and engineers. Those are professional, somewhat formal examples of domains with their own jargon, but you can create your own! Among a select group of people, you can create jargon, or your secret code, that only people in your club understand. We all do this all the time. You probably know of some word usage that only your family understands. Using *dee* and *deepa* as synonyms for grandma and grandpa is a good example. These are clearly the mispronunciations of a family's first child that were considered cute enough to stick.

Jargon is a serious complication for non-English speakers who are trying to learn the language. Here's a true story that influenced my use of jargon. At a presentation in Korea, I was simultaneously translated while speaking to a rather large audience. The audience had the option of wearing headphones so that the people who couldn't comprehend me, the English speaker, could listen to a translation in Korean.

What this entails is rather complex. In a soundproof box at the back of the room, two translators listened to me in English and translated into Korean. This is one of the hardest jobs in the world; it takes two people because they need to alternate every 10 minutes or so. The translators usually go over the presentation material in advance to get a feel for the word usage and the technical terms that might be difficult to translate. The translators emphasized how important it was for me to speak slowly and methodically and to avoid the use of American jargon because it just does not translate well.

This was the first time I had ever been translated. I was fascinated and somewhat anxious. A colleague of mine spoke first. He is a brilliant speaker, but he talked fast and used a tremendous amount of engineering jargon and folksy humor. The Korean audience seemed riveted, even though he did not adjust his speaking style much. Even his jokes received an authentic laughing response, although slightly offset by the few-second delay of translation. One joke in particular seemed like it should have been complete nonsense outside the United States nerd programmer community. It was something about "getting hosed by overusing go-to statements and ending up with spaghetti code." Even to English-speaking nonprogrammers, this phrase should have been almost unintelligible.

After my colleague finished, I went to the soundproof room to compliment the translators and assure them that I would speak more slowly and without all the funny business. The translators were dripping with sweat; they looked like they had just gone three rounds with Muhammad Ali. I told them I was amazed with their ability to translate the "getting hosed" joke. The younger translator looked at me and smiled. He said, "Well, I told the audience that this joke does not translate into Korean. Please laugh now." Wow! Right there, I swore off all humor in my international presentations.

Some of my favorite examples of jargon come from my government contracting days where we had many obscure but concise terms that had sophisticated and verbose meanings. Here are two good examples of jargon that I encountered early in my career.

C-Student's Revenge. Contractors and consultants use this term to characterize the frustrating experience of dealing with an ignorant client. It is a snarky description of the feelings of some snobby know-it-alls when they have to subordinate themselves to someone with less informed judgment. I have heard many government contractors use this term, as well as general contractors who are getting paid and controlled by clients who know very little about the service or technology they are buying. Notice how *C-Student's Revenge* captures well a concept that took me a few sentences to explain. This is the real value of jargon: to create a shortcut word or phrase that has clear meaning within a certain context.

Horse-Apple Pancakes. My second example comes from an old joke. For many written compositions, acceptable quality is an elusive standard. In many team efforts, such as scripts or business proposals, there is sometimes an unwritten team rule that if you critique some piece harshly, you must write a better alternative yourself. Much material starts getting deemed "good enough" because you know that if you criticize it, you must improve it, thereby taking on more work. The term *horse-apple pancakes* is jargon for "I don't really like it, but I have nothing better to offer."

Where did this come from? Here is the old joke that was the source of this beautiful jargon.

Some lumberjacks working a secluded camp in the boondocks had trouble sharing the everyday chores, especially cooking. While they all loved to eat, none of them wanted to do the cooking. They had a camp rule that anyone who complained about the food had to take over the cooking immediately. One lumberjack named Fred finally got so fed up with the current cook's tasteless cuisine that he decided he would enjoy a tour of cooking duty to show his fellow lumberjacks that it could be done well. He stood up and announced: "This food is awful!" The lumberjacks all pointed at him and said, "Your turn, wise guy."

Fred undertook his new responsibility with pleasure and served up some of the best food they had ever eaten in a lumberjack camp. But after a few months, he started missing the lumber activity, the smell of fresh cut trees, and the male camaraderie in the forest. So he started cooking with less spice, overcooking or undercooking meats, and fixing dishes that he knew some of his buddies hated. After days of half-hearted attempts to get someone to complain, he was staring at the corral thinking of new schemes when one of the horses let loose with a load of horse apples. "That's it!" he said to himself. He collected a bushel of dried horse apples and mixed them up in pancake batter with just the right consistency. He added fresh blueberries to make the pancakes visually appealing, and served them for breakfast. The lumberjacks dug in enthusiastically. Fred could see their consternation as the flavor sank in and they swallowed hard. Finally, after a few tense moments, the previous cook stood up and stated firmly, "These pancakes taste like crap!" As the other lumberjacks looked at him, he added, "and they're delicious!"

In the early 1990s, David Burke published three great works on slang and jargon used in America. *Street Talk 1, Street Talk 2,* and *Biz Talk 1* are excellent references for people learning English as a second language and even for native speakers. These books provide insight into just how much our everyday conversation and our business discussions depend to some degree on jargon.

Acronyms

The use of acronyms has exploded in the past 30 years as technology has permeated everyone's life and the jargon of the technical and business worlds has become more commonplace. An acronym uses the first letter(s) of each word in a common string of words to create a pronounceable new word, such as NATO. Nowadays, most abbreviations formed by collecting the first letters of a string of words— whether they are pronounceable or not—are commonly called acronyms: USA, IBM, DVD, ATM, PIN, IRA, BYOB, RSVP. Some words that started out as acronyms are now accepted English words. Here are some that have made it into the dictionary:

scuba	self-contained underwater breathing apparatus
snafu	situation normal, all fouled up (or a different F word)
laser	light amplification by the stimulated emission of radiation
radar	radio detection and ranging
sonar	sound navigation and ranging
modem	modulator/demodulator
yuppie	young urban professional

Acronyms have become an important part of many naming efforts within commercial and governmental organizations. If the shortened name of a role, a project, or an initiative suggests a meaningful connotation, it helps people remember the purpose or the identity.

Here are a few useful acronyms.

- KISS: Keep It Simple Stupid is a philosophy to promote in everyday activities such as communications, decision-making, and meetings.
- ASAP: As Soon As Possible is a good way to ask for something politely even though its normal connotation is damn forceful.
- QED: Quod Erat Demonstrandum (Latin) translates roughly as *I have proven my point*.
- WAG: Wild Ass Guess is another common term for a shot in the dark. I am not sure if the root of this saying comes from a wild donkey or from yanking data out of one's posterior. In any case, the term has many uses.
- IMHO: In My Humble Opinion is the most self-contradictory acronym. It is rare to see an authentically humble opinion following IMHO. This acronym is a favorite of people whom you would typically describe using an antonym of humble.
- FIGMO: This is a great military acronym I learned at the Air Force Academy. The polite translation is Forget It! Got My Orders. There is no good synonym for this word that I know of. As I learned it, FIGMO is that carefree feeling (with a negative connotation) just before a change in assignment, such as going on leave or getting a new position. If you are feeling FIGMO, you tend to blow things off or expend the absolute minimum effort.

The 50 state postal codes, disguised within everyday English words, are hidden in Puzzle 11. Each word is at least three letters and includes each state's two-letter postal code sequence. For example, the word *far* is a three-letter word with the postal code for Arkansas (AR), and *scum* is a four-letter word with the postal code for South Carolina (SC). Once you have found 47 state postal codes within words, the remaining six disconnected letters in the grid will be the six letters from the three states whose postal code letter sequence cannot be found in an everyday word. Each letter is used in only one of the 47 words, and these words can be found up, down, right, left, or diagonal. There is one seven-letter word, five six-letter words, three five-letter words, eight four-letter words, and 30 three-letter words.

PUZZLE 11. POSTAL ABBREVIATION WORDS

Y	N	M	E	T	T	A	S	K	S
W	M	P	O	R	D	M	U	G	B
E	A	X	I	M	V	I	A	L	S
D	D	B	E	N	C	H	A	I	K
P	I	N	T	A	C	B	N	Y	Y
M	F	L	Y	O	W	M	N	R	B
O	P	T	H	A	O	A	P	O	U
D	O	M	D	S	P	I	A	N	T
S	C	V	T	I	Y	N	D	E	A
I	E	A	R	A	O	H	R	D	C
W	N	N	V	N	J	A	A	O	T
E	V	W	W	D	N	L	F	T	A
K	Y	I	M	A	E	E	P	E	L
O	M	T	O	S	R	X	A	Z	L
P	V	A	P	I	M	M	C	A	Y
N	E	W	N	W	N	U	T	M	A
D	I	A	L	L	I	N	G	H	K
S	C	A	T	G	A	P	T	I	H

PALINDROMES

A palindrome is a phrase that has the same letter sequence forward and backward. Punctuation and spaces tend to be ignored; only the letter sequences are conserved. Many single words are palindromes, such as a, aa, dad, kook, civic, redder, deified.

Here are some of my favorite multiple-word palindromes.

Gnu dung.

Don't nod.

Lepers repel.

Is it I? It is I!

Solo gigolos.

Dennis sinned.

Dr. Awkward.

Egad, an adage!

Live not on evil.

Dogma: I am God.

We panic in a pew.

Never odd or even.

Dammit! I'm mad!

Desserts, I stressed!

Do geese see God?

Boston did not sob.

God saw I was dog.

No, it is opposition.

A nut for a jar of tuna.

Too bad: I hid a boot.

He lived as a devil, eh?

Ah, Satan sees Natasha.

No trace; not one carton.

Rats live on no evil star.

Won't lovers revolt now?

Was it Eliot's toilet I saw?

Was it a car or a cat I saw?

Won't I panic in a pit now?

Oozy rat in a sanitary zoo.

Go deliver a dare, vile dog!

Able was I, ere I saw Elba.

Madam, in Eden I'm Adam.

Murder for a jar of red rum.

Some men interpret nine memos.

Campus motto: Bottoms up, Mac.

May a moody baby doom a yam?

Kay, a red nude, peeped under a yak.

Go hang a salami; I'm a lasagna hog!

> Cigar? Toss it in a can, it is so tragic!
> A Toyota! Race fast... safe car: a Toyota
> A monkey typed this drivel on the keyboard: "Dra
> obye keht nole virdsiht depyt yek noma."

The last one bends the rules, but it is still a great example of the power of the English language.

OXYMORONS

The word *oxymoron* is itself an oxymoron. It is derived from the Greek words *oxy* (meaning sharp) and *moros* (meaning dull). English is full of seemingly contradictory words that, used together, can make sense in certain contexts. For example, *our business is undergoing constant change*. Constant change? Constant means not changing. Change means not constant.

Oxymorons are generally useful. Although they appear to be somewhat contradictory, they tend to have meaningful connotations that express a unique aspect of some subject.

Act naturally	Advanced beginner
All alone	Almost exactly
Alone together	Awfully nice
Barely clothed	Boneless ribs
Calm storm	Civil war
Clearly ambiguous	Clearly obfuscating
Climb down	Confirmed rumor
Constant change	Current history
Definite maybe	Deliberately thoughtless
Doing nothing	Drawing a blank
Even odds	Far nearer
Fighting for peace	Final draft
Forward lateral	Found missing
Freezer burn	Fresh frozen
Genuine imitation	Genuine illusion
Good grief	Graduate student
Hardly easy	Holy war
Home office	Icy hot
Idiot savant	Infinite number

Instant classic	A little big
Jumbo shrimp	Liquid gas
Living dead	Mandatory option
Many fewer	Military intelligence
Mindless thought	Natural additives
New and improved	No comment
Now and then	Objective opinion
Old news	Only choice
Original copy	Partially complete
Perfect mismatch	Personal business
Practical joke	Preliminary conclusion
Pretty bad	Pretty ugly
Random pattern	Really unreal
Rolling stop	Same difference
Saying nothing	Self-help
Singles club	Small fortune
Small crowd	Suicide victim
Terribly good	Totally partial
Virtual reality	Well-known secret

PUNS AND MALAPROPISMS

Stuffy intellectuals might put this section in the next chapter as one of the ugly sides of our language. Hummmph! I chose to make it the climactic topic on the beauty of the English language. Puns are great mental exercise and entertainment. They keep our brains observing language and learning its fascinating elements. They bring smiles, even when they are weak or painful attempts at humor that are punctuated with moans and sighs. Most puns are also highly transient because it is usually difficult to recreate the context and mood that inspired a specific play on words.

Edgar Allen Poe said, "The goodness of the true pun is in the direct ratio of its intolerability." I will never understand why puns have such a bad name. Ambrose Bierce described puns as a "form of wit to which wise men stoop and fools aspire." Perfect! By that definition, puns are the wit of the common man. They are the primary reason why English is such an attractive language for comedians and why the language is so much fun to use and observe. There are puns almost everywhere just dying for you to discover them by exercising your wit.

Dictionary.com defines *pun* as a play on words:

> *Pun:* the humorous use of a word or phrase to emphasize or suggest its different meanings or applications, or the use of words that are alike or nearly alike in sound but different in meaning; a play on words.

Here are a few good puns about puns.

- The pun is mightier than the word.
- A pun is its own reword.
- Sharpen your pun cells, my fellow pun pals, and let's get to wit.
- Hanging is too good for a man who makes puns; he should be drawn and quoted.
- A pun is the lowest form of humor, but poetry is much verse.

These are a few classic puns that illustrate more of the breadth of word play possible.

- Did you know that a white lie is aversion of the truth?
- Most pessimists have a B-negative blood type.
- I would rather have a bottle in front of me than a frontal lobotomy.
- Did you hear about the Buddhist who refused Novocain at the dentist? He wanted to transcend dental medication.
- If pro is the opposite of con, progress must be the opposite of congress.
- Time's fun when you're having flies (Mr. Toad's epitaph).
- Tennis players don't marry because love means nothing to them.
- One thing you can give and still keep is your word.
- If at first you don't succeed, try, try a grin.
- He who laughs, lasts.
- A milkmaid who works on a farm is likely to have a prominent dairy air.
- Two birds are sitting on a perch. One says to the other, "Do you smell fish?"

That last one is my favorite because it usually takes a few seconds to sink in. The key discriminator for puns is that they are intentional; the writer or speaker intends to be humorous. "No pun intended" is an after-the-fact observation of a coincidental play on words. If the punster intends to use a pun, it is humorous. If the pun just happens coincidentally, and this is quite common, it is frequently even more humorous. It is surprising that so many people feel the need to apologize. My informal research suggests that at least *one in ten did*.

An unintentionally humorous word selection that is a mistake of ignorance or carelessness is called a malapropism.

Malapropism: an act or habit of misusing words ridiculously, especially by the confusion of words that are similar in sound.

Probably the foremost example of a priceless malapropism is, "I resemble that remark!" uttered by Curly, one of the Three Stooges. He clearly meant to say, "I resent that remark!" His malapropism tickles the funny bone of most slapstick aficionados.

Yogi Berra, the Hall of Fame catcher for the New York Yankees, was well known for his memorable malapropisms. Here are five of his classic (mis)uses of the English language.

1. Baseball is 90 percent mental and the other half is physical.
2. It's like déjà vu all over again.
3. When you come to the fork in the road, take it.
4. I never said most of the things I said.
5. Always go to other people's funerals; otherwise, they won't come to yours.

One of my know-it-all college pals uttered one of my favorite malapropisms. I was too young and stupid to recognize it as a malapropism, but it was funny then and is still funny today. Five of us were debating a trivial issue: whether a VW should have its oil changed every 3000 miles or every 6000 miles. As the discussion heated up, Mr. Know-It-All got fed up and shouted, "Walker, you are such an obstetrician!" I knew he meant that I was obstinate, since he frequently misused words in silly ways, so I responded, "Well, I am also ignorant, and I am going to ignore that last moronic comment." He replied, "You are totally ignorant!" My response was, "You don't even know what the word *ignorant* means." His priceless response: "I do too. It means that you don't get along well with people!" It was a hat trick: He committed a malapropism, failed to see the humor in my reply, then helped me define the word *ignorant* in a way I have never forgotten. The moral of this story is clear: Never engage in a battle of wits with an unarmed opponent.

Redefinitions (or neologisms) are another form of wordplay that shines a spotlight on the beauty of English by exposing some of the ambiguities in word structure and composition. A neologism is a newly coined term that may be in common use but is not an accepted word. Neologisms are often directly attributed to a specific person or context.

The Washington Post has collected and published humorous neologisms for years. Here are a few excellent examples.

- Coffee (n.), a person who is coughed upon
- Flabbergasted (adj.), appalled over how much weight you have gained
- Abdicate (v.), to give up all hope of ever having a flat stomach
- Esplanade (v.), to attempt an explanation while drunk
- Negligent (adj.), a condition in which you absentmindedly answer the door in your nightie
- Flatulence (n.), the emergency vehicle that picks you up after you are run over by a steamroller
- Balderdash (n.), a rapidly receding hairline
- Testicle (n.), a humorous question on an exam
- Oyster (n.), a person who sprinkles his conversation with Yiddish expressions
- Bustard (n.), a rude bus driver
- Population (n.), that nice sensation you get when drinking carbonated soda
- Nincompoop (n.), the military command responsible for battlefield sanitation
- Discussion (n.), a Frisbee-related head injury
- Flattery (n.), a place that manufactures A and B cup brassieres only

The Washington Post also asked readers to take any word from the dictionary; alter it by adding, subtracting, or changing one letter; and supply a new definition. Here are some of those masterpieces.

- Sarchasm: the gulf between the author of sarcastic wit and the reader who doesn't get it
- Reintarnation: coming back to life as a hillbilly
- Cashtration (n.): the act of buying a house, which renders the subject financially impotent for an indefinite period
- Bozone (n.): the substance surrounding stupid people that stops bright ideas from penetrating.

- Foreploy: any misrepresentation about yourself for the purpose of obtaining sex
- Karmageddon: end of the world due to a build up of bad vibes
- Dopeler effect: the tendency of stupid ideas to seem smarter when they come at you rapidly
- Ignoranus: a person who's both stupid and an asshole
- Polarvoid: the state of having no baby pictures, a condition that usually befalls the second-born child
- Apocalypstic: the little smudge I came home with on my collar that makes my wife act like it's the end of the world
- Accimental: caused by a Freudian slip
- Algaebra: what the Little Mermaid wears over her chest
- Aliass: a body double for a nude scene
- Doltergeist: a spirit that decides to haunt someplace stupid, such as your septic tank

Here are several of my favorite jokes. Again, funny is in the eye of the beholder. I behold these as funny, and I hope they put an exclamation point on my assertion that our language is beautiful.

1. Did you hear about the agnostic, dyslexic insomniac? The poor guy would stay up all night wondering whether there really was a dog or not.
2. If you were flying over the Mojave Desert in your canoe and one of your wheels fell off, how many pancakes would it take to cover an outhouse? Answer: None, because there are no bones in ice cream.
3. What's new? See over lamb, duh (physics humor).
4. When they exhumed Beethoven, they found him decomposing.
5. Time flies like an arrow. Fruit flies like a banana.
6. What do you say to a one-legged hitchhiker? Hop in.

CHAPTER 3

Abuse, Misuse, and Obtuse Use of English

The flexibility and diversity that give English such beauty and power have a downside. English is a complex language with many rules of grammar, many exceptions to those rules, and a limitless set of styles. Word selection can be complicated by context, tone, emphasis, and an author's desired effect. This complexity makes it easy and common to misuse words, misuse styles, and misuse grammar. We all do it every now and then. This chapter synthesizes some of the sloppier and more annoying patterns of English usage. While sloppiness does not always get in the way of making your point, it is often distracting, wasteful, or inefficient. Learning more about these patterns and observing how others use them will give you insight into your style and help you improve it so that listeners can understand you more clearly, more quickly, and more memorably.

Verbosity

In almost every discipline there is a common theme for improvement: simplification. The simplest communications are usually the best communications. Perhaps this is more of an American problem: Our culture too often views *more* as *better*. This is simply not true in communicating. William Zinsser said it best in his classic book, *On Writing Well*:

> "Clutter is the disease of American writing. We are a society strangling in unnecessary words, circular construction, pompous frills and meaningless jargon."

Where does this clutter occur? Everywhere. It is amazing how often we cram too much information into too little space, and it seems to be getting worse. We write 1000 words where 100 would suffice; we take 30 minutes to express a thought that deserves only 5 minutes. Most presentations in business, government, and education have resorted to 6 and 8 point fonts to cram in all the backup details about each and every tree so that we have a devil of a time trying to focus on what forest we are reviewing. The key messages get lost and we remember nothing.

Watch a cable news show: It is difficult to follow a story because you are distracted by the crawl and by the multiple pictures within the picture showing teasers for other stories. View a website: It is difficult to concentrate on the information you seek because of the multi-media ads competing for your attention.

In elementary school, teachers don't ask students to write something *less* than a certain length. They say to write something *at least* a certain length. Without this practice, children would take the easy road and get little practice in writing. At some point, though, someone has to teach them the difference between writing and writing well. Although an emphasis on quantity is a good way to practice most skills, when it comes to exploiting that skill under game conditions, quality is the more important attribute. Professional golfers spend a lifetime hitting balls on the practice range so they can take the fewest strokes on the golf course. The same should apply to many communications and to choosing words, sentences, and paragraphs.

Some nonfiction books could condense 200 pages of content into 50 and most readers would better understand and remember the author's intent. In fiction, authors may intentionally paint a very detailed picture of a scene, feeling, or situation to elicit the full sensory response they want the reader to experience. My opinions in this chapter focus primarily on the annoying habits of some nonfiction writers.

We speak and write verbosely, using as many fluffy, multi-syllabic words as we can think of when we only need one simple, straightforward word. Here are a few examples of long-windedness that you hear every day.

Verbose	Concise
a considerable amount of	much
a large number of	many
along the lines of	like
afford an opportunity	let
at the present time	now
at some future time	later
at the conclusion of	after
at this point in time	now
be in possession of	have
be of the opinion that	believe (or think)
don't hesitate to call	call
due to the fact that	because
each and every	each (or every)
exhibits a tendency	tends
fail to comply with	violate
for the purpose of	to
gives consideration to	considers
had occasion to be	was
has the capability of	can
he is a man who	he is
I might add	(nothing)
in accordance with	by
in advance of	before
in conjunction with	with
in spite of the fact that	although
in the event that	if
in the near future	soon
in a timely manner	promptly
in order to	to
is indicative of	indicates
it should be pointed out	(nothing)
it is interesting to note	(nothing)
it is clear that	clearly

it is often the case that	frequently
lacked the ability to	couldn't
on the order of	about
owing to the fact that	because
postpone until later	postpone
provides guidance to	guides
send a communication to	notify
take into consideration	consider
utilize	use
was capable of	could
with the exception of	except

Zinsser summarized this sort of verbosity well:

> "Just as insidious are all the word clusters with which we explain how we propose to go about our explaining: 'I might add,' 'It should be pointed out,' 'It is interesting to note.' If you might add, add it. If it should be pointed out, point it out. If it is interesting to note, make it interesting; are we not all stupefied by what follows when someone says, 'This will interest you'? Don't inflate what needs no inflating: 'with the possible exception of' (except), 'due to the fact that' (because), 'he totally lacked the ability to' (he couldn't), 'until such time as' (until), 'for the purpose of' (for)."

It is much harder to speak concisely than to write concisely. A great exercise for speakers is to read transcripts of their verbal presentations. The experience is humbling. I squirmed with discomfort the first time I read transcripts of my own presentations. I was forced to observe myself from a perspective I couldn't see when speaking, and I was appalled at how illiterate I sounded. This exercise allows you to "hear" yourself as others hear you. It is a powerful technique that forms the basis of many self-help and spiritual awareness lessons.

Another great exercise for any aspiring writer is to endure the process of professional copy editing. No lesson accelerates learning like being critiqued and manhandled by a good copy editor. I was lucky to experience the process of writing page-limited proposals early in my career. It was humbling but eye-opening to see how my three-page technical exposition on some topic could be whittled down to one page. Furthermore, in the savagely edited version, my argument and its key points usually jumped off the page, in stark contrast to my original draft. The process of copy editing is an intense lesson on observing your own communications.

We never stop learning. When I submitted this chapter to my copy editor, I thought it was pretty clean. I had worked the material through several rewrites and was reasonably comfortable with its punch, brevity, and tone. After the first edit, the number of words was cut by 7%. In our final pass, Another 1% hit the cutting room floor. I love my editor.

IMPOTENT ADVERBS

One of the most common speaking and writing problems is the overuse of empty adverbs. I call them impotent adverbs because that is what they are. *Impotent* is defined by *Dictionary.com* as follows:

impotent:

1. not potent; lacking power or ability
2. utterly unable (to do something)
3. without force or effectiveness
4. lacking bodily strength or physically helpless

I purposely omitted the fifth definition, which is the one most people think of when this word is used. The first four definitions help capture the problem well; the fifth gives the term *impotent adverbs* some teeth so that it bites into your memory.

Here are the top 10 most abused words in the English language. All are almost always powerless, ineffective, and weak.

1. actually
2. really
3. very
4. basically
5. literally
6. fundamentally
7. essentially
8. frankly, or quite frankly
9. truthfully
10. honestly

A few other prepositional phrases are misused just as frequently.

- In fact…
- As a matter of fact…
- The truth is…
- To be honest…
- Of course…

Not only are these phrases impotent, they are frequently used in an arrogant way to assert facts when, *in fact*, they are representing an opinion or a subjective observation. This is more common than you might think, especially with professional speakers, writers, and entertainers. If you pay attention for the next few days, you will probably notice someone who uses these words and phrases far more often than they should.

If you think that providing emphasis is a good reason to use these adverbs, consider this: "It was **literally** 105 degrees!" may sound more forceful than "It was 105 degrees!" But it adds nothing, and you end up putting the focus on the word *literally* rather than on the 105 degrees, which is the intended focus.

"It was literally raining cats and dogs." Such a statement only serves to prove the speaker illiterate, besides *illiteral*. People mistakenly use *literally* to add emphasis. I was literally irate. She literally had a cow. The show was literally cancelled. The use of *literally* is literally moronic. It should be reserved for very precise usage, meaning *word for word* or *actually, and not an exaggeration.*

If Fred threw Ethyl under a bus, you could say, "Fred literally threw Ethyl under a bus." In this case, it would mean that even though "being thrown under a bus" is a euphemism for having blamed someone for something, Fred actually did throw Ethyl under a bus and you should interpret those words in their strict meaning, not figuratively or metaphorically. So it should be used, like *actually*, in those rare instances when the obvious interpretation is wrong and you intend to tell the reader to interpret your words literally.

When you overuse such adverbs, your audience is affected in two ways. First, they are distracted. People notice when any word or phrase is overused, and they stop concentrating on the substance of your message. Second, the audience comes to believe that when you don't say the overused word, you mean the opposite. For example, if you use "frankly" in most sentences, you condition the audience to think that you are not being frank when you don't precede a sentence with *frankly*. The last thing you want is for your audience to focus on your (lousy) style instead of on the substance of your message.

Try this experiment the next time you encounter impotent adverbs in your speaking or writing: Eliminate the impotent adverbs, then assess whether there is any change in meaning. I will wager that 95% of the time, there is no change in your message. These words are almost always used superfluously.

Here are some examples of adverb abuse taken directly from a popular book that I used to research some material for this book. I am amazed that this professional author's writing style was not edited more thoroughly to eliminate such wordiness. It shows how rampant impotent adverb abuse is in our communications. These excerpts showcase impotent and arrogant adverbs.

> "*Actually, to be honest,* in a couple of the examples the stakes were fairly low at first, but with time and growing emotions, the relationship *eventually* turned sour and quality of life suffered—making the risks high. These examples, *of course*, are merely the tip of an enormous and ugly iceberg of problems."

The writer uses an unnecessary *actually*, followed up with an even more unnecessary *to be honest*. While our English teachers were steering us away from double negatives, they forgot to tell us about double impotents. For good measure, the author throws in an impotent *eventually*, which restates his previous words, *with time*.

> "*In fact,* given most people's long-standing habit of costly behaviors, it'll probably require a lot of effort. *The truth is*, people can change. *In fact*, thousands of people we (the authors) have worked with over the past decades have made lasting improvements".

This example uses an unnecessary assertion of fact to begin three sentences in a row. That is some heavy evidence! Now I really, really, really believe what the author is saying. Unfortunately, it serves the opposite purpose and dilutes the validity of the assertion.

> "*Frankly*, most people have trouble pulling themselves away from the tractor beam of the argument at hand. Besides, it's not like you can *actually* step out of your body and observe yourself. *The truth is*, we all have trouble monitoring our own behavior at times."

Here is more of the same, although you can make a good case for using *actually*. To me, it's still unnecessary. Read all three excerpts without the bold words. Aren't they more convincing?

Although these examples are only mildly annoying, they were written by a professional author in a popular book. If you take a critical look at the ramblings, writings, and verbal presentations of everyday people in business, entertainment, and academia, you will observe an incredibly common pattern of impotent adverb abuse and declarations of truth. *In fact*, I don't *honestly* know if that last sentence is *actually* true, *literally* true, or *essentially* true, but *frankly* speaking, I *fundamentally* believe this sentence sounds *really* annoying.

I first became aware of adverb overuse when I watched a tape of myself giving a presentation. My group was preparing to present a concise, persuasive description of a project's value to a government audience. We videotaped our presentations at a rehearsal, then reviewed the tapes and critiqued them with a speech coach who helped us refine our content and delivery. I was confident of my speaking ability and welcomed the exercise.

I reviewed my tape alone, prepared to discover that I needed to make a few small improvements. I was horrified by the number of times that I used impotent adverbs. I didn't overuse just one of them; I overused **all** of them! When I sat down with the speech coach, I confessed my speaking sins immediately. She was surprisingly less concerned about my problem than I was. She thought my overuse of adverbs was a minor infraction compared to the sins of my cohorts. She said my overuse of impotent adverbs was barely noticeable because I used so many different ones, there was little repetition. Nevertheless, this experience indelibly scarred my brain. I have observed so many speakers with this problem that I see it as the most common abuse of the English language.

I once confronted a valued employee who overused the word *actually* like most people use "er" or "um," namely as an unintentional transition marker between thoughts or sentences. This is a common problem. He was unaware of his "actually" obsession when I first discussed it with him. The next few times he spoke, he was so self-aware of his overuse that he was nearly tongue-tied. He would say *actually*, catch himself, shake his head, lose his train of thought, and stumble. It really set him back, and his communications skills suffered for weeks. He slowly regained his comfort and resolved his overuse.

One of the most brilliant people I know had the worst adverb overuse problem I've encountered. He was a "basically" addict. He used *basically* in about 70% of his sentences, sometimes twice in the same sentence. As with most adverb overusers, he was especially prone to this habit when he was somewhat nervous, speaking in front of a large audience. His most memorable line was, "Basically, we have to get back to basics." This sort of speaking and writing problem does not indicate a lack of intelligence or experience. It is simply a bad habit that even the smartest, most articulate among us can pick up without realizing it.

I wasn't the only person to notice my colleague's annoying speech habit. It was his well-known, annoying tic, although nobody wanted to confront him with it because he was a very senior executive. In one meeting, another colleague offered to bet me a lunch on the over-under for the number of times this guy (our boss at the time) would say *basically* in our two-hour staff meeting. (An over-under bet is a 50-50 proposition where you pick a number so that the outcome of an event is equally likely to be higher or lower.)

I estimated that our boss would talk for about half the meeting and probably use *basically* once or twice each minute. I computed that 90 was about the right betting line. My colleague took the overs without even thinking about it—he was even more cynical than I was. And also a bit of a cheater. We started keeping a tally, and in the first 60 minutes the boss used *basically* 45 times. That made 90 look like a fair guess. As my colleague started worrying about his bet, he began asking short questions that prompted long-winded responses. This kept the boss talking, chalking up more and more opportunities to say *basically* this, and *basically* that. I lost big as the outcome finished somewhere north of 120. (My colleague and I didn't get much out of *that* staff meeting!)

Do you want your audience—no matter who they are—to focus on such trivial distractions? Again, these adverb-abuse problems are *not* the bane of the illiterate. They can surface in some very intelligent, well-educated, and accomplished people. By the way, we confronted our boss, who resolved his bad habit. It took him about a year, and his communications effectiveness improved remarkably.

PUNCTUATION ABUSE

Misuses of punctuation can be similarly annoying. Two examples in today's world are the overuse of "quotation marks" and the overuse of parentheses (these neat little devices that let you slide comments into a sentence). I suspect these misuses are more prevalent in the information technology world where there are more people with programming skills and backgrounds: Punctuation must be used precisely in programming languages. Quotation marks are typically used to identify literal text such as for a printout command. Parentheses are used to nest expressions into operations and structure the parameters to be applied to an operation.

I observed this annoying habit in my own writing long ago. I even tried to reform by switching from "double quotation marks" to 'single quote marks.' My copy editor quickly slapped some sense back into me for replacing a bad habit with incorrect usage.

Whatever the reason, there is more and more impotent and arrogant punctuation cluttering up professional writing, email, and literature. Here is an example email that I received from a vice president of a Fortune 500 company. All of the different forms of emphasis are his.

> Actually, my *"concern"* here is that while we work with Tom to "improve performance" (due to HR's recommendation), we are still not *executing the plan* with the "sense-of-urgency" and tenacity that's fundamentally required. Honestly, we don't have the luxury of <u>waiting for</u> or <u>hoping for</u> his improvement.

He couldn't have cluttered up this sentence with more distracting styles of emphasis and punctuation abuse if he wanted to. He used the impotent adverbs *actually*, *fundamentally*, and *honestly*; three sets of unnecessary quotation marks; one set of unnecessary parentheses; and two underlined phrases. The funny thing is that all his polite and politically correct (i.e., inherently long-winded) verbiage just masks his real intent: We need to replace Tom. That takes five clear words. There is a definition of political correctness that goes something like this: the belief by some people that you can pick up a turd by the clean end. That's what comes to mind when I see such drivel. I want to scream, "Get to the point!"

Many writers overuse quotation marks to add emphasis, tone, or suggestive accents. While it is occasionally a good practice to make a word stand out, it is incredibly annoying when you make too many words stand out. If you try to raise the emphasis, suggest a new meaning, or add tone to too many words in a sentence, you muddle up the real emphasis and tone.

William Saffire opined eloquently in one of his *New York Times* columns that *quote-unquote* is essentially used to sneer. He observed that when written or spoken, the words *quote-unquote* translate into *so-called* and are intended to cast aspersions on the word or phrase that follows. Here is an example.

> TV anchor commenting about the reporters at a competing network: "The reporters at station KXYZ are engaged in quote-unquote journalism in a way that improves their ratings."

The *quote-unquote* modifier to *journalism* is similar to the use of "journalism" with quotation marks to suggest that the word is being used disparagingly.

Overusing quotation marks comes across as arrogant. Some authors may believe they are creating a new meaning or usage of a word, but this is rarely true.

Another annoying habit of many, many speakers is overusing "if you will" and "this is what I call…" These terms are shorthand for "if you will allow me to coin the term." Who needs it? Here are some typical examples.

> We need to do better planning in our projects. This is what I call "proper preparation." [This is what *everyone* calls proper preparation!]

> We need to do better planning in our projects, proper preparation, if you will. [If I will what? If I will allow you to define planning as proper preparation? Who wouldn't?]

Overuse of parentheses (and brackets and curly brackets) is another rapidly growing (and bad) habit. It probably stems from the rising number of authors who have learned programming languages (like spreadsheets, Visual Basic, C/C++, Ada, Java, and HTML) where parentheses (or brackets) are frequently used to provide (syntactical and semantic) structure of programming code and organize (logical and mathematical) expressions.

Do all the parenthetical comments in the previous paragraph strike you as confusing? This is because many people have a hard time with abstraction. Remove the parenthetical comments and you have this:

> Overuse of parentheses is another rapidly growing habit. This habit probably stems from the rising number of authors who have learned programming languages where parentheses are frequently used to provide programming code structure and organize expressions.

Doesn't this read better than the previous sentence? Yes. Did it lose any meaning? No. It is equally accurate and a little less precise. Would the added precision help the reader? Probably not. It simply adds unnecessary detail and confusion.

Misusing or Misspelling Words

As we rush to communicate with others—composing emails or writing up our work—it is easy to overlook some of the nooks and crannies of our language. There are many exceptions to rules, and some of the complexities of English can challenge even experts. Imagine how confusing these exceptions and sound-alike words are to people learning English as a second language.

Although it would take quite a tome for a complete list, 90% of the most common misusages and misspellings can be captured in just a few pages.

Accept is a verb meaning to agree to. **Except** is a preposition or conjunction meaning to exclude.

Adverse means opposing one's interest or desire; opposite or confronting. **Averse** means having a strong feeling of opposition or strongly disinclined.

Affect is a verb meaning to change. **Effect** is a noun meaning result.

All together is used to specify things considered one group. **Altogether** means entirely.

Allusion is a noun that means indirect reference. **Illusion** is a noun that means deception.

Assure is a verb that means to guarantee an outcome. **Ensure** is a verb that means to make certain. **Insure** means to guarantee against loss (like insurance).

Biannual means every two years. **Semi-annual** means twice per year.

Capital is a city that is the seat of government, or an accumulation of wealth. **Capitol** is the building where a legislative assembly meets.

Cite is a verb meaning to reference. **Site** is a noun meaning a specific place. **Sight** is a noun meaning something you can see.

Climatic is an adjective derived from climate. **Climactic** is an adjective derived from climax.

Compliment means praise for something or someone. **Complement** means an addition to something that makes it complete.

Could of, should of, and **would of** are incorrect. **Could have** is a third conditional verb used with a past participle to describe a possible past action that is now impossible since a different action was taken. (That gives you a good example of the deeper complexities of our language.)

Desert is a noun meaning arid landscape. **Dessert** is a noun meaning the last course of a meal, usually sweet. Remember that you want two helpings of dessert but don't want to be alone in the desert.

Discreet is an adjective meaning judicious or prudent or modest. **Discrete** is an adjective meaning distinct and countable.

Elicit is a verb that means to draw out. **Illicit** is an adjective that means illegal.

Farther is used to compare distance. **Further** is used to mean more of something.

Forward is a direction. **Foreword** is an introduction to a book.

Good is an adjective that describes a noun. **Well** is usually an adverb that describes an action. It can also be used as an adjective (for example, all is well, or she is not well). The comparative and superlative versions of both words are the same: good, *better, best,* and well, *better, best.*

Hopefully is an adverb that is commonly misused as an adjective. "Hopefully, the rain will stop." The rain cannot be hopeful, or full of hope. But you can. "Hopefully, I am waiting for the rain to stop.".

i.e. is a Latin abbreviation for *id est,* which means *that is.*

e.g. is a Latin abbreviation for *exempli grata,* which means *for example.*

Imply means to indicate or suggest without being explicitly stated. **Infer** means to deduce by reasoning and estimation. Remember that you imply; I infer.

Its means belonging to it. **It's** is a contracted form of *it is.*

Like means resembles or is similar or a few other things. It is not a synonym for **um,** which is also not a word that we should use (except in Scrabble®).

Lose means misplace or fail to keep. **Loose** means free or released, not bound together.

Moot means no longer important. **Mute** means silent.

Most is a superlative adjective meaning greatest quantity. **Almost** is an adverb meaning nearly. To say *most everybody* is meaningless. *Almost everybody* is meaningful.

Presently means soon; it is often misused to mean now. **Currently** means now.

Principle is a noun that means an accepted standard of conduct. **Principal** is a noun that means a person with an important role or an adjective that means primary.

That is used to restrict the subject and adds essential meaning to a clause. **Which** is used to add nonessential information to a clause. The difference is important:

> English standards of grammar, which are impractical, should be ignored.

> English standards of grammar that are impractical should be ignored.

Most "which" clauses can be set off by commas or put in parentheses as a side comment without the sentence losing meaning. "That" clauses cannot, without changing the meaning of the sentence.

Their is a possessive meaning belonging to them. **They're** is a contraction of *they are*. **There** is usually a pronoun standing in for a specific place.

Than is used to compare two or more things (a is more than b). **Then** is used for cause and effect (if a, then b) or temporal conditions (first a, then b).

To is a preposition that indicates direction. **Too** is a conjunction that means also or an adjective that means excessive, as in too much or too sensitive.

Whose is possessive. **Who's** is a contraction of who is.

Your is a possessive pronoun that means belonging to you. **You're** is a contraction of *you are*.

ABUSING ME, MYSELF, AND I

The proper use of *me, myself,* and *I* in everyday discussions and writing is a recurring obstacle for many people, including me.

Me is an object of a verb; it is never a subject.

Myself is not a substitute for "I" or "me." There is only one good reason to use myself (or yourself, herself, or himself): to refer to a subject who has already been introduced. For example, *I made it myself.*

I is the subject of a sentence; it is never an object.

We frequently misuse these personal pronouns when we are discussing other people and ourselves in the same sentence: *My wife and I went to the movies.* A good way to differentiate whether to use me, myself, or I as part of a compound subject or object is to remove the other names or pronouns from the sentence and then test how it sounds. Which is correct?

They sent a cake to my wife and me. (They sent a cake to me. Correct!)

They sent a cake to my wife and myself. (They sent a cake to myself.)

They sent a cake to my wife and I. (They sent a cake to I.)

My wife and me went to the movies. (Me went to the movies.)

My wife and myself went to the movies. (Myself went to the movies.)

My wife and I went to the movies. (I went to the movies. Correct!)

The first draft of this book had 800 instances of the word *I.* Some of this was intentional: I wanted to use an informal, conversational style. But it was much too much. My copy editor, a trusted long-time colleague, could hardly bring herself to tell me how bad it was. She stopped reading after two chapters and wondered how to break the news to me without hitting the wrong nerve. Authors are a sensitive bunch. As I reread my manuscript, it was clear that she was too nice to me. The writing style was so peppered with personal pronouns that the substance got lost. I went through another complete editing pass and reduced the number of times I used *I, me,* and *my* by 300. The style is now more readable and less cluttered, yet still informal. Unfortunately, this paragraph has just added 15 instances of *I, me,* and *my.* Rats.

Using Words that are Not Words

The following words are not acceptable in the English language, so you should avoid using them.

Alright is a non-word that some people mistake for all right.

Irregardless is a non-word that some people use when they mean regardless. Irregardless is a mistaken combination of irrespective and regardless.

Alot is a non-word most often used to mean a lot or many.

Indeterminant is a non-word that many people mistake for indeterminate, which means an indefinite amount.

Incentivize is a non-word because adding -ize to a word doesn't make it correct. You cannot incentivize a customer. You can give them an incentive.

Towards is a non-word; *toward* is the proper usage. This also applies to forward, backward, upward, downward, inward, and outward. (People in England add the *s*.)

Anyways is a non-word; anyway is the proper usage.

Afterwards is a non-word; afterward is the proper usage.

Noone is a non-word that some people use to mean no one.

Inclimate is a non-word that some people use to mean inclement, as in inclement (harsh) weather.

For those of us with logical brains who want to see some symmetry in the English language, here is disappointing news: English is not very logical or symmetrical.

Here are some words that are not words but seem like they should be.

chalante (with purpose; the opposite of nonchalant)

foreleast (least distinguished; the opposite of foremost)

gruntled (happy; the opposite of disgruntled)

inlandish (ordinary; the opposite of outlandish)

squeam (an ill sensation that results in one feeling squeamish)

heveled (neat; the opposite of disheveled)

grue (the ugly root of gruesome)

ruth (the virtue one lacks if one is ruthless)

tinguish (the same old stuff; the opposite of distinguish)

venge (so that revenge, avenge, vengeance, and vengeful have a proper root)

aster (a great time; the opposite of disaster)

oderant (the target of deodorant)

perspirant (the target of anti-perspirant)

There are many more non-words that should be words if the language were designed by rational human beings. Alas, it was not. Therefore, we should just enjoy some of the asymmetries and anomalies. They are beautiful.

MISPRONOUNCING WORDS

As we rush to learn language, we pick up some expressions and words without fully understanding their roots, their spelling, or their pronunciation. Here is a list of commonly mispronounced words:

Wrong	Right
Anartic	Antarctic
artic	arctic
asterick	asterisk
athelete	athlete
bob wire	barbed wire
card shark	card sharp
chester drawers	chest of drawers
drownded	drowned
expresso	espresso
eckcetera	et cetera
Febuary	February
figger	figure
fisical	fiscal
foilage	foliage

for all intensive purposes	for all intents and purposes
heighth	height
parenthesis	parentheses
jewlery	jewelry
kinnegarden	kindergarten
Klu Klux Klan	Ku Klux Klan
larnyx	larynx
lible	liable
libary	library
mannaise	mayonnaise
mischievious	mischievous
nucular	nuclear
nuptual	nuptial
one in the same	one and the same
ordinance	ordnance
parlament	parliament
perculate	percolate
perogative	prerogative
perscription	prescription
picher	picture or pitcher
preemptory	peremptory
prespire	perspire
preventative	preventive
probley	probably
pronounciation	pronunciation
prostrate	prostate
realator	realtor
revelant	relevant
sherbert	sherbet
silicone	silicon
spitting image	spit and image
supposably	supposedly
supremist	supremacist
tack	tact
take for granite	take for granted
tenant	tenet
tongue and cheek	tongue in cheek
verbage	verbiage

The Department of Redundancy Department

The communications we encounter every day are filled with redundant junk and clutter. Here are some typical silly word choices we hear on television or see in print advertising.

Receive this free gift as an added bonus! (Would anyone ever charge you for a gift? Bonus means something added so is an added bonus something added *added*?)

This new invention is unbelievable! (An invention is a new idea, so this is a *new* new idea?)

The actual facts show otherwise! (Actually, facts are always actual.)

And at work, everyone has heard things like this:

Let me give you a brief summary (unlike the long-winded summary you gave yesterday).

My final conclusion is... (unlike the three other conclusions you reached without concluding).

We made a significant breakthrough (unlike the insignificant progress we previously called a breakthrough so it would sound more important).

There was an unintentional error (unlike the intentional errors we introduced so that we could show more progress by eliminating errors).

Okay, okay. Some of us are obsessed with eliminating tautological pleonasms. Here are definitions of these two words, from *Dictionary.com*:

tautology:

1. Needless repetition of an idea, especially in words other than those of the immediate context, without imparting additional force or clearness, as in "widow woman."
2. An instance of such repetition.
3. *Logic.* (a) compound propositional form, all of whose instances are true, as "A or not A." (b) an instance of such a form, as "This candidate will win or will not win."

pleonasm:

1. The use of more words than are necessary to express an idea; redundancy.
2. An instance of this, as *free gift* or *true fact*.
3. A redundant word or expression.

Tautological pleonasm is itself a pleonasm; it is also tautological. Although this may seem like an esoteric topic, dozens of pleonasms are commonly used in everyday communications. They have permeated our language and become entirely too acceptable. We don't need to change this; we can certainly laugh about it every now and then, and recognize a silly pleonasm from a rare, useful one.

William Zinsser addresses this topic in detail when he writes about reducing clutter. Here is a choice excerpt that summarizes his view on this ugly part of our language.

"Take the adjective 'personal,' as in 'a personal friend of mine,' 'his personal feeling' or 'her personal physician.' It's typical of hundreds of words that can be eliminated. The personal friend has come into the language to distinguish him or her from the business friend, thereby debasing both language and friendship. Someone's feeling is that person's personal feeling—that's what 'his' means. As for the personal physician, that's the man or woman summoned to the dressing room of a stricken actress so she won't have to be treated by the impersonal physician assigned to the theater. Someday I'd like to see that person identified as 'her doctor.' Physicians are physicians, friends are friends. The rest is clutter."

In the list below, the unnecessary words are shown in parentheses. They can almost always be deleted without losing any meaning.

Some significant classes of pleonasms are excluded, such as:

- There were three in number (four in number, five in number…).
- They were red in color (blue in color, puce in color, taupe in color…).
- Eleven a.m. Thursday morning (or any specific time with morning, afternoon, or evening attached).

A

(absolutely) essential	(absolutely) necessary
(actual) experience	(actual) facts

adequate (enough)
(advance) planning
(advance) reservations
add (an additional)
(added) bonus
(aid and) abet
alternative (choice)
(anonymous) stranger
(armed) gunman
ask (the question)
attach (together)

advance (forward)
(advance) preview
(advance) warning
add (up)
(affirmative) yes
(all-time) record
(and) etc.
(annual) anniversary
ascend (up)
assemble (together)
autobiography (of a life)

B

bald(-headed)
(basic) fundamentals
best (ever)
blend (together)
bouquet (of flowers)
(brief) moment
burn (down)

balsa (wood)
(basic) necessities
bitter (in taste)
(boat) marina
brief (in duration)
(brief) summary
(burning) embers

C

cacophony (of sound)
cancel (out)
cash (money)
circle (around)
classify (into groups)
close (up)
(closed) fist
collaborate (together)
commute (back and forth)
(completely) eliminate
(completely) filled
(component) parts
connect (together)
confused (state)
(constantly) maintained
could (possibly)
curative (process)

cameo (appearance)
(careful) scrutiny
cease (and desist)
circulate (around)
close (down)
(close) proximity
(co-equal) partners
combine (together)
(completely) destroyed
(completely) engulfed
(completely) surround
(conclusive) proof
connect (up)
consensus (of opinion)
continue (on)
crisis (situation)
(current) status

D

depreciate (in value)

(desirable) benefits

disappear (from sight)

during (the course of)

descend (down)

(different) kinds

drop (down)

E

each (and every)

eliminate (altogether)

(empirical) observation

empty (out)

enclosed (herein)

enter (in)

equal (to one another)

estimated at (about)

evolve (over time)

(exact) same

extradite (back)

earlier (in time)

emergency (situation)

(empty) hole

(empty) space

(end) result

(entirely) eliminate

eradicate (completely)

evacuate (out)

(exact) replica

(exposed) opening

(extreme) hazard

F

(face) mask

(false) pretense

(fellow) classmates

few (in number)

(final) conclusion

(final) outcome

(first) conceived

first time (ever)

follow (after)

(former) graduate

(free) gift

(from) whence

(frozen) tundra

(full) satisfaction

(future) plans

fall (down)

(favorable) approval

(fellow) colleague

filled (to capacity)

(final) end

(first and) foremost

first (of all)

fly (through the air)

(foreign) imports

(former) veteran

friend (of mine)

(frozen) ice

full (to capacity)

fuse (together)

(future) recurrence

G

gather (together)

grow (in size)

(general) public

H

(harmful) injuries

heat (up)

(hot) water heater

(head) honcho

(hollow) tube

hurry (up)

I

(illustrated) drawing

input (into)

integrate (with each other)

introduced (for the first time)

indicted (on a charge)

integrate (together)

introduced (a new)

(invited) guests

J

join (together)

(joint) collaboration

K

killed him/her (dead)

(knowledgeable) experts

kneel (down)

L

lag (behind)

lift (up)

limited (only) to

(live) witness

look (ahead) to the future

later (time)

(little) baby

(live) studio audience

(local) residents

look back (in retrospect)

M

made (out) of

(major) feat

may (possibly)

meet (with each other)

merge (together)

mix (together)

(mutually) interdependent

(major) breakthrough

manually (by hand)

meet (together)

(mental) telepathy

might (possibly)

(mutual) cooperation

N

nape (of her neck)

(natural) instinct

(new) beginning

(new) innovation

(new) recruit

nostalgia (for the past)

(native) habitat

never (before)

(new) construction

(new) invention

none (at all)

(now) pending

O

off (of)

(old) cliché

(old) proverb

open (up)

(originally) created

(original) source

output (out of)

(over) exaggerate

(old) adage

(old) custom

(open) trench

(oral) conversation

(original) founder

(other) alternatives

(outside) in the yard

(overused) cliché

P

(pair of) twins

(passing) fad

(past) history

(past) records

penetrate (through)

period (of time)

(personal) opinion

plan (ahead)

(Please) RSVP

(polar) opposites

postpone (until later)

(pre)board

(pre)record

(present) incumbent

previously listed (above)

progress (forward)

protest (against)

palm (of the hand)

(past) experience

(past) memories

penetrate (into)

(perfect) circle

(personal) friend

pick (and choose)

plan (in advance)

plunge (down)

(positive) identification

pouring (down) rain

(pre)heat

(private) industry

present (time)

proceed (ahead)

(proposed) plan

pursue (after)

R

rarely (ever)

reason (why)

re-elect (for another term)

reflect (back)

reiterate (again)

reply (back)

return (back)

rise (up)

reason is (because)

recur (again)

refer (back)

(regular) routine

repeat (again)

retreat (back)

revert (back)

round (in shape)

S

(safe) haven

scrutinize (in detail)

share (together)

shiny (in appearance)

(single) unit

slow (speed)

(small) speck

soft (to the touch)

spell out (in detail)

square (in shape)

(still) persists

(sudden) impulse

same (exact)

(serious) danger

(sharp) point

shut (down)

skipped (over)

small (size)

socialize (together)

speeding (too fast)

spliced (together)

start (off or out)

(still) remains

(sum) total

T

tall (in height)

(temper) tantrum

(three-way) love triangle

(tiny) bit

(total) destruction

(truly) sincere

(twelve) noon or midnight

(two polar) opposites

tall (in stature)

(temporary) reprieve

time (period)

(tired) cliché

(true) facts

tuna (fish)

(two equal) halves

U

(ultimate) end

(ultimate) outcome

undergraduate (student)

(unexpected) emergency

(unintentional) mistake

(usual) custom

(ultimate) goal

(unconfirmed) rumor

(underground) subway

(unexpected) surprise

(unnamed) anonymous

V

various (different)

(very) unique

(veiled) ambush

visible (to the eye)

W

warn (in advance)

whether (or not)

write (down)

weather (conditions)

(white) snow

RELATIVE ABSOLUTES

Some words represent absolute things or ideas; some words represent relative concepts. Here's the difference: An absolute is something that cannot be modified; for example, a certain extreme state or condition. It is the epitome of what we mean when we say, "It is what it is." These important words represent absolutes:

absolute	not relative; only has one state, measure, or meaning
best	most extreme element with some good quality
better	good in some higher degree
dead	not alive or functional
equal	exactly the same
eternal	forever, without beginning or end
false	factually incorrect
fatal	deadly
final	conclusive
finite	bounded, not infinite
identical	exactly the same
immortal	lives forever
infinite	unbounded, not finite
irrevocable	granted forever
opposite	the other side of a binary condition
parallel	not converging or diverging; exactly the same direction
perfect	cannot be made better
pregnant	with child
relative	not absolute; has a spectrum of states, measures, or meanings
round	circular
square	at exactly right angles
straight	without a bend or curve
supreme	extreme, of the highest quality, degree, importance, etc.
total	complete, 100% of something
true	actual, real, correct
unanimous	in complete agreement
unique	one of a kind
worse	bad in some higher degree
worst	most extreme element with some bad quality

Absolutes tend to have only one distinct meaning. Most of the time, an absolute is the end of some binary scale. You can frequently define an absolute by saying it is the opposite of the other end of the binary scale, as *truth* is the opposite of *falsehood*. Some absolutes have multiple meanings, but in general, they cannot be modified with adjectives and adverbs like most, least, more, less, very, not very, or almost. Modifying absolutes as though they were relatives is a common abuse. We frequently hear phrases like these:

> It was the most unique.
> She was very pregnant.
> That is more true.
> We need to make this more square.
> The vote was more unanimous.
> This poison is less fatal.

These absolutes provide a large source of pleonasms. Put *absolutely* or *relatively* in front of any of the words listed above and you get a pleonasm.

Double Negatives

We all learned in school that we shouldn't use no double negatives. A double negative is created when two negative terms are used in the same clause. Logically, a double negative resolves to negating a negation; therefore, it resolves to a positive. In other words:

negative one times negative one = positive one ($-1 \times -1 = +1$)

The Yale Book of Quotations, edited by Fred Shapiro, contains a great quote by the philosopher Sidney Morgenbesser. He listened to a speaker saying that although in many cases two negatives make a positive, he could think of no case in which two positives make a negative. To this, Morganbesser replied, "Yeah, yeah." This is nice example of the importance of tone in delivery. Only humans can invent ways to circumvent the purity of mathematics and create a double positive that translates into a negative.

Double negatives usually occur in informal speaking and vernaculars. Here are a few classic rock and roll double negatives with which almost everyone is familiar.

> I can't get no satisfaction. (The Rolling Stones meant, "I can't get any satisfaction," but these words translate logically into *I can get satisfaction*, which we all know is true.)

We don't need no education. (Pink Floyd meant, "We don't need any education," but these words translate logically into *we need education*, which we all know is true.

You ain't seen nothing yet. (Bachman Turner Overdrive meant, "You have not seen anything yet," but these words translate into *you have seen something*.

I ain't gonna work on Maggie's farm no more. (Dylan meant, "I ain't gonna work on Maggie's farm any more," which nobody misinterprets.)

There are many common double negatives that are proper English. However, there are positive ways to say exactly the same thing with no confusion.

Don't go without me! (Wait for me!)
I am not dissatisfied. (I am satisfied.)
I don't dislike that person. (I like that person.)
It is not infinite. (It is finite.)
I am not independent. (I am dependent.)
I won't ask you to not go. (Please leave.)
It is not unusual. (It is common.)
I don't disagree. (I agree.)

In most of these cases, the reasonable-looking double negatives are used by people who can't bring themselves to say the positive form because it feels too strong to them. They resort to the double negative form, which feels softer. My favorite is the expression, "I don't disagree." We have all heard this a jillion times in business meetings, where it is almost always secret code for, "I don't totally agree, but I don't want to say I don't agree." The speaker usually follows this up with a sentence that begins with the word *but*. Try stopping someone right after they say, "I don't disagree," and ask, "But do you agree?" The person will usually squirm and stall, think over their answer, and respond either "Yes, but…" or "Well, partly," and then state the points that they don't agree with.

I found my all-time favorite example of a double negative about 15 years ago in the sports section of a newspaper. A Cal Berkeley alumnus had just been traded to an NBA basketball team that had the worst record in the league. Asked about his team's chances in the upcoming year, he was quoted as saying, "We are going to turn this team around 360 degrees." Although this is not a double negative, it is a great example of a statement that has the same effect. This alumnus meant to turn the team around 180 degrees. He doubled the negation unintentionally, ignorantly setting the team on the same dismal path as the year before. I was not happy that my alma mater had not produced a basketball player who was not illiterate.

Triple and quadruple negation can also occasionally be seen. It results in total obfuscation of the author's real intent. The last sentence of the previous paragraph is a good example, as is my parenthetical comment regarding Dylan, above. While double negatives are frowned upon in English, the French commonly use two negatives to make a stronger negative, particularly in informal French. The Romance languages and Greek and Slavic languages routinely use double negatives. If you are a native English speaker and converse with non-English speakers using either spoken or written communications, you may notice that they use double negatives in their English. Imagine how hard it is to learn English as a second language when your native tongue routinely uses semantic structures that are considered incorrect in English.

PUZZLE 12. COULD JEFFERSON WRITE?

The preamble to the Constitution of the United States is a good example of a one-sentence paragraph. While it may be a rather long sentence (due to its list of intents), it is a well-structured thought with crisp, meaningful words. It stands alone as a strong paragraph.

We the people of the United States, in order to form a more perfect union, establish justice, insure domestic tranquility, provide for the common defense, promote the general welfare, and secure the blessings of liberty to ourselves and our posterity, do ordain and establish this Constitution of the United States of America.

Of all the abuses presented in this chapter, there are two specific instances that show up in one of America's most revered paragraphs. Can you find them?

Many of the examples of English abuse sprinkled throughout this book have been the works of very accomplished people. Perhaps it is insane for me to suggest that our preamble could have been written better. Perhaps I should strike the word *perhaps* from that last sentence. This paragraph has stood the test of time. My nitpicky judgments on some potentially poor usage are made more than 230 years later, when the usage models for some words have evolved quite a bit. Nevertheless, this is a great retrospective poser for pedantic language observers.

CHAPTER 4

Synchronize With Your Audience

Communicating more effectively tops the list of organizational development needs year after year. It is emphasized and highlighted in feedback from every employee survey, leadership workshop, and management training session. Whenever managers or management consultants confer, they discuss the need for more effective communications, but then what? The how, why, when, what, and where are left to be dealt with later and usually by short-term, unsustained, and shallow efforts. You can't significantly improve your communications skill with one quick-hitting lecture or book, or even a longer term curricula, it needs to be a long term self-motivated pursuit.

I attended excellent public schools in the suburbs of Los Angeles, then elite institutions of higher learning (the U.S. Air Force Academy, Cal Berkeley, UCLA, and the University of Michigan, Ann Arbor). I have worked at successful companies that are standouts at investing in employee education, including TRW, Rational Software Corporation, and IBM. Surprisingly, I can't remember my education or professional training courses allocating much time to improving communications. And they certainly didn't spend much time motivating me to care, or making it fun and relevant.

Why are students, employees, supervisors, parents, spouses and teachers so lackadaisical in improving their communications? One hypothesis is that communicating more effectively is hairy, personal, and introspective. It requires people to get outside their heads to evaluate objectively what they need to do to improve. It also takes objective and personal critique and forces us to make judgments about style. In my experience such objective self-reflection is rare, limited to the few truly egoless people who can do it well. For a great treatment of this topic, see Eckhard Tolle's *A New Earth, Awakening to Your Life's Purpose.*

Adjust to Your Context

We could blame our schools and parents for ineffective teaching, but we students were equally at fault: We were so smart in our teens and twenties that we didn't listen well to our instructors or parents. My father, who earned a PhD in astronautics from the California Institute of Technology, was an expert in the benchmark of hairy stuff, better known as rocket science. Although he was a gifted writer and communicator, he never emphasized to me the importance that those skills played in every facet of life. Or maybe he did, and I wasn't listening. My mother, a voracious reader, writer, and lover of crossword puzzles, *did* emphasize the importance in her words and her actions, but my brain was not wired to listen as I went through my formative years. That was my loss, because she was right.

I was naturally gifted in math ability, so science and math became my self-proclaimed identity. Most of my clique had no use for the more social skills of English, and we put minimum effort into our English courses and into developing our communications skills. Our future was certainly some sort of engineering or scientific pursuit. English, literature, writing, speaking, and teamwork exercises were for others, not for engineering studs like us. How naïve we were.

This is one lesson that we need to teach better as parents, as educators, and as professional coaches of the people we supervise: There are few growth paths in this world that don't require strong communications skills. That is just as true if your career is in engineering as it is in sports, journalism, medicine, law, or finance.

As I started working as a systems and software engineer, I realized that building software was much more about communications than it was about engineering. Good writing and good speaking were clear differentiators in my superiors and the engineers who were the most valuable to our organization. They could sell an idea; they could convince and influence others; and they could build teams. Most of all, they could save time and money by avoiding scrap and rework caused by miscommunications. I developed a passion for the English language, including the power inherent in its effective usage and the humor associated with both its intentional and its unintentional misuse.

Communications involves the exchange of information between a transmitter and a receiver. Although this is a nerd engineer's viewpoint of a non-engineering concept, I think the physical analogy works well. Consider the following examples of communications where there is an obvious mismatch between the transmitter and receiver.

- An AM radio owner wants to listen to FM music stations.
- A radio station transmits in French, even though there are few French-speaking people within its range.
- A professor delivers a graduate-level talk to a middle school class.
- An amateur sits down at a poker table with five professionals, who are licking their chops.
- A southern conservative talks politics with a Cambridge liberal.
- A woman from Venus chats with a man from Mars.

These situations involve obstacles to a meaningful exchange of information between the parties. The differences between transmitter and receiver are so stark that we know the information exchange will be rough and erroneous because the transmitters and receivers are not adjusted to each other's context. No one who values their time would attempt any of them, except the last one. John Gray's classic, *Men are from Mars, Women are from Venus*, is an enlightening treatment of the different contextual perspectives between men and women. It provides a great analysis of male-female communications and the importance of synching up your transmissions with the receivers of the opposite sex.

For high-quality communications to occur, the transmitter and receiver must be in synch. In everyday life, this can be hard to achieve. Nevertheless, you should do whatever you can to get better in synch, whether you are the transmitter or the receiver. This is especially true for stressful communications like a father/daughter talk about a touchy subject or a yearly personnel performance review, and for high-stakes communications like an interview, a sales presentation, or a PhD oral exam. The transmitter generally has more responsibility for knowing the receiver's preferences than vice versa. The person doing the speaking or writing is in control of the words, style, delivery, and tone. That person can adjust to the context of the audience best, whether it is a one-on-one conversation or a one-to-many presentation. If you are on the receiving end of a communication—reading a newspaper, magazine, book, or internet site—adjusting to your context means knowing the transmitter's frame of reference.

Consider what it takes to do the *New York Times* crossword puzzle. For the first few years, it was quite difficult for me because I didn't understand the style of Will Shortz, the editor (transmitter). I did hundreds of puzzles before I learned what to expect from him and his biases in editing crossword puzzles. Understanding his style made a huge difference.

Whenever you listen to a presenter or a commentator, or read a nonfiction work, it is extremely important to understand the author's perspective and background in order to understand the author's biases and to qualify or interpret the information for your use.

Here are a few transmitters with obvious biases:

- A political party leader giving a speech on why their candidate is the best choice.
- A product salesperson describing the pros and cons of competing products.
- A child's parent discussing their child's accomplishments.
- An alleged criminal providing an alibi.

What is the likelihood of getting objective and fair assessments from these transmitters? Zip. Although these are extreme cases, most people transmit and communicate with their own innate biases. Everyone communicates within the larger context of their personality, their background, and their immediate specific purpose for communicating.

William Zinsser summarized the perspective of most receivers well:

> *Who is this elusive creature, the reader? The reader is someone with an attention span of about 30 seconds—a person assailed by many forces competing for attention. At one time those forces were relatively few: newspapers, magazines, radio, spouse, children, pets. Today they include a galaxy of electronic devices for receiving entertainment and information—television, VCRs, DVDs, CDs, video games, the Internet, email, cell phones, Blackberries, iPods — as well as a fitness program, a pool, a lawn, and that most potent of competitors, sleep. The man or woman snoozing in a chair with a magazine or a book is a person who has been given too much trouble by the writer.*

The main point is simple: Know with whom you are communicating and adjust your communications to your receivers and transmitters. This is true whether you are engaged in personal conversations such as talking to your spouse or speaking at an Alcoholics Anonymous meeting, or engaged in professional exchanges such as delivering a professional sales presentation or presenting a yearly performance assessment.

Adjusting to your context is an important aspect of more leisurely forms of communications as well. For example, many games require competitors to do battle through their communications skills. Adjusting to your context in sports and games translates into knowing your opponents.

I was a student of the game of poker throughout my teens, twenties, and thirties. I read every book I could find, wrote computer programs, and played in home games with friends. I also played in the card rooms of Gardena and San Jose, California, with both amateurs and pros. This was during the 1970s and 1980s, long before poker became the popular game it is today. Great poker players had not begun disclosing the secrets of the game, so there were few books with top-notch poker guidance. But the great players all knew that their skills in transmitting and receiving, both accurately and deceptively, were far more important than knowing the mathematical odds and logically deducing the other opponents' cards from the sequence of playing and betting. They knew that poker is a game of communications skills more than anything else.

One basic poker strategy is to play good hands like they were mediocre and to play mediocre hands like they were good. The key to making this strategy work is to communicate with the other players through your mannerisms and actions. However, communicating to players who know how to communicate well, versus players who are oblivious to communications, adds some challenging complexities to the game. Today's books on poker strategy have matured and improved. They spend much more time on how to read other players (receiving) and playing your cards with varying styles (transmitting).

I am also a lifetime student and fan of baseball. Many people have a superficial understanding of the game and think baseball is a rather boring spectator sport. With a deeper understanding of how much communicating goes on inside the game, baseball becomes a fascinating spectator sport. *Inside baseball* is a term used across the media nowadays to describe the depth of understanding that practitioners inside a particular domain have, compared to outside observers.

George Will synthesized the best description of *inside baseball* in his classic book, *Men At Work, The Craft of Baseball.* His macro- and micro-analysis of communications between batter and pitcher, pitcher and catcher, fielder and batter, and coaches and players provides an exceptional case study on how communications give the better players and teams a significant edge in what most people think is simply a contest of athletic ability.

This excerpt from Will's book summarizes this relatively misunderstood aspect of America's favorite pastime.

> *Thinking infielders who want to cheat must do so at the last minute, lest they telegraph to the hitter the kind of pitch that is coming. Kubek recalls that Rick Burleson of the Red Sox lacked quickness, so he moved two steps to his right on off-speed pitches to right-handed hitters and two steps to his left on fastballs — and he moved too soon. He moved as soon as the catcher gave the sign to the pitcher, before the pitcher started his motion. Kubek says that Mickey Mantle feasted on Red Sox pitching during the season when Jimmy Piersall was the Red Sox centerfielder. Piersall was a fine outfielder but he, too, moved too soon. The Red Sox shortstop would signal with his glove behind his back indicating a fastball (no glove meant a breaking ball). Piersall would move and Mantle would sit on whatever pitch was coming.*
>
> *Of course an intelligent outfielder can use disinformation against an observant batter. When Tony Gwynn briefly became a center-fielder after five seasons (and two Gold Gloves) in right field, he discovered a way to mislead hitters. From center field he could see the catcher's signs, so he would shift "wrong" before the pitcher started his motion, then he would quickly move back to where he really wanted to be. His hope was that the batter would make a mistaken inference from his first move.*

In these few paragraphs, Will summarizes the extent to which communications go on inside baseball. His book is packed with many other examples of communications—both information and disinformation—within the game. Just as poker is much more than a game of odds and card playing, baseball is much more than a game of hitting, pitching, and fielding. Communications play a crucial role, and knowing your opponents or, in other words, adjusting to their context and communicating better than they do are crucial to success.

We play a lot of roles in our lives—parents, colleagues, supervisors, subordinates, friends, coaches, trusted advisors, and strangers—so we use a broad spectrum of behavioral and communications styles. Behavior and communications are highly integrated. Others perceive our behavior—shown by our actions, words, facial expressions, and emotions—as we communicate our intentions, feelings, and judgments. Our communications, oral and written, are a significant aspect of how we form relationships with other people.

ASSERTIVENESS AND RESPONSIVENESS

A lot of my thinking on synchronizing with your audience stems from two books that are extremely pragmatic and useful in building teams and supervising people:

1. *Personal Styles and Effective Performance*, by David Merrill and Roger Reid (1983). This book summarizes research into personality styles and is well matched to my experience with being supervised and working with other colleagues in the software engineering field.
2. *First Among Equals*, by Patrick McKenna and David H. Maister (2002). This book builds on the Merrill-Reid work and provides guidance on building and coaching diverse teams of capable professionals.

Merrill's fundamental conclusion is that people's behaviors can be grouped roughly into four different styles, based on their relative tendencies on two different scales: assertiveness and responsiveness. These scales are roughly comparable to humans' basic instincts and how they will react when things get tense or heated; namely, fight or flight.

Low: Flight		High: Fight
Assertiveness: Ask/read/listen	←→	Tell/write/speak
Responsiveness: Reasons/controls	←→	Emote/act/react

Assertiveness captures a person's instinctive interaction style. Less assertive people tend to speak more slowly and softly with fewer words. They are more relaxed and avoid direct eye contact. More assertive people tend to speak quickly and loudly with more words. They may lean forward and use direct eye contact.

Responsiveness captures a person's instinctive reaction style. Less responsive people are more independent, indifferent, and objective. They speak monotonously about things or actions and use statistics and data. They tend to be more formal, rigid, and under control. More responsive people are more subjective, concerned with relationships, and care what others think. They speak with inflections and state opinions. They tend to be more informal, casual, and animated.

By combining the two dimensions of assertiveness and responsiveness into four quadrants, Merrill defined a useful mapping of social styles that contains roughly equal numbers of people in a randomly selected population with no predominance of any race or gender in any given quadrant. In other words, about one-fourth of any random group of people will probably fall into each style. Figure 4-1 (adapted from Merrill's presentation) summarizes these styles.

FIGURE 4-1. *Social Style Summary*

Less responsive, guarded

Analytical Style Asks and Controls *Thinks*	**Driver Style** Tells and Controls *Acts*
Negative **Positive** Critical Industrious Indecisive Persistent Stuffy Serious Picky Exacting Moralistic Orderly	**Negative** **Positive** Pushy Strong-Willed Severe Independent Tough Practical Dominating Decisive Harsh Efficient

Less assertive, indirect ← → **More assertive, direct**

Amiable Style Asks and Emotes *Feels*	**Expressive Style** Tells and Emotes *Shows*
Negative **Positive** Conforming Supportive Unsure Respectful Pliable Willing Dependent Dependable Awkward Agreeable	**Negative** **Positive** Manipulative Ambitious Excitable Stimulating Undisciplined Enthusiastic Reacting Dramatic Egotistical Friendly

More responsive, unguarded

Here are a few people—both fictional and nonfictional—who epitomize these styles.

Amiable: Oprah Winfrey, Edith Bunker, Ghandi, Billy Graham
Analytical: Jimmy Carter, Martha Stewart, Sherlock Holmes, Eckhart Tolle
Driver: Hillary Clinton, Vince Lombardi, George Patton, James Bond
Expressive: Bill O'Reilly, Ellen DeGeneres, Richard Feynmen,
        Ralph Kramden

The social styles summarized in Figure 4-1 can be roughly observed in everyone. Table 4-1 presents some general attributes that help to differentiate the social styles. These characteristics simply describe the observable behavior through people's verbal and physical styles of communicating. There is no inherent judgment that less or more of either assertiveness or responsiveness is good or bad. They do not depict what a person intends or what they are thinking or feeling. There are successful and unsuccessful people on both ends of both spectrums, with roughly equal distributions. The adjectives used to define each style include both negative and positive connotations. There is no best style. This research paints people with some broad brushes, and almost everyone exhibits a mix of these styles in various proportions. However, almost everyone has a predominant style.

TABLE 4-1. *Rough Generalities of Social Styles*

	Amiable	**Analytical**	**Driver**	**Expressive**
Values	Compatibility Contribution	Precision Quality	Results Impact	Recognition Compliments
Motives	The team	The process	The win	The show
Strengths	Listening Teamwork Follow-up	Planning Predictable Organization	Managing Leader Pioneer	Persuading Enthusiasm Visionary
Weaknesses	Sensitive Slow to act Stagnant	Unresponsive Perfectionist Critical	Poor listener Impatient Insensitive	Sloppy Competitive No follow-up
Failure mode	Resignation	Withdrawal	Autocratic	Attack
Aspires to	Acceptance	Accuracy	Control	Renown
Annoyed by	Insensitivity Impatience	Chaos Impropriety	Inefficiency Indecision	Routines Insignificance
Reaction to stress	Submissive Indecisive	Withdrawn Headstrong	Dictatorial Critical	Sarcastic Superficial
Decision making	Consensus Risk-averse	Deliberate Facts	Decisive Confident	Spontaneous Risk takers
Fears	Change	Criticism	Manipulation	Obscurity
Comforts	Friendship	Preparation	Control	Spotlight
Time	Present	Past	Present	Future
Pronoun	We	It	I	Me
Attractive professions	Service Social worker Teaching	Engineer Lawyer Accountant	Management Military Executive	Entertainment Entrepreneur Design

Adapted from McKenna and Maister.

A critical skill in life is the ability to observe one's own behavior. *A New Earth*, by Eckhart Tolle, provides a compelling treatment of the human ego and the importance of gaining objectivity by understanding your ego, then stepping outside its influence to be an objective observer. One of the skills necessary to step outside your ego is to observe others objectively in various situations and judge whether you would act the same way or not. These judgments can help you understand yourself and see how other people judge your behavior. If there is a big difference between your judgments and other people's judgments, trust theirs first. Your ego is a powerfully polluted filter.

There is always tension when people communicate. In general, when two people of the same style communicate, there is less tension and more comfort. When opposing styles communicate, there is typically more tension and less comfort. Is either good or bad? Merrill's research and my own experience suggest that too much comfort or too much tension leads to less productive communications and results. A balanced tension leads to more effective communications and results.

One key to using this research is to become an objective observer of other people's styles, as well as our own. It is very difficult for most people to categorize themselves. We look at the positives and negatives; we see things that we want to be and that we don't want to be. However, your behavior is not necessarily aligned with your intentions and your desires. Perception is reality, and how others perceive you—through your observable behaviors and communications—is usually more meaningful than how you perceive yourself. Behavior is what we communicate, namely, what we say and do. This is different than our intentions. We can all remember situations where people misinterpreted our intent based on what we said or did. Although we frequently defend our actions and words, we almost always do so from our own transmitter frame of reference without considering the styles and preferences of the receivers.

It is much easier to categorize other people. As you observe others, you will agree with certain behaviors. When you disagree, it will usually be because they act differently than you would in the same situation. These comparisons help us understand and form opinions about other people, and understanding their social styles will help you adjust your communications to affect them in a more positive way.

The descriptions of social styles identify dominant tendencies in a widely varying population. Nobody is all one style. We all have a mix of styles, where one style is dominant. It should not be surprising that analytical people flock to engineering roles more than expressive people, because their tendencies are well matched to the roles. Similarly, it is not surprising that a person in a management role will be perceived as more of a driver, because that role demands that a person accentuate that style. Any style can succeed in any role.

Amiable

Amiable people want you to know them and they want to participate. They appreciate the time you invest in them and in the mutual sharing of personal information. Expect them to take things personally. Their feelings and your feelings will be just as important to them as facts and realities. They care about whether you care about them, the team, or others. Showing empathy and listening attentively establish comfort.

Use collective pronouns like *we* and *us* rather than *I*, *me*, or *you*. Use anecdotes and stories where people succeed or fail because of their actions or words. Describe benefits to the organization, the family, or the group. Folklore, traditions, and cultures are positive contexts for channeling a message. Deadlines and urgency will create discomfort, as will force, authority, and mandates. Give them time to talk things through.

Amiables are generally supportive, easy to talk to and coach. Reinforcing their desire for teamwork, good relationship building, and open communications is useful. Recognition will be welcome and valued. Providing feedback on the team, rather than on each team member, is usually easier for them to accept because they tend to be uncomfortable when the spotlight is on them as individuals. They usually need to be coached toward being more assertive and feeling confident to initiate things, whether it is their ideas, their actions toward objectives, or challenging others when their opinions differ.

Analytical

Analytical people want you to know the facts. They appreciate your preparation and ability to prove your case, or to show them supporting evidence. They don't take things personally and are generally cautious about opening up their personal lives or offering subjective opinions on gray-area topics. To them, facts and realities are more important than feelings and relationships. Showing risk aversion, historical precedent, and details establishes comfort.

Use objective case studies, tables, graphs, and data to establish a story line. Describe benefits to the quality of any product or service. Sequencing, credibility, and cause and effect relationships will capture an Analytical's attention. Past experience, scientific proof, and logical arguments are positive contexts for channeling a message. Gut feel, unsupported estimates, and half-baked or risky ideas will create discomfort. Give them time to think things through.

When they are being coached, Analyticals want a framework. Use an agenda; back up your assertions with facts and precedents; frame improvements with timeframes and measures of some sort. Reinforcing their desire for quality, accuracy, logic, and data is useful. Recognition will be welcome and valued. Providing feedback on the product and the results of their actions is usually easier for them to accept because they tend to be uncomfortable when the spotlight is on gray areas like behaviors, actions, and customer satisfaction. They usually need to be coached toward being more declarative, taking calculated risks, and opening up to other people. Living in the gray world of decisions that are not black and white is particularly hard on an Analytical. Coaching them to become comfortable with delivering an idea, product, or opinion before it is fully baked is a key to growth. They need to accept that completion may be achieved faster by exposing incomplete work for earlier correction and feedback.

Driver

Drivers want to succeed and accomplish tasks. They appreciate when you get to the point as soon as possible because they tend to be inattentive listeners. Expect them to focus on results and outcomes (what and when), not process or people (how and who). The quickest solution to a problem will dominate a Driver's concern, and they will be tempted by shortcuts. They care about achievement and results. Showing decisiveness and a "let's get it done" attitude establishes comfort.

Use results and outcomes as the main focus of your communications. Describe benefits to the outcome (sooner, better, more impact) of the present task. Brevity and efficiency are welcome, while substantial proof and supporting evidence are unnecessary and will cause drivers to lose patience and attentiveness. Create comfort by considering timing and urgency, and the ramifications of action or inaction. Get to the point, discuss risks and rewards, and request a rapid follow-up if necessary.

Drivers are generally unhappy with the status quo and want to see something change. They like to be given alternatives for moving forward so they can decide the best course of action. Reinforcing their desire for achieving results is useful. Recognition will be welcome and valued. It is usually easier for them to accept feedback on the plan and objectives because they tend to be uncomfortable when the spotlight is on the process or the people. They usually need to be coached toward being better listeners and accepting competing opinions for further analysis rather than reacting prematurely. They like to be recognized for achievement and given credit for leading a team to a positive outcome.

Expressive

Expressives want you to know what they have contributed and experienced. Tell them something that happened to someone, and they will have a story about what happened to them. They appreciate the time you invest in them and in understanding their perspectives. Expect them to take things very personally and to exaggerate the plusses and minuses of most situations. Their gut feelings will trump facts and realities. They care about their future. Creativity, empathy, and acknowledgement of their instincts will make them comfortable.

Focus the communications directly on an Expressive's specific context. Describe the benefit to yourself or to the Expressive himself. Excitement, radical change, and significant objectives are positive contexts for channeling a message. Process compliance and detailed plans will create discomfort; so will force, authority, and mandates. Feel free to make it their idea, or to shape an idea so that they have ownership in its creation. Summarize any follow-ups if necessary; be specific.

Expressives are frequently difficult to coach. They are often unaware of how they rub others the wrong way or just don't care. Reinforcing their importance to the team or family or group is useful. They value this recognition best when it is done publicly. Providing constructive feedback is best done informally and off the cuff rather than in a more formally arranged setting. Expressives tend to be comfortable when the spotlight is on them as individuals. They usually need to be coached to sit on emails for a day before sending them, looking before leaping, and being more conscious of consequences. They also need help learning to consider other people's opinions and put themselves in other people's shoes.

DIVERSITY AND VERSATILITY

Pigeonholing people into four different social styles may make some people feel uncomfortable. Even so, it helps us address our audience from their perspective, especially in one-on-one situations. Categorizing people forces us to think about the diversity of transmitters and receivers. It is not necessary to create the perfect set of pigeonholes. It is important for people to realize that their style of communications—both receiving and transmitting—should be adjusted dynamically to the situation at hand. This is what Merrill calls versatility.

In this definition of social style, there are both positive and negative connotations in the descriptions of each style. The more versatile you are, the more endorsements you will get from other people, regardless of your style. Endorsement means that you evoke the use of positive connotations of your social behaviors. People approve of your behavior when it brings them comfort and they understand that you have accommodated their needs as well as those of others.

Versatility represents a person's ability to adapt to those around them and effectively form diverse relationships. It is not about how well you get along with people; it is about how well you relate with people so that both parties come away from an encounter feeling better about themselves: It is the ability to create win-win relationships.

Assessing your versatility or that of others is a function of several factors, including the following:

1. Other people's attraction to you as a trusted advisor
2. Consistency of attraction across diverse groups (e.g., church, work, softball team)
3. Consistency of what people say about you, both directly to you and to others
4. People's attraction across a spectrum of colleagues, subordinates, and superiors (independent of position power)

Merrill uses a simple scale to measures a person's concern for tension in a relationship or communication. On one end of the spectrum is concern for one's own tension. On the other end is concern with other people's tension. No matter which social style is involved, most people don't trust people who exhibit behaviors on the extremes at either end of this spectrum. Most people experience the most comfort when they perceive a roughly balanced view of tension between transmitter and receiver. Table 4-2 provides some example descriptions of people across this spectrum of versatility.

TABLE 4-2. *The Range of People's Concerns with Various Tensions*

More concern with my tensions	Balanced	More concern with others' tensions
How it should be… I am right. I am sticking to my guns. Take it or leave it. You are wrong. You know where I stand.		Let's look at a few alternatives. You win; let's do it your way. I will do whatever it takes. It depends. We can work this out. How can I help?
Apprehensive Deterministic Blunt Argumentative Critical	Resourceful Flexible Tactful Reasonable Perceptive	Provocative Individualistic Polished Compromising Unbiased, open minded

We can establish the most effective channels of communications by letting other people know our tensions and making sure that others know we are trying to understand and accommodate them in a balanced way. How can we improve this balance? The four simple steps may seem similar to advice from a million other self-help sources.

1. Know yourself, your tendencies, styles, and competencies.
2. Exploit your strengths and avoid your weaknesses.
3. Observe other people and their responses to your transmissions.
4. Give to others and accommodate their preferences without sacrificing your values.

This is the basic lesson of adjusting to your context. It may seem more observable in one-on-one relationships and communications. However, giving to others—by adjusting your communications specifically to another person or team in the context of small groups, large groups, or even public audiences—gets noticed and establishes more endorsement of your versatility and better receptivity to your further communications. This is the essence of what people mean when they say that a speaker really connects with the audience.

The books referenced earlier—by Merrill and Reid, and by McKenna and Maister—are worth reading. They contain great discussions and examples of interpersonal relationships and communications styles and provide much more depth in usage scenarios.

ONE-ON-ONE COMMUNICATIONS

Adjusting to the context of your receiver is particularly important when communicating one-on-one with other people. The next few sections provide specific examples of how to communicate better with people who have various social styles. Treatment of these topics is intentionally brief. Once you open your eyes to the diversity of communications styles you need to be aware of, and the need to alter your style based on the context and situation, your ability to communicate will blossom.

1.   Consciously try to adjust your transmissions to the styles of the receivers.
2.   Adjust your presentations to your audience.
3.   Adjust your conversations to the people with whom you are conversing.

When you fail to communicate well, it is easier to see what part of the miscommunication was your fault and how to improve it. Although some people seem to be born with this innate ability to adjust, most of us must learn it from experience.

Your Style

Before you can improve your ability to communicate with others, you need to have an objective appreciation of your style. Very few people are good at assessing themselves because they are not what they think they are or would like to be. Our social styles are formed early in life as we build our values and witness the reinforcement of behaviors by our parents, friends, and social experiences.

Accepting ourselves for what we are and understanding our own biases and tendencies are critical to improving our ability to transmit and receive. It is normal for people to review the social style generalities presented earlier and deny that one or another could be the social style that fits them best. Why? Most people have the strongest negative feelings (pet peeves) about things that are natural to their social style because they are acutely familiar with the negative tendencies inherent in the style as their own shortfalls and failure modes. People compete most with people like themselves. For example:

*   Drivers are frequently frustrated with overly competitive people and control freaks like themselves.
*   Perfectionists can drive Analyticals crazy because their idea of perfect may be different.

- People looking to get more credit than they deserve irritate Expressives, who compete for the spotlight.
- People who obsess about what others might think can annoy Amiables, who have a different idea about how others will think.

The moral of this story: A mirror is an important, yet deceptive, tool. As you assess your style, be objective. Get outside your head and look at the way your family, your close friends, and your colleagues would describe you. They would be much more objective than you are about assessing your style. Give more weight to your positive connotations of style rather than the negative connotations when assessing yourself. The negatives of your dominant style will likely be more objectionable to you than the negatives of your other less dominant styles. If you can't pick a specific quadrant, at least pick one of the four halves (north, south, east, or west) that represents two dominant styles. This will help you differentiate tendencies and biases that need adjusting when communicating with other styles.

Their Style

It is not always possible to assess accurately the people we are communicating with. You may not know them well enough, or your audience may be a mix of people where there is no dominant style. Nevertheless, it is still beneficial to consider the person or the audience either by doing preparatory research or by assessing initial reactions as the conversation or communication unfolds. For something like a casual dinner party conversation, there is no need for research For an interview, a prepared speech, or a purposeful letter to a potential business partner, where something significant is at stake, this research and adjustment can make the difference between communicating well and laying an egg.

Communicating with others effectively requires sensitivity to the behavioral preferences of others, tolerance of their differences from your preferences, and compromise by adjusting your style to best suit their needs. If you become better at observing how your behaviors and communications affect others, you can better avoid conflicts and miscommunications that create tension. This will allow you to avoid wasted efforts in defending your words and actions and to channel your energy more efficiently into better relationships, teamwork, and results.

TRUSTED ADVISORS

One of the objectives in many endeavors, including personal friendships and business relationships, is to become a trusted advisor. Whether your company is a trusted advisor to your client, or you are a trusted advisor to another person, this is a powerful label. What does it really mean? Here is my version (derived from the words of David Maister) of the characteristics of a trusted advisor:

- Has my interests at heart
- Is consistent and dependable
- Gives me a meaningful perspective
- Helps me think through my decisions
- Is calm and unemotional
- Is constructive in criticism
- Doesn't pull punches
- Puts our long-term relationship ahead of any single issue
- Provides reasoning for his judgments and conclusions
- Acts human, not like an actor in a role
- Is savvy in ways I am not
- Is honorable, with values I trust
- Seems to understand me and like me

Okay, this is too long-winded. The true differentiating attribute of a trusted advisor is **someone with whom you can communicate comfortably**. My main goal is to give you a framework for more comfortable communications between you and your receivers. Table 4-3 summarizes ways to adjust your style when communicating with others.

Let me take the concept of trusted advisor one step farther, by talking about trust. When people define trust, they usually relate it to integrity. However, the more complete meaning of trust gets lost.

> *trust*: reliance on the integrity, strength, ability, surety, etc., of a person or thing; confidence. (*Dictionary.com*)

The most important dimension of trust is that it gives you confidence. Integrity is one dimension of confidence, but competence is another. You don't trust a friend to give you medical advice (unless they are a competent M.D.) and you don't trust an M.D. to be your divorce lawyer. Trusted advisors come in many flavors. Integrity and communications effectiveness apply to them all, but competence is context-dependent.

As we build trusted relationships with other people, both as advisors and as people we advise, our paramount need turns out to be a feeling of safety. When you package integrity, comfort in communicating, and competence into a purposeful relationship, you feel safe. A person's competence gives you confidence in their opinion, but the person's integrity and ability to communicate comfortably without tension is what makes an individual, an audience, or an organization feel safe and motivates them to elevate you to the position of a trusted advisor.

TABLE 4-3. *Adjustments You Can Make to Various Social Styles*

Situation	Amiable	Analytical	Driver	Expressive
Initiation	Get personal	Query facts	Query results	Ask opinions
When you agree...	Endorse the person over the outcome	Endorse the process and checkpoints	Endorse the results over the person	Endorse the ideas and creativity
When you disagree...	Express and acknowledge differences	Seek a deeper understanding	Stick to facts and expected outcomes	Don't argue; look for alternatives
Focus the discussion on...	Teams and people	Facts and process	Results and rewards	Importance and excitement
Emphasize...	Getting along; the **who**	Getting it right; the **how**	Getting it done; the **what**	Getting recognized; the **why**
De-emphasize...	The big picture	The risks	The details	The status quo
Commit your help by...	Stating your role in supporting any needs	Detailing the next steps	Trusting things will get done	Offering to help
Conclude with...	Understanding and warm thanks	Interest in an even deeper understanding	Expectations for interim results	Requesting frequent follow-ups

CHAPTER 5

Presentations: Accuracy and Precision

This chapter is a compilation of loosely connected topics whose common thread is two words that most people associate with science and mathematics, not writing or speaking. Communicating **accurately** with the right level of **precision** is a discriminating strength of most great communications. Conversely, communicating inaccurately or with too much or too little precision is a recurring fault in many ineffective communications. This balance, underappreciated by most communicators, is an instructive topic for some important observations on speaking and listening. While this chapter focuses mostly on presentation style, it is equally applicable to writing.

Although there are many different reasons why written and oral communications succeed or fail, there is one pattern of failure that dominates all others: information overload. Providing excessive detail can obscure your message, just as superfluous precision can obscure your reasoning about some mathematical relationship. Let's look at this topic a little more precisely by starting with some definitions.

accuracy: mathematics. The degree of correctness of a quantity or expression.

precision: mathematics. The degree to which the correctness of a quantity is expressed.

In mathematics and scientific measurement, accuracy and precision are related yet quite distinct. Accuracy indicates how close to the truth a specific measurement is; precision indicates how much certainty or uncertainty there is in that measurement. Sometimes the units of measure give you a good indication of precision. Here are a few examples.

- You have a scale that weighs a person to the nearest kilogram. That is accurate enough for most purposes, but it is imprecise. If you want to measure gold dust or pharmaceuticals, you will need a more precise scale to find the amounts to the nearest gram.
- If a person asks me how old I am, I can answer 54 years (accurate), or 19,890 days (more precise), or 28,641,600 minutes (even more precise). In this case, the less precise measure remains accurate for a longer time; the more precise measure becomes inaccurate quickly.
- If a person asks me how far I live from Boston, I can answer 40 miles (accurate) or 220,202 feet, or 41.705 miles. The latter two are very precise and also somewhat silly. They imply that you know where Boston is to the nearest foot (to the front door of city hall?) and where your home is to the nearest foot (to the property line? your front door? the doormat?).

Here is another example. Suppose you are in London with your family and you ask what time it is.

- Your mom looks at her watch and says, "It is almost 3 o'clock."
- Your dad looks at his watch and says, "It is 9:51, but I am still on U.S. time."
- You look up at Big Ben (which you know to keep accurate time). It says 2:50.
- On his computer, your nerd brother has access to a highly refined cesium clock used to measure precise time intervals. He hits a button and tells you that it is now precisely 2:50:50.397.

Your mom is accurate but imprecise. Your dad is inaccurate but precise. Big Ben is accurate and precise enough for almost any purpose. Your brother is a pest (as always) and confuses you with a long string of numbers. He is very, very precise, and gives you much more detail than you need. By being overly precise, he becomes ever more inaccurate as time passes. The longer it takes him to tell you the time, the more time elapses since he hit the button.

What does this wide range of responses have to do with writing or speaking? We encounter this sort of information spectrum every day in business meetings, academic lectures, storytelling, church sermons, and newspaper articles. People use 5 or 10 mushy words trying to be precise, when one carefully selected word would more accurately describe their thought. They confuse you with 10 digits of precision when they need only one or two. They give you 20 pages of fluff to explain something that could be covered in a few meaty paragraphs.

Right now you're probably saying to yourself, "Joe Blow is exactly like that." So are most of the rest of us! We feel compelled to explain the whole situation, or to provide years and years of context, or to describe how every person at the party reacted, or to say whatever it takes to describe every tree until the audience has forgotten the forest.

If someone asks me how old I am and I give my answer in minutes, or if someone asks me how far I live from Boston and I give an answer in feet, have I communicated more effectively? These extreme examples illustrate an important point.

> When you communicate with more precision than is necessary, you confuse or lose your audience.

Most presentations are called *briefings* for a reason. They are intended to be brief, which usually means *accurate* yet *imprecise*. To give an effective briefing, you need not present every bullet on every page and every word in every sub-bullet. In my experience, oral presentations in the business and academic worlds show three common failure patterns.

1. Information overload: preparing written presentation material that is overly precise
2. Oral tedium: presenting every aspect of the prepared material too precisely
3. Too much foreplay: presenting too much context (being overly precise describing the problem) and not enough substance (being under-precise describing the solution)

AVOID INFORMATION OVERLOAD

The best presentations are pretty sparse. They do not fill every bit of white space with data, words, cute clip art, frilly backgrounds, and eye-catching multi-media elements. There is a time and place for all these elements, but most presentations don't need them. If you are producing a documentary film of an important construction project, you don't need special effects, action scenes, and nudity to tell the story. Similarly, if you are presenting your team's budgetary status, you don't need clip art, PowerPoint animations, and distracting background graphics.

Although there are occasionally good reasons for very detailed and polished presentations, too often people feel compelled to be complete and precise in every presentation on every topic. These tendencies simply lead to turd polishing and unsatisfactory communications. The self-defining jargon I just used is a memorable term for adding lots of details and frills in an attempt to make relatively weak or low-quality messages look better. Turd polishing, practiced both in writing and speaking, is usually obvious to an audience and is somewhat insulting. Most audiences are too polite to challenge you when they see such material, but they will turn on their BS filters and start interpreting everything you say with more skepticism. Here are a few ideas for improving the preparation and style of your presentation and avoiding information overload.

Use Illustrations and Pictures

A picture is worth 1000 words. Try to explain in words what the face of a clock looks like, how Celsius translates into Fahrenheit, how your net worth has changed over the past 10 years, or the beauty of the Aurora Borealis. These are far easier to convey with a simple illustration, equation, graph, and photo, respectively. These are all more memorable than strings of words.

Figure 5-1 is a relatively simple graphic that I have used for more than 20 years, in numerous variations, to explain some complicated topics in software management. I include the graphic in my presentations while explaining the topic verbally. If I were to present just the graphic or just my spoken remarks, the audience would be hard-pressed to grasp and remember what I was talking about. A meaningful graphic provides a framework for words to be reasoned through, making complex topics understandable and memorable. The figure provides an incredible amount of information in a simple graphic that compares and contrasts three project profiles. I could easily use 1000 words to explain the concepts that are well-painted with the illustration.

FIGURE 5-1. *A Picture Worth 1000 Words*

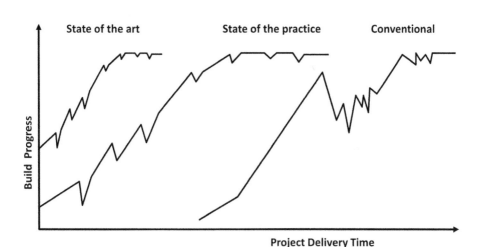

Simple graphics, combined with a strong argument, are vital to presenting a topic with impact. For a great treatment of the power of simple graphics, see Dan Roam's book, *The Back of the Napkin*. This should be a must-read for classes or seminars on speaking and presenting. Roam tackles visual thinking and presents compelling techniques for solving problems and communicating ideas with simple pictures that anyone can draw.

Graphics and illustrations can be misused. Not all graphics improve clarity and make your message more memorable. Complex illustrations awash in boxes, lines, and arrows have become increasingly popular in presentations. Presenters throw every symbol and box they can find onto one drawing, with lines and arrows contorted in every conceivable way, trying to portray a wide spectrum of concepts such as cause and effect, process flow, relationships among parts of a system, state changes, organizational hierarchy, and sequences of activities: Ouch! I'm getting a headache!

While some complex graphics can be effective, most are simply background structures for depositing boatloads of text with a low signal-to-noise ratio. [Signal-to-noise ratio is a term for the power ratio between a signal (i.e., meaningful information) and the background noise (i.e., clutter and random background information).]

Good presentations have a clear signal—namely, your message—and a low level of noise. Leave out the clutter, details, irrelevant clip art, unnecessary boxes and arrows, and false precision unless it amplifies your signal.

Figure 5-2 shows a graphic in which a rather simple message has been completely obfuscated by a plethora of arrows and text. It is a good example of illustrations that confuse more than they clarify. Such diagrams can be found everywhere in today's presentations.

FIGURE 5-2. *Overdoing Arrows and Text*

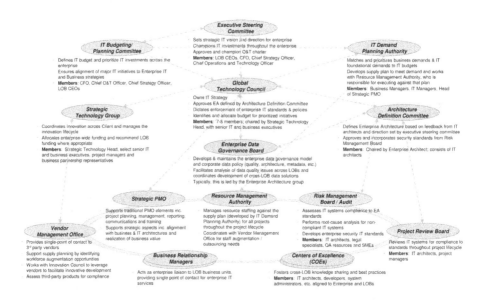

The graphic might be useful to show that the relationships among the 14 teams are well understood, but throwing in all the explanatory text clouds that message. When you see almost 500 words of 7-point type shrunk down to explain 14 bubbles, the only thing your brain registers is, "I don't get it." By the way, 500 words typically fill an 8 ½ by 11 page of text, single-spaced. To the audience, it is all noise.

Use Mathematics

Mathematical formulae are another powerful dimension of graphical representation that people hesitate to use. For example, here is a verbal explanation of the relationship between Celsius and Fahrenheit:

To convert Fahrenheit (F) to Celsius (C) or Celsius to Fahrenheit, first add 40 to the number. Next, multiply by 5/9 or 9/5. Then subtract the 40 you just added to yield the final result. You can remember whether to use 5/9 or 9/5 for the conversion if you remember that F (for Fahrenheit) begins with the same letter as *fraction*. Because 5/9 is a fraction, this is the number you use to convert Fahrenheit to Celsius. While 9/5 is also a fraction, it can also be expressed as a whole number plus a fraction (1 4/5). So to convert Celsius to Fahrenheit, use 9/5.

I created this description by *simplifying* a 135-word description I found on a website down to 104 words. It is still a fogbank compared to a simple mathematical formula that is clearer and more memorable.

Celsius $\qquad\qquad T_C = 5/9\ (T_F - 32)$

Fahrenheit $\qquad\quad\ T_F = (9/5\ T_C) + 32$

Anyone with grade school math can understand and remember these equations. Why are people so afraid to use mathematical representations to describe concepts that are based in mathematical terms?

Figure 5-3 shows a simple graphic I have used for years to represent an important set of messages about software economics (clearly an esoteric topic).

FIGURE 5-3. *Simplified Software Economics Equation*

$$\text{Cost} = (\textbf{Complexity})^{(\text{Process})} * (\textbf{Team}) * (\textbf{Automation})$$

Complexity	Process	Team	Automation
• Volume of human-generated stuff • Quality/performance • Scope	• Methods • Maturity • Agility • Precedence	• Skills/experience • Collaboration • Motivation	• Tools • Process enactment • Data management

This simple equation ($\$ = C^PTA$) has only four terms. Over the years, however, I heard from numerous people in marketing and sales that no one would understand it because it uses an exponential equation. Their inclination was to dumb down the message so that everyone would get it, including them. The error in this thinking is that a topic like software economics is not presented to uninformed people. This message is for savvy professionals who are likely to spend millions of dollars to improve their organization's capability to develop software products. These audiences have no trouble understanding a simple equation with an exponent.

In the hands of a savvy presenter, the equation provides a great framework to make the key point: These four terms are in priority order. Reducing complexity has the most impact, followed by improving the process, then improving the people, and, lastly, improving the tool automation. All the advanced mathematics within the empirical models and the underlying details about how to characterize each of these parameters are unnecessary because the equation serves to lay out a credible and accurate foundation for the subsequent discussions on those four key themes of improving software economics.

Make Things Memorable

In preparing a presentation, start with the end in mind: Think about what you really want the audience to remember. In time, it will be hard for people to recall your message out of a flood of sentences and words. Pictures, graphics, and other high-value briefing elements are more memorable. Design some mnemonic, graphic, logo, or illustration that captures the essence of your message and build your briefing around it.

You will still use many words when you craft your message. The key is to select words that people will remember. This is especially important in titles, thematic statements, and conclusions. Using words with teeth improves your communications effectiveness significantly. Consider the following example, still indelibly etched in my memory.

In the 1980s, there was a general perception among software engineers that jobs as designers and coders were cool and attracted the A players in most software organizations. The B players had to settle for the un-cool positions: testers and quality assurance engineers. There were good reasons for this view, partly because of the manual processes used at the time in software engineering. Designing and coding were creative, high-leverage activities; testing and quality assurance roles were more mundane and mostly involved paper-pushing.

Despite their less attractive responsibilities, the test and quality assurance roles had tremendous power at certain points in the software engineering process. They could halt a whole project if certain intermediate milestones were not met or documents were not approved. The A players resented this power held by the B players.

I was one of those snooty designers who looked down on the quality assurance caste as a lower form of life that slowed the engineering process. At a large industry conference in the 1980s, I scanned the program to choose the presentations that interested me the most. I usually selected the cool design and management topics, which routinely drew larger audiences than the un-cool test and quality assurance topics. But I couldn't pass up "Software Quality Assurance, The Sphincter of Software Engineering." The presenter had grabbed my attention with his witty and unexpected title.

I wasn't alone: It was one of the best-attended sessions at the conference. I've remembered the title because it nailed the topic in a memorable way. Better yet, the author delivered a good message, and I made a commitment to follow through on it. He presented the quality assurance process (not the people) as flawed and proposed that a better process would naturally attract better people, which would benefit everyone.

Avoid False Precision When Using Numbers

It is almost standard practice nowadays for presentations to use precise numbers that are computations from a spreadsheet or averages from a lot of surveys, or that are calculations from various models, plans, or estimates. In many cases, authors use numeric representations that imply much more precision than they should. Even though we know our planning process is only accurate to within 20%, we present multi-year contract prices for uncertain business endeavors down to the dollar (for example, $1,650,745). We claim that customer satisfaction has improved 23% when our survey is based on subjective assessments of 10 different customer satisfaction questions where the answers vary from 1 (very satisfied) to 5 (very dissatisfied).

These are examples of false precision. We don't know the estimated cost down to the dollar. If we know our $1.65M price to the nearest 20%, it is likely somewhere between $1.3 and $2 million. Presenting a number that has seven digits of precision is dishonest. At least present the price as $1.6M or $1,600,000 so that it portrays an uncertain estimate and does not deceptively imply more precision. Similarly, a more accurate way of presenting the improvement in customer satisfaction is to say that it has increased one full unit in our five-unit scale, or to round the number to 20%, thereby implying only one digit of precision.

An appreciation of basic statistics is also crucial to accurate communications. This topic is under-emphasized in our schools compared to its importance in everyday communications. Presenting relative and absolute measures makes a big difference in communicating information credibly. For a pragmatic treatment of this topic, see *How To Measure Anything* by Douglas Hubbard.

Most numeric measures take on two forms: an absolute value (a quantity of something) or a relative value (a measure of one quantity relative to another quantity). Relative values, usually presented as percentages, are commonly used to express two things:

1. A proportion: how much one subset measure is, relative to the total measure. For example:
    - 48% of our employees are women.
    - 30% of our product sales were to first-time customers.
    - About 20% of this book's pages are devoted to puzzles.
2. A rate of change: how much a measure has changed since a previous benchmark. Examples:
    - We added 10% more female employees in 2009.
    - Product sales were down 22% over last month.
    - Version 2 of this book increased its puzzle pages by 12% over Version 1.

These are valuable and very common measures in communicating objective information. Numeric quantities provide clear and meaningful representations. Here is a sampling that illustrates how vague some words can be. A specific numeric representation would paint a picture with more clarity and meaning.

Word	Numeric Ambiguity
numerous	10 items if describing your to-do list; 19,000 if speaking of fans at a stadium
many	jillions, referring to stars in the sky; two if speaking about ex-wives
jillions	infinity in some cases; inconceivably large for the context
hardly any	not zero, but much fewer than expected
a few	more than 1 but less than 5
several	less than 10 but more than a few
giant	10 to 13 meters if referring to squid; 1 inch if referring to ants
tall	over 5'10" if referring to a human; more than 50 stories if referring to a building

jumbo	181 to 200 per kilo when describing olives;
	3 inches if referring to shrimp
genius	IQ > 120 in absolute terms, or anyone smarter than you
idiot	3rd grade mental capability, or an inebriated genius

It is no secret that objective and quantified measures are a critical aspect of communicating clearly. However, many communications use numbers inappropriately and lose credibility through exaggeration, false precision, inappropriate units, or other forms of deceptive misusage. Hubbard defines a measurement as follows:

measurement: a set of observations that reduce uncertainty where the result is expressed as a quantity

Although you won't find it in a dictionary, this is the essence of how the scientific community defines measurement. Scientists realize that reducing uncertainty is necessary and sufficient to make a measurement useful, especially as they look at things they don't understand well such as the infinitely large and infinitesimally small. A measure does not need to eliminate all uncertainty to be useful. Given this definition, the value of percentages is easy to see: A percentage adds some further context—namely, a measure relative to some other known measure—so that you can put the measure into a perspective that further reduces uncertainty. Percentages let you add context by comparing one measure to another known value.

Everyone knows that percentages are useful. But it is important to be wary of games people can play with numbers to purposely spin information in a positive or negative way. When someone makes a comparison using only a percentage or only absolute numbers, without enough context, be suspicious. Using one without the other can paint a biased picture. This sort of spinning is most acute in selling and politics, where the bias is in favor of one product or one party or one position on an issue.

When a person is selling a product or an idea, it is natural to present a positive bias that reflects well on their perspective. While the best scientists, teachers, and judges may epitomize some of the exceptions to this statement, there are still enough counter-examples that we must be wary of the natural bias of our human nature. We all need to remember that rose-colored glasses are built into human reasoning and communications.

Here are a few generic examples of bias and ambiguity in the use of percentages.

- Sales grew 15% over last month. If last month's sales were terrible, this number may paint an overly rosy picture.
- You added 15 new hires to your organization last month. If the goal was 45 new hires, 15 is not very good performance compared to plan.
- Your GPA went up 20%. If your last GPA was 2.1 and your new GPA is 2.5, this may fall short of your parents' expectations of a B average.
- Your 401K account was up 21% over last quarter. If the rest of the markets were up 40%, your performance was relatively weak.
- Sales of product A were up 100% and product B only 10%. If product A's sales last period were only $100,000 and product B's were $10,000,000, these data are potentially misleading.
- The Dodgers won 6 more close games (decided by 1 run) this year than last year. This number is more significant if they won 10 close games last year than if they won 60.
- Politician X voted to cut taxes 90% of the time. If politician X voted yes 27 times on trivial tax-cutting bills and voted No on 3 significant tax-cutting bills, this measure may completely obfuscate his stance on tax cutting.
- 66.7% of doctors recommend this remedy for this affliction.

The last one is particularly interesting. With three digits of precision, you get the feeling that there must be a pretty thorough analysis behind that claim. But what if some advertising drone asked three doctors their opinions and two responded positively? That would make 66.7% an accurate but potentially misleading answer. A more honest measure would state that two out of the three doctors asked recommended the remedy.

There are several ways to present numbers, and it is important to communicate them honestly. It is also important as an audience or a listener to be skeptical when the numbers presented fail to tell the whole story.

A useful metaphor for presenting information honestly is evident in how *truth* is defined in the American justice system by emphasizing three aspects:

1. The truth: Be accurate.
2. The whole truth: Be precise enough and include everything relevant.
3. Nothing but the truth: Don't be overly precise or add anything irrelevant.

Providing a measure is usually the primary dimension of *the truth*. Providing a credible measure with the appropriate backup context (like both the percentage and the absolute numbers) is necessary to tell *the whole truth*. And using accurate data with the right level of precision ensures that you are not misleading people with additional detail that obfuscates the truth. I think a statistics class should be part of every high school core curriculum. Understanding estimates, random variables, expected values, and standard deviations is crucial to many decisions and is a core skill for communicating honestly.

There is one common use of percentages that makes little sense. Has a boss or a coach asked you to give 110%? The use of numbers over 100% is silly. When someone asks you to give 110%, they are referring to your total capacity (either all your heart, all your energy, all your time, or all of something). In that context, isn't it erroneous to request someone to give 110% of some quantity where all of that quantity is equal to 100%? Either the boss/coach is a moron (they don't understand percentages), or the boss/coach thinks the employee/player is a moron. In my view, it is a mathematical oxymoron.

Have Empathy for the Audience

Not everyone is expert at composing graphics and tables and presentations. Not everyone is a good writer. However, we all consider ourselves experts at being part of an audience. We watch TV, listen to the radio, watch movies, read books, listen to conversations, and act as an audience several times a day. What do you like in a presentation? Most people like pictures (not descriptions), brevity (not long-winded stories reliving every detail), facts (more than speculation), provocative challenges (rather than whitewash that offends the fewest people), debate among alternatives (rather than obvious bias), and clarity (rather than ambiguity). As we prepare a presentation, we should ask ourselves whether *we* would want to listen to it. We are our own best critics, so we should try to evaluate our presentation from the audience's perspective.

To have empathy for the audience, we must consider who is in the audience, what their motivations are in being there, and what we want them to remember. Here are a few key questions to consider as you prepare any communication.

Who is in my audience? Would you give the same physics lesson to 8th graders as you would to graduate students? Would you present your employment background to your date as you would to a prospective hiring manager? Would you write the same autobiography for general consumption as you would for your family? No, no, and no. The composition of your audience can substantially affect the way you communicate. Because your message is for them, not just for you, you should tailor your message, style, tone, and content to maximize its effective reception by the audience. This is not always easy, but it is always worth considering. Most audiences are mixed and very difficult to pigeonhole into a typical listener. Don't let that stop you from examining the common characteristics that most of the listeners will have. There are reasons these people are all reading or listening to your communications. What are some common themes that brought them into your audience?

Why are they here? Within every audience, there are many different reasons for these particular people to want to listen to your topic. Attendance may be required, such as a mandatory meeting or an assignment by a teacher. Some may want to attend because the title of your talk is so intriguing, or because you are known to the audience members to have an interesting opinion, or because their trusted friend or colleague said, "You will enjoy this." The reasons they want to be there may vary widely.

- They expect to agree with you and want to reinforce their opinion.
- They expect to disagree with you and want to understand an opposing opinion.
- They know nothing about the topic but want to learn.
- They know something about the topic but want to learn more.
- They are accompanying a friend with one of the reasons given above.

Whatever the reason, you need to consider why your audience is there and attempt to satisfy their motivation. If they are there to learn something, you'd better present something new that they didn't already know. If they are there to be entertained, you'd better show some flair. If they are there expecting you to sell them something, you'd better demonstrate some empathy and credibility for how you can add value to their life in exchange for money. If they are there to scout you as their competition, you'd better impress them with your credibility and worthiness to compete. If they are there to see one of their colleagues honored, you'd better honor them in an honest and upbeat way. And if they are there to honor a loved one who has passed away, you might want to help them feel positive about that person's transition.

If the audience is required to be there, your job is more challenging, but pretty simple: Make them happy they came and fulfill their requirement as effectively and efficiently as possible.

What do I want them to remember? You want every audience to remember that your presentation was worth their time. Even if they decide to leave early or stop reading your written piece before finishing it, you want to help them make that decision by providing your key points early in your communication. This is why we are taught that good writing and good presentations do three things: tell them what you are going to tell them, tell them, then tell them what you just told them. I don't recommend following that advice verbatim, but there is some wisdom in it.

1. Tell them what you are going to tell them: Use a catchy, meaningful title and a concise introduction.
2. Tell them: Keep the body of your message concise and punchy. Be accurate and use the right level of precision to make your points.
3. Tell them what you just told them: Summarize concisely and memorably, reinforcing what you want them to remember.

Practice Sequential Translation

When you present in foreign forums where the audience does not understand enough English to appreciate your presentation, you may have to resort to translation. There are two forms of translation: simultaneous and sequential. Simultaneous translation involves the audience wearing headsets like you would see at a United Nations meeting. Remote translators are listening to you and simultaneously translating for the audience as you walk through the presentation. In such circumstances, it is imperative for speakers to speak slowly and with good diction, avoiding jargon, accents, and colloquialisms.

Sequential translation is a different experience. It can provide more fidelity in the translation and much more room for interaction with the audience than simultaneous translation. The speaker presents a few sentences and waits while they are translated for the audience. The presentation moves at roughly half the pace of normal, forcing the speaker to present each slide in half the usual time or to present only half the material. This has proven to be a great mechanism for training people to be concise and hone verbal presentations down to the bare essentials to make the key points. This is what every presenter should do in every presentation, and going through the process under game conditions is a great exercise. Each time the translator is translating what you just said, you can focus on what the next key point should be and how to say it concisely. If you can set this up as the method for practicing, rather than doing a typical dry run, you will benefit.

Prevent Oral Tedium

A good speaker can make good material more understandable and more memorable. A good speaker can make weak material tolerable by using the audience's time effectively to emphasize the highlights and ignore the weak stuff. A presentation might be interesting, compelling, and earth-shattering, but the audience won't know this without someone emphasizing the important points and leading them through the material.

A poor speaker with good material can distract the audience from understanding it. A poor speaker with weak material can torture an audience by forcing them to waste time. The combination of a bad presentation and a bad speaker who insists on addressing every bullet and reading every word on every page is deadly. How many times have you sat through a presentation that was not a briefing, but rather a prepared speech, with sentences or paragraphs extracted from some written prose and pasted into PowerPoint slides? Aaauuuggghh!

Having fidgeted through a jillion ineffective presentations (and delivered a few myself), I have observed some recurring characteristics of speakers that annoy audiences. Here are some tips for avoiding these bad habits.

1. Don't spend a lot of time introducing yourself, your role, or how much experience you have. These preliminaries may be necessary to get people into the audience, but once they are there, they want to hear your message, not your resume.

2. Don't read your presentation material. This is another good reason to use graphics. You must explain them, and they can't be read like bulleted words. The audience can read, and they expect you to add something to the presentation as a speaker. Narration is a waste of their time and they will resent it.

3. Use a laser pointer only in the rarest circumstances where you need to point to a specific detail that is not easily seen on a graphic. Most speakers use a laser pointer as a crutch to point at the words they are reading on the slide. Don't insult the audience by pointing at words

as you read them. Laser pointers should be banned. They distract the speaker and the audience in most presentations.

4. Only use humor if you are comfortable with it and it fits into the context of your talk. The last thing you need to communicate clearly is the uncomfortable feeling you experience when a joke flops. When I first started public speaking, I was presenting in front of 1200 people at a large industry conference. I started off with a joke that I thought was funny and pertinent. The silence in the room after my punch line was so *loud*, I could barely continue. That incident left an indelible scar; I didn't tell a joke during a presentation for 10 years.

5. Don't act. Be yourself, speak with some inflection, use hand gestures if they feel comfortable, and move around if you need to. If I have a choice, I speak from the audience's right-hand side. Perhaps I am not an ambidextrous speaker; I don't know, but I am more comfortable on the right. Whatever it takes, get comfortable on stage and be yourself.

6. Don't sacrifice accuracy and credibility by substituting (false) precision.

7. Don't overuse adverbs like *actually, basically, fundamentally*, and *frankly*. Consciously work to eliminate annoying speaker idiosyncrasies like too many *ums*, or saying "…right?" at the end of each sentence. Don't use "I would argue…" or "It should be noted…" or "It is interesting to note…" Just argue, note it, or make it interesting.

Get to the Point

It is unusual to face an audience filled with people who are completely ignorant about the topic being presented. Therefore, you probably don't need to spend half your presentation introducing the context and the problem that you are addressing. Most people in an audience want to hear your recommendation, perspective, or approach, not a rehash of why this topic is important. If they didn't already think it was important, they wouldn't be in the audience.

Spending too much time on the context/problem is one of the most common characteristics of ineffective presentations. Speakers invariably try to squeeze more material into a presentation than can be briefed effectively in the time allocated, and they tend to start presentations much more slowly than they finish. The natural tendency of most speakers is to spend 60% of their allocated timeslot on the first

50% of the material. Consequently, the material that follows the context/problem—what the audience came to learn—gets short shrift.

Here's a simple example of what can happen. Suppose you have one hour to present a topic. This is the typical sequence of events.

1. You know that you can present about 20 slides in an hour. You budget 5 slides for the introduction/context, 5 slides for alternative solutions, 5 slides for tradeoffs, and 5 slides for the selected solution, impacts, and conclusions. You figure the first 10 slides are easy and will take about 2 minutes each to present. The last 10 slides are meatier and may stimulate questions, so you budget 4 minutes each for them. This feels about right: 20 minutes on the context, 40 minutes on your main message.

2. You are comfortable with the intro and alternatives material, and you have plenty of detail. You end up with 15 slides on those topics and only 9 slides on the last two topics. Now your briefing is 24 slides, but you figure you can easily cram that into the time slot.

3. As you present the familiar, comfortable front-end material, you spend more time than planned. Rather than 2 minutes per slide, you spend 3 minutes per slide. Since you have more slides of that comfortable context material, you end up consuming 45 minutes, or 75% of your time slot, on context. Now you only have 15 minutes, or 25% of your one-hour time slot, to discuss your main message.

This scenario unfolds in four out of five briefings I attend (including many of my own, early in my career). Even speakers with the best intentions can fall into this easy trap. If some members of the audience want to discuss the front-end material, you are vulnerable to presenting more context than necessary.

Here are a few suggestions for avoiding this trap.

•   Assume that your audience is reasonably smart on the context. Purposefully minimize introductory material. If the audience asks questions, fill them in verbally or offer to provide more context as a follow-up. Most people forgive you for treating them like they are more knowledgeable than they might be. Audiences are less forgiving when you waste their time with basics that are already well known.

•   Build your main message first, and then add only the context and introductory material you need to make your point. Too many people start with what they know well rather than starting with the main message they want the audience to receive.

- Begin your briefing with a few simple slides that you can present quickly, setting a pace for the presentation. It is extremely common for presenters to spend 15 minutes on the first slide of a 30-slide presentation, mired down in some hairy topic and setting a slow pace. Once you dig this hole, it is difficult to recover. It is hard enough to speak clearly when you are comfortable with the topic and the timing; a speaker who feels rushed has tremendous difficulty communicating effectively.

- Don't be afraid to pause in the middle of your briefing to check your timing, collect your thoughts, and adjust, or to let an important point sink in. Audiences appreciate it when a speaker pauses occasionally. This is generally viewed as an attribute of good and great speakers.

There are many good reference books filled with techniques for better speaking. Most of these tips are obvious, or they are easy to say and hard to do. There is only one way to get comfortable at public speaking: Do it. It is easy to speak to others when you have confidence in what you are saying. It is hard when you fear that they know more about your presentation topic than you do. In general, it is rare to be asked to speak in front of an audience that is more expert than you are. PhD oral exams and assignments in speech classes are two obvious exceptions. If you get nervous before speaking, as most people do, remind yourself that you probably know this topic better than anyone in the audience. That thought can be very comforting and help you to relax.

The best way to combat fear is proper preparation. Rehearsing alone in dry runs can be mildly helpful but is no substitute for a live audience. So if you are going to rehearse, try to find an audience, even a small one, to listen and critique. Being prepared with an honest presentation that makes its points in a memorable way should give you confidence and reduce your fear.

CHAPTER 6

Selling an Idea

Selling is persuading someone to buy something. The *something* may be a product, a service, an agreement, an exchange, a plea, an observation, or a story. You may simply be trying to persuade someone to believe you, or you may be asking them to exchange a wad of money for a product or service. You want, and sometimes need, to be persuasive. What does this take?

Everyone needs to sell, and sometimes the act of selling something or persuading someone escalates into a high-stakes communication. When we are young, we may want to sell our parents on letting us stay up past curfew to attend that special concert with our friends. Or we may want to convince them that our preferred college choice (a remote, well-known party school) is better than their preferred college choice (a local, nerdy school). As we move into our professions, the need for selling occurs frequently.

Dan Roam's book, *The Back of the Napkin,* provides an excellent discussion of some fundamentals of observing, articulating, and selling ideas. He frames his visual thinking analysis with four steps: look, see, imagine, and show. *Looking* is collecting raw information as a visual sensor. *Seeing* is the act of observing, mentally processing that information, and filtering, sorting, pattern matching, and prioritizing standout images. *Imagining* is using our brain's ability to process the physical things we see and transform them into logical models, patterns, and cause-and-effect relationships. It is thinking about what we don't see, and reasoning about why the things we do see are what they are. It is what sets humans apart from other life forms. *Showing* is the way we communicate our mental picture to ourselves and to others in order to inform and persuade.

When it comes to seeing and showing, Roam recommends the 6Ws model (see Table 6-1) for organizing information and communicating our thoughts to others. His central thesis is, "For every one of the six ways of seeing, there is one corresponding way for showing; for each one of these six ways of showing, there is a single visual framework that serves as a starting point."

TABLE 6-1. *Visual Frameworks*

What We See	Description	What We Show
Who and what	Objects	Portrait or image
How many	Quantities	Chart
When	Positions in time	Timeline
Where	Positions in space	Map
How	Causes and effects	Flowchart
Why	Logical conclusions	Graph

Even though Roam might have called this the "Four Ws + 1 and two Hs" model, the 6Ws is more memorable. Most of us relate questions to words that begin with *w*, and this set of interrogatories is a great framework for observing and analyzing a situation, a problem, or a solution. They also help us compartmentalize our observations into multiple aspects so that we observe and communicate a more complete picture.

With some minor extensions of this model, these dimensions are a good framework for reasoning about selling. My extensions are as follows. First, separate out the *who* and the *what*. The reason for this is that selling is an action: You want to sell something to someone. The *who* now allows you to capture observations about the someone, and the *what* allows you to capture observations about the something. Second, add a *which* question that can be used to characterize the sort of language you should use to make your proposal. *Language* does not refer to whether you should speak in English, Portuguese, or Mandarin. It refers to the tone and shades of your sales pitch that will appeal to your intended audience. This includes the jargon you might use (demonstrating some savvy in the field), the maturity level of the audience (expert, skilled, amateur), the style of the audience (analytical, driver, amiable, expressive), and other sorts of presentation attributes that attract the audience to your sales pitch.

With these extensions and a few wording changes, we now have an 8W model.

1. To whom are you selling?   Understand the audience.
2. Why would they buy?   Understand their motivations.
3. Where do they live or operate?   Understand their domain and environment.
4. How will they realize value?   Understand how they operate.
5. When are results expected?   Understand their timeframes.
6. How much value will be realized? Understand the impact for them.
7. Which language should you use?   Understand their channels of communications.
8. What should you sell them?   Understand how you both benefit.

A seller should answer these questions before delivering a value proposition. I have found this approach to be a best practice among the many exceptional salespeople with whom I have worked in my life. They intuitively know they must *show* their client multiple dimensions of information so that the client can *see* the value of their product, idea, or solution. This maximizes the persuasiveness of their sales argument. Knowing this, sellers spend time diagnosing their client's needs so that they can understand the whole picture from the client's point of view. This is the point of Roam's book, although he captures it in a beautiful treatment of visual thinking and communicating with pictures.

We can use this 8W model in a somewhat abstract way to examine the breadth of the solution space that most sellers must be able to navigate. Most product lines span a broad spectrum of client contexts. How broad? This is a simple problem to analyze with the 8W model. You can do a coarse analysis of your marketplace by estimating the number of different client contexts in which you sell. Table 6-2 summarizes some examples of distinct answers to the eight questions, using very generic answers just to demonstrate the variety of contexts.

TABLE 6-2. *Examples of Answers to the 8W Model Questions*

Diagnostic Dimension	Examples of Distinctly Different Client Contexts
To **whom** are you selling?	Executives, managers, practitioners Professionals, skilled artisans, amateurs Parents, teachers, children
Why would they buy?	Cost savings, time savings, quality improvement Necessity, luxury Best value, best reputation, best quality, best price
Where do they live or operate?	Locally, nationally, globally Commercial, government, academia, family Financial, industrial, entertainment, technology
How will they realize value?	Automation, process improvement, simplification Prestige, efficiency, usefulness, longevity
When are results expected?	Immediately, days, weeks, months, years Single instance, multiple instances, continually
How much value will be realized?	Small, moderate, large, very large, extra large 10% to 50% more or 10% to 50% less $100s, $1,000s, $1,000,000s
Which language should you use?	Analytical, driver, amiable, expressive Jargon, formal, informal Technical, financial, emotional
What should you sell them?	Products, services, knowhow Sports equipment, clothing, housewares Raw data, filtered data sets, analysis

If you quantify the number of distinct possibilities in each dimension, you can make a rough guess of the number of different value propositions with which you might be confronted. If all the dimensions were independent and all permutations were possible, the number of different possibilities would be surprisingly large. If each dimension had just three distinct answers, there would be 6,500 different value propositions. Although my assumptions are weak—the dimensions are not all independent and the categorization of distinct contexts is usually rough and arguable—the conclusion is strong. There are almost always a very large number of possibilities, and you can't afford to have canned sales pitches available for all of them. Consequently, most salespeople need to be good diagnosticians, which requires keen observation skills.

Many sales organizations sell a broad product line with diverse usage models. They must create highly customized value propositions where the number of distinct possibilities is in the millions. Many global system integrators, defense contractors, software product companies, and retail companies have very capable sales forces dealing with this challenge of very context-dependent value propositions. Searching out that one sharp needle in this haystack of possibilities is the exciting detective work that motivates many sellers. To stand out, they must understand the customer's context by diagnosing the answers to the first seven questions of the 8W model, and then synthesize a solution from their product line by asking themselves the eighth question.

This discussion has dealt with professional selling. What does it take to communicate persuasively in a one-on-one situation like a conversation with your mother or a one-to-many situation like a presentation to colleagues?

Value-Based Selling

The verb *to sell* can take on many different meanings. Here are the *Dictionary.com* definitions for *sell* when it is used as a verb with an object:

1. To transfer (goods) to or render (services) for another in exchange for money; dispose of to a purchaser for a price: He sold the car to me for $1000.
2. To deal in; keep or offer for sale: He sells insurance. This store sells my favorite brand.
3. To make a sale or offer for sale to: He'll sell me the car for $1000.
4. To persuade or induce (someone) to buy something: The salesman sold me on a more expensive model than I wanted.
5. To persuade or induce someone to buy (something): The clerk really sold the shoes to me by flattery.
6. To make sales of: The hot record sold a million copies this month.
7. To cause to be accepted, especially generally or widely: to sell an idea to the public.
8. To cause or persuade to accept; convince: to sell the voters on a candidate.
9. To accept a price for or profit from (something not a proper object for such action): to sell one's soul for political power.
10. To force or exact a price for: The defenders of the fort sold their lives dearly.
11. Informal: to cheat, betray, or hoax.

The first 10 definitions boil down to two core meanings: to exchange something for money, or to persuade someone. The eleventh definition is also an important one, with a negative connotation. We will discuss that later.

If you are going to exchange something for money, you have to create a value proposition that has at least equal value to the client for the money they are going to give you in return. In many situations, the value to the client is intangible. Nevertheless, you need to monetize your offer so that the client believes that what they need or want is worth the price you are asking. To gain agreement for the transaction, a seller must do two things: create a value proposition, and persuade the client that the value proposition is credible or better than available alternatives.

The most important lesson in selling is that value is in the eye of the beholder. I chose these exact words for two reasons. First, the value of most things we want to sell is as immeasurable as beauty, which is the well-known basis of the statement. Second, beauty and value can only be measured from the observer's perspective, or in this case, that of the buyer. We all have different tastes in art, food, pets, and friends. Their beauty/value is subjective, different to us than to other people. Sure, there are some things that most people agree are beautiful, at least within a given culture, but to varying degrees. You would be perplexed if you tried to quantify the difference between your appreciation of Pink Floyd and mine. I think Zion National Park is twice as beautiful as the Grand Canyon. Do you?

For most things that people are trying to sell, there is no formulaic definition of value that allows a seller to say that this thing is worth this price. Although sellers may present such arguments, buyers rarely agree. Everyone has seen commercials where a vendor offers their product at a discounted price, adds in a few sweeteners, and claims that you pay only $19.95 for this $79 value. Sellers imply that the "value" is the list price of their product plus the list prices of the sweeteners. This may make sense to them, but we know better. The true value to us is what we are willing to pay for it based on our own sense of values.

Creating a value proposition is another exercise in understanding the receiver before beginning to transmit. This is the basis of one of the habits in Stephen Covey's *The Seven Habits of Highly Effective People*. Seek first to understand, then to be understood. This is particularly important in selling because a buyer wants to trust a seller. When money changes hands, the stakes escalate. The communications between buyer and seller become the make-its (trust builders) or the break-its (trust destroyers).

Persuading

Persuasive communications are communications whose specific purpose is to gain agreement on something. Here are some examples.

- A lawyer's closing statement to a jury on the guilt or innocence of a defendant
- A job interview
- A politician's speech requesting your vote
- Pickup lines in a bar conversation with a new acquaintance
- An essay on a college entrance exam
- A parent's plea to improve their child's grades and study habits

The 8Ws model provides a solid framework for the various aspects that a receiver is likely to see in the value proposition, idea, or suggestion that you transmit. If these are the aspects that people observe, these are the aspects that you should consider and communicate.

There are several synonyms for *persuasive*: trustworthy, influential, logical, charming, and articulate. These synonyms are the positive reactions that you want your message to cause in the audience you are trying to persuade. However, each of these attributes has a diversity of meanings to different people. For example, *articulate* means concise and expressive to me. To someone else, it might mean thorough and analytical. *Charming* means humorous and clever to me; to my wife, it means gentle and thoughtful. Like beauty, these attributes vary somewhat with the beholder. Once again, as the stakes of the communications increase, the need to understand your receiver and address their style preferences in your communications also increases. Some specific examples of persuasive communications illustrate how the 8W framework can be used to facilitate the planning and execution of a persuasive argument.

First Example: A communication from a subordinate to a superior

Suppose I'm a teenager and I want to sell my parents on letting me get my driver's license earlier than they want me to. In my family, children weren't allowed to drive until they were 17 years old, even though our state allowed children to drive at 16. My parents believed that teenagers were just not mature enough at 16 to be trusted with the responsibility of an automobile. I failed to "sell" my parents to change their minds. If I could go back and redo my approach, armed with the wisdom of the intervening decades, here's the analysis I would perform.

To **whom** are you selling? My parents are reasonable, but they are not going to bend the rules without a good reason. My rotten brother screwed me over by setting the wrong precedent 2 years ago when he got his license. Within a week, he had permission to stay out late. He went someplace different than he had told my folks and got ratted out by nosy neighbors. So now my parents are going to be biased against my request by mistrust. They constantly harp that privileges come with increased responsibility, and my lame brother didn't make my case easy to sell.

Why would they buy? They are not going to let me get my license early unless I can demonstrate that I am more trustworthy than my brother. If they think I am more responsible than he was when he was younger, they might see the value of my proposal.

Where do they live or operate? We live in a rural community where I have many transportation needs. My folks and my brother have to drive me everywhere. Because they are willing to do this, however, my parents think that a driver's license is a luxury for me, not a necessity.

How will they realize value? My folks and my brother would see some benefit in not having to drive me around. My parents would save time, and they would be spared frequent arguments with my snobby brother who doesn't like being seen with me.

When are results expected? As soon as I get my license, they will have more freedom. This will give them less hectic lives between my 16th and 17th birthdays. I have already saved enough money to pay for my insurance, which I know is a precondition in our family for getting a license. So there should be no timing issues.

How much value will be realized? It is hard to quantify the value of allowing me to get my license early. It would save my parents some time; I estimate about 10 hours a week. That should be worth a lot to them. They could spend more time at the gym, or cooking together, or doing other things for which they wish they had more time. The biggest value to them would be to see me demonstrate increased responsibility in exchange for this early privilege. How can I quantify that? Maybe I could demonstrate my willingness to be more responsible by offering to take the trash to the dump every weekend (dad hates that errand) and take on half of the snow shoveling. My lazy brother would love this, since he has all that responsibility now. If I can offer some benefit to everyone in the family, I have a better chance of selling my idea.

Which language should you use? My dad's style is pretty analytical, and my mom's style is a driver. So I need to use some facts and data to satisfy my dad and make sure that he knows I have a well thought-out proposal. I will have to promise some definitive results to satisfy mom and give her some control over my destiny. I know they will be predisposed against my proposal, thanks to my brother. I will need to emphasize that I am different from him and that this decision should be based on the merits of my proposal, not on his past mistakes.

What should you sell them? After noodling through the seven dimensions discussed above, I am prepared to make a persuasive proposal to my parents. Here is what that might look like in its simplest form.

> Mom, Dad, I want to ask you for something that is really important to me. I've been thinking through the pros and cons for a while, and I would like you to listen to my whole story before you make a decision.
>
> My request is for you to allow me to get my driver's license next month. I understand your reasons for wanting me to wait until my 17th birthday. But getting my driver's license has great value to me, and I would like to offer something of even greater value to you and my brother. In exchange for this privilege, I will enthusiastically take on more responsibility for household chores to demonstrate my maturity. I will make the weekly trip to the garbage dump and I will take on half the snow shoveling duties.
>
> I did a rough analysis, and I estimate that you will free up 10 hours a week by not having to drive me around. That would give you more time to go to the gym or cook together or do other fun things. I have saved the money for my insurance, and if things don't turn out better from your perspective, you could take away my driving privilege at any time. What do you say?

That proposition would not succeed in every household, but I think it might increase the probability of a *yes* answer over the usual approach that most teenagers take. Even if I fail to get the answer I want, I will have impressed my parents with a respectable attempt and built some further trust that will pay off in the future.

Here's a more complicated example.

Second Example: A professional sales scenario

Suppose you are selling software tools for website construction. The value proposition for your products is pretty simple: The software tools provide a 20% performance improvement in website construction by automating a lot of coding and testing. The cost of your product runs about 5% of typical labor costs for a year. Therefore, your customers could save 15% on labor costs or perform 15% more work for the same labor using your products. That sounds like an easy sale, but it is not. Some industry background explains why.

Performance improvement in many businesses, such as software development, is frequently measured using some function of productivity. Productivity is not always easy to measure in creative activities like software development, movie production, or book writing. Productivity is defined as some measure of cost per unit output. Let's say that this book has 200 pages and required 2000 hours to produce. That is a productivity of 10 hours per page or $1000 per page if you assume that I make $100 per hour.

You can write many pages of a chapter, program several software components, or script several scenes of a movie and appear productive. For example, I drafted this 200-page manuscript in about 600 hours, by my estimate. As I write this sentence, that was more than a year ago and I am still revising, editing, and even adding new material that was not in my original manuscript. Until you start copy editing and integrating chapters, or testing and integrating software components, or shooting and integrating movie scenes, and then exposing them to an audience of readers, or software users, or movie goers, you are not sure how much progress you have made.

Even though I had a draft manuscript more than a year ago, I knew that I was only about 50% complete. Creative disciplines tend to require several iterations, extensive teamwork, and significant scrap and rework to achieve a suitable end product. The necessary revisions and the amount of work remaining are frequently difficult to estimate. Because productivity, interim progress, and interim quality are difficult to measure in such creative endeavors, the related industries don't put much trust into such measures.

The performance measurements in most software organizations are more like the sleight-of-hand statistics quoted by politicians than the matter-of-fact statistics quoted by engineers and scientists. Politicians have a well-deserved reputation for being disingenuous, and they have track records similar to software organizations for under-delivering on committed productivity improvements. Disingenuous means "deceptively calculating" or "smart but dishonest." The software industry is full of cynical customers because their experience with software productivity improvements—internally as well as externally from vendors—is plagued by hyperbole and spin. It is difficult to sell your software tool product line in a market where there is mistrust.

Another key challenge in selling software tools is that the client initially sees only an increased cost. The productivity improvements (if there are any) won't pay for themselves until many months or years later. Asking customers to spend now and benefit later is a tough sell. Most clients won't buy unless they have rock-solid confidence in your value proposition. You must make productivity improvements more credible and demonstrable, and thereby earn more trust than your competitors. Otherwise, your selling efforts will look just like those of your competitors: long-shot propositions with no compelling evidence that you can improve on the customer's status quo.

This situation confronts a jillion sales professionals every day. Their product lines range from $20 items sold to individuals to multi-million dollar products sold to multi-national organizations that have thousands of people distributed across the world collaborating over the internet. The 8W model provides a good framework for diagnosing both simple and complex customer situations. Table 6-3 captures an example of how this could unfold for a very complicated sale.

The table only hints at the different perspectives you would use to communicate with the three key constituents: executives, managers, and practitioners. In many selling situations in today's technologically complex world, it may take 6 to 9 months for a sales team to diagnose the client's situation. Until they have this complete context, they cannot fully prepare to make a proposal that is persuasive and has the right value to compel the client to buy.

TABLE 6-3. *Example of an Industrial Strength Selling Situation*

Diagnostic Dimension	Elaboration of Client Context
To **whom** are you selling?	We need to gain buy-in from the executives, managers, and practitioners.
Why would they buy?	Executives: Financial benefits, such as higher profits, lower costs, corporate growth Managers: Improved morale, ability to attract better people Practitioners: More creative and productive work, less overhead and tedium
Where do they live or operate?	Executives: In several countries and in a competitive market Managers: At a specific work site with an existing labor pool Practitioners: Collaboratively over the web in cyberspace
How will they realize value?	Executives: Increased revenue through more attractive products Managers: Increased team productivity and less personnel turnover Practitioners: More output per hour, less boredom
When are results expected?	Executives: 15% improvement within a year, 5% improvement each quarter Managers: Monthly improvements in operational efficiency and hiring Practitioners: After one month of training and transition
How much value will be realized?	Executives: 10% increase in profits, 20% increase in market share Managers: 10% more team productivity, 10% higher bonuses, promotions Practitioners: 20% less dog work, 20% more output per hour, good raises
Which language should you use?	Executives: Financial, business results Managers: Operational, teamwork, operational efficiencies Practitioners: Technical, demonstrable, features
What should you sell them?	Executives: Financial leverage Managers: Team productivity leverage Practitioners: Individual productivity leverage

SELLING IS NOT ABOUT WINNING

Dysfunctional selling practices are rampant throughout the world today, especially where people are selling stuff with intangible, or difficult to quantify, value.

Dysfunctional buying practices have evolved to defend against dysfunctional selling practices. The world of buying and selling has devolved into a world that is driven by mistrust. This can be a very frustrating world to live in.

Let's Get Real or Let's Not Play by Mahan Khalsa is one of the books that has helped me advance my professional sales skills. Khalsa lays out an insightful rationale on why professional sellers struggle with prospective clients and why clients struggle with prospective sellers. Here is his memorable description of the problem:

> *With due respect to sales professionals, the notion of sales and selling carries a lot of negative baggage. It is the second oldest profession, often confused with the first. No matter what you put in front of or in back of the word "selling" (consultative, solution, visionary, creative, integrity, value-based, beyond), it still ends up with the sense of doing something "to" somebody rather than "for" or "with" somebody.*

The perception that sellers are preying on you (they win, you lose) rather than trading with you (you both win by receiving good value in the exchange) is the source of mistrust that drives our perceptions and fear of sellers. To be blunt, this perception is often deserved. It is a rare human being who will negotiate for the fairest exchange rather than an outcome where they come out ahead. When the value of something is intangible and difficult to quantify (a piece of art, a manuscript, or some other collectible), fairness becomes a very elastic measure. This adds complications because the people negotiating with each other have no consistent measurement standard on which to base their arguments.

Trust is the recurring theme for successful selling. This topic is well covered in Stephen M. R. Covey's classic, *The Speed of Trust*. His essential point is that trust speeds up everything and reduces the cost of everything. If you look at your life, you will see that his assertion holds up well. In cases where you detest some process that wastes your time, you can usually find mistrust as the root cause of your dissatisfaction.

- If employers trusted employees to spend company money as if it were their own, they wouldn't need spending limits, detailed expense reports with receipts, expense audits, and other administrative procedures on which companies spend money and employees waste time.
- Our tax system is expensive for the government to administer because citizens are not trustworthy in paying their fair share. People cheat on their taxes because they don't trust the government to fairly administer the tax system and spend their money wisely.
- Have you gone through an airport security line recently?

I may not think these things are fair to me, but most of them are necessary because enough people are untrustworthy and will take advantage of situations if they are given the chance. Corporations, governments, and even families create costly mechanisms for us all to protect against the untrustworthy actions of a few.

A Self-Assessment

I spent a lot of time trying to decide how to conclude this chapter. Finally, I asked myself, "What are you trying to sell the reader?" Eureka! I should close with a practice-what-you-preach example. So in conclusion, I'm using the 8W model in Table 6-4 to communicate how I view my target audience and how I want to communicate the value of this book. If it's persuasive enough, it will provide a foundation for the material on the back cover.

TABLE 6-4. *To Whom are You Selling?*

Diagnostic Dimension	Elaboration of Client Context
To **Whom** are you selling?	People who want to communicate better Young adults who want practical lessons Professionals who want to build advanced skills
Why would they buy?	Deep insights delivered in simple, thought-provoking lessons Years of lessons learned packaged in 200+ entertaining pages A reference book of reusable knowledge, puzzles, and observations
Where do they live or operate?	English-speaking countries Schools and workplaces Communications workshops and adolescent leadership camps
How will they realize value?	Observing their own communications patterns Observing the communications strengths and weaknesses of others Solving puzzles and relishing their observation skills
When are results expected?	Aha! moments in every chapter Immediately upon observing other people's communications styles Over time, improving the effectiveness of their communications
How much value will be realized?	A huge, colossal, gargantuan, mammoth amount Heaps more than the cost of the book, or about $100,000*

Which language should you use?	An informal style suitable for everyone
	Occasionally advanced, occasionally humorous, always useful
	Practice what you preach
What should you sell them?	An entertaining mix of communications topics, including:
	Educational tidbits, principles, patterns, trivia
	Puzzles, anecdotes, know-how, worldly wisdom

* *This is my context-independent, rough order of magnitude, wild-ass guess of the value that the typical reader will realize in 2010 dollars. If you have a better guess, use it.*

Yikes! I'm sure trying to fulfill a tall order! The information I captured in Table 6-4 certainly persuaded me to reconsider and refine many of the topics as well as the presentation of this book. I hope it provides you with more use and more entertainment value than the price you paid for it and the time you invested in reading it.

CHAPTER 7

Interviews

Interviews are an acute example of one-on-one communications. Because they are the epitome of a critical conversation where the stakes are high for both parties, they provide a great case study for effective communications. This chapter contains observations on communicating in interviews and suggests some provocative techniques for improving your effectiveness as an interviewer or an interviewee.

Few decisions in business are as crucial as hiring the right people. Most businesses run on the backs of employees, and interviews are one of the key filters in the hiring process. For an interviewee, the stakes are even higher. Few endeavors matter more to our livelihood than the employment we seek. Your job, the company, and the people you work with have a significant impact on your overall pursuit of happiness.

So how serious and prepared are most interviewers and interviewees? In my experience, both parties are complacent and unprepared. Most interviewers get the same value in the first 5 minutes as they do in 60 to 90 minutes. The initial impression gained during the first 5 minutes, mostly framed by appearance, is the predominant differentiator. How did I learn this? As I started managing people and gaining experience in hiring, I began each interview with these three questions:

1. How would you grade the interviews you have already experienced?
2. Have your previous interviews for this job helped you learn more about this opportunity?
3. Do you think the interviewer learned much about your ability to perform in this role?

I repeatedly heard that most interviews spent two-thirds of the time on the applicant's resume, long-term goals, and outside interests. Most interviewees gave their interviewers a B. They were hesitant to give lower grades because they didn't want to insult anyone, but they did not get much out of the interviews and thought that the interviewers didn't either. There was little deep insight into whether the applicants could perform well on the available job, the interviewer's main goal, or whether this opportunity was in the best interest of the applicant, the interviewee's main goal.

As I gained more responsibility for hiring, I made it clear to all the people who did preliminary interviews for me that I would be the last interviewer and I would ask the three questions listed above. As my interview teams realized that their interview techniques were being graded by the applicant and were visible to their boss, it was amazing how much more effective they all became at discerning good hires from poor hires.

RESUMES

First impressions in the hiring process start with a resume (or CV, *curriculum vitae*). When screening any candidate, be wary of the multiple-page, here-is-everything-I-have-done-since-birth resume. In my experience, there is an inverse correlation between the length of a person's resume and their accomplishments. People with one-page resumes tend to have accomplished more than people with three-page resumes. Big accomplishments are easy to state concisely and require little explanation.

Here's how Sandy Koufax's resume might read:

- Three-time winner of the Cy Young award
- Youngest player inducted into the Baseball Hall of Fame
- Pitched four no-hitters, including one perfect game
- World Series record of 4-3, with a .95 ERA in 57 innings
- Averaged more than one strikeout per inning over his entire career

Wow! Why say more? Why add nuggets that can't hold a candle to those boulders? I have seen many accomplished people's resumes. Almost all the ones that communicate well are concise and focus on the significant stuff.

However, there are not many Sandy Koufaxes out there, nor people with huge accomplishments in their respective fields. Most of us have a typical range of good solid qualifications, educational degrees, awards of various value, and past experience. How someone puts together their resume provides a clue to their ability to communicate. Capturing a life-time of qualifications and accomplishments in a brief description is a high-stakes communications exercise.

Here is a definition from *Dictionary.com*:

> *resume*:
> 1. a summing up; summary
> 2. a brief written account of personal, educational, and professional qualifications and experience, as that prepared by an applicant for a job.

Notice the emphasis on *summary* and *brief*. Most resume-writing guides recommend that you confine yourself to one page. Amen to that advice. One page is plenty of space to get hiring managers excited about talking to you. If they want more information, they will ask for it or schedule an interview. Sending someone a multiple-page resume is a clear signal that you cannot communicate concisely or have little concern for doing so.

Here are some ideas for creating a crisp resume that will make a positive impact.

1. Fit on one page, without resorting to the size type used on postage stamps.
2. Put lists in priority order, with the most important entries first.
3. Define your current role and responsibilities succinctly.
4. Briefly describe your pertinent jobs and responsibilities for the past 5 to 10 years.
5. List titles and employers for experience from 10 or more years ago only if the experience is especially relevant to the role for which you are applying.
6. Be honest; don't inflate titles, responsibilities, education, or awards.

One of my former employees recently applied for a job in another part of the company. The hiring manager, one of my peers, wanted a reference from me because he knew the guy had worked for me in the past. He forwarded the guy's resume to me, a four-page monstrosity that is a case study of everything to do wrong. This applicant is no dummy; he is an accomplished professional. The gist of his resume is summarized below.

Current Role: Chief Engineer
- Followed by 20 bullets, with two sentences for each bullet describing activities performed

Previous Roles
- 13 different roles dating back 25 years, with an average of 10 sentences describing activities performed in each role

Publications
- 10 different presentations at public conferences
- 5 white papers, available internally but unpublished

Awards
- 9 certifications/awards

I knew this guy and his history pretty well. I knew that Chief Engineer was an inflated title. Although he listed all the activities he performed, he did not describe his responsibilities. At least that was honest, because he was a lone staff person who was not responsible for a budget, a team, a design, or a project. His long-winded list of activities made it impossible to determine whether he had accomplished anything. (A truism that I think applies to progress reports, performance assessments, and resumes: The longer it takes to describe what you have done, the less likely it is that you have done anything significant.) Then he went into almost as much detail about his previous jobs, going back 25 years. Who cares? Anything he did more than 5 years ago was probably stale experience in today's high-tech world anyway. He described the job he performed when he worked for me with enough exaggeration and flair that I came close to torpedoing his candidacy. It is a bad idea to candy-coat or puff up your resume, especially if you are applying to an organization where you previously worked.

His list of publications and presentations included every public talk he had ever given, in chronological order rather than order of importance. "Numerous technical presentations at industry conferences," which conveys public speaking ability, would have been preferable. Only significant publications should be included, such as books or articles in respected industry journals.

He listed a patent under awards, which was good, but it was only in process, which carries less weight, and it was buried near the end of the list. Other awards, for which I knew the context, were mostly trivial. The few that were meaningful lost significance by being listed with the minutia.

We rehired the guy, but only because he was the best candidate among a weak group. The moral of this story is the same as for many other stories in this book: Be honest, be concise, choose your words carefully, and communicate clearly when the stakes are high.

Some Ideas for Interviewers

Interviews are critical conversations. You have limited time and a specific purpose: to discern the relative qualifications of an applicant versus other applicants. Don't waste time looking for the perfect candidate; look for the best candidate from the pool of applicants. The later you are in the interview process, the more effective and discerning you can be because you have context from the other candidates and need only to discover whether this person is better or worse for the job than your frontrunners.

With limited time for face-to-face interaction with an applicant, usually an hour, the interviewer needs to be direct and prepared. Most interviewers do little preparation for an interview other than reading a candidate's resume. Here are some good ways to prepare.

- Go in with an agenda of no more than five topics, each with a purpose. Discuss these before meandering into side topics that might arise.
- Pre-arrange with the hiring manager a purpose for your interview. Does the boss want you to examine technical skills? Past experience? Personal values? If the hiring manager doesn't have an integrated plan for an applicant's sequence of interviews, your question may result in one being created, which is a good practice.
- Control the agenda and feel fee to cut off a candidate who becomes verbose. Get to the discriminators and look for reasons to end the interview (showstoppers that can't be overcome) or to keep going (discriminating assets, experience, or skills that match the role well).
- Personal priorities must be assessed by someone in the interview process, even though they are best confirmed by trusted references who have worked with the candidate for some time.

- Integrity: Without this, nothing else matters.
- Motivation: Passion for your company's mission is the best indicator of long-term retention.
- Culture fit: Topics such as teamwork, customer empathy, sales savvy, context-dependent thinking, adaptability, attention to quality, creativity, and others that vary among organizations but are critical for both parties to discuss.
- Skills: Problem solving, communications, time management.
- Experience: In today's world of rapidly evolving technology, only the past 5 years of experience are probably relevant for the day-to-day skills in many roles. However, the longer term experience may be important to assess maturity, domain knowledge, career path continuity, and other important factors.

Reaching some of these topics and having a meaningful discussion about them is a challenge. One key is to use open-ended questions, such as, "What sort of culture are you looking for?" This is far better than stating, "Teamwork is important at our company. What is your view of a good team?" This leading question will get exactly the response you ask for, whether the candidate believes it or not. When you get a response to an open-ended question, it is easy to dive into the candidate's understanding and determine whether the candidate aligns with your needs.

You also need to be an attentive observer, like a world-class poker player in a high-stakes game, examining the candidate's every word and action. Does the candidate use plural pronouns (*we* and *our*) or personal pronouns (*I* and *me*)? Does the candidate emphasize team achievements or personal contributions? Is their body language timid, confident, or phony? Feel free to point out what you notice and get the candidate's reaction. You may gain tangible insight into how this person reacts to stress or how they deal with a sensitive topic, such as someone confronting them with their body language.

Too many interviews are too polite and too gentle. Consequently, you only learn about a candidate's persona under the best conditions. One thing I learned in the military, reinforced throughout my life, is that you don't really know your partners and colleagues and teammates until you see them under stress. The strong and weak points of most people's personalities, skills, and judgments become obvious when they are subjected to stressful situations such as boot camp, survival training, challenging physical exertion, or high-stakes competition. So why not apply this to interviews? Stress is extremely effective at exposing strengths and weaknesses, enabling you to discern the real candidate from their interview façade.

Here are a few techniques for adding stress to an interview.

- As discussed earlier, ask the candidate to rank or grade their previous interviewers. Most people are stressed when they are required to judge others. This is especially true when the interviewee knows that the current interviewer knows the other interviewers well and the interviewee does not.
- Take an opposing view to something they say. Exaggerate your perspective enough for them to realize that they have hit a negative nerve. Observe how they reconcile the situation.
- Give them 5 minutes to do an exercise that cannot be done well in that amount of time. Walk out of the room. This will cause stress, allowing you to assess their time-management capabilities.
- Raise the stakes of the interview by stating your biggest concern with their resume, or the most challenging part of the role that this person will struggle with, based on your understanding of their background and the needs of this role.

There are many other possibilities. The point is to force the candidate from a comfortable place to a stress-filled place during the interview. The role you are hiring for is probably not stress-free, and you will learn more about how this candidate might react to stress and observe more of their true colors by seeing them deal with stress first-hand in an interview setting.

Control the interview. You shouldn't speak more than 25% of the time. Be sure that you get to your whole agenda. Tackle the hard things first and look for discriminators. Stress the candidate in at least one interview. Don't overlap with other interviewers unless a topic is so important that you need multiple perspectives, or you are following up because previous interviewers had concerns. Don't waste their time, and don't let them waste yours.

A Typical Interview Scenario

Here is a template for my typical interview. This layout usually allows me to get a meaningful opinion of a candidate in less than 90 minutes.

1. **Homework**: In preparation for the interview, have the candidate read a short paper, a newspaper article, or a specific excerpt from a book that is relevant to the role for which you are hiring. Provide two or three questions that you want the candidate to be prepared to answer during the interview. I sometimes ask one of these questions and then a totally different question that they are not prepared for.

2. **Agenda**: Lay out your plan of topics and questions for the interview.

3. **Get context**: Assess the candidate's view of previous interviews (stress accurate assessment).

4. **Apply stress**: Give the candidate a relevant 10-minute assignment to do in 5 minutes. Leave the room. When you return, have the candidate present their opinion briefly.

5. **Evaluate:** Discuss the stress test results and homework results with the candidate. Assess their time management and communications skills, as well as the quality of their response to your assessment.

6. **Go deep**: Take one important topic from the homework relatively deep to gauge the candidate's knowledge.

7. **Go broad**: Determine the candidate's passion for your organization's mission or their understanding of your organization's strengths/weaknesses.

8. **Problem solving**: Present a tough relevant situation such as a customer conflict, human resources issue, technical issue, or team dynamics challenge. Assess the candidate's organized reasoning toward a solution.

9. **Summarize**: Ask the candidate what grade they think you will give them as a result of this interview. Assess whether they have read you and the situation accurately. Tell them your grade and explain how you arrived at it.

10. **Follow up:** Ask the candidate to follow up with an email that assesses their day of interviews.

This approach may look daunting to interviewers and frightening to interviewees. Good. Here are the benefits I have realized with this approach.

- Over the years, numerous employees have told me that they had nothing but respect for the tough interviews they went through to join our organization. Universally, the feedback from those we hired was, "Wow! This organization cares about the people they hire. I definitely want to be a part of this team and I am happy to see such scrutiny in hiring."
- We scared away numerous candidates who were frightened to be subjected to such scrutiny. Unlike qualified candidates, who are likely to be confident and not fearful of this process, wannabes who cannot reach the performance bar you are setting are likely to be frightened away. This represents significant savings and efficiency in your hiring process.
- The quality and efficiency of hiring and interviewing have improved dramatically. Interviewers and candidates who know that the interview process is scrutinized and somewhat transparent take it much more seriously.

Some Favorite Questions for Interviewers

An interview can go in a jillion directions. The candidate, the team, the boss, the domain, the job, the economic situation, and the organizational culture are all widely variable. Here is a repertoire of questions that have worked well for me in exposing strengths and weaknesses in various candidates.

1. Your resume is long-winded. Can you differentiate the big accomplishments from the noise?
2. What are the top one or two attributes you look for in a supervisor?
3. What are the top one or two attributes you look for in a teammate?
4. If you were a hiring manager for this role and could ask only one question of an interviewee, what would it be? (This is a great question for a hiring manager because it will expose the interviewee's understanding of the role and priorities regarding values.)
5. Who do you think should be selling themselves more: you to us or us to you? (This is a good framework for understanding some internal motivations.)
6. Have you ever fired anyone? Why, and how did it turn out? (This is another good question for management candidates.)
7. Have you ever made a hiring mistake? What went wrong? How did you resolve it, and how could you have prevented it?
8. What topic, relevant to this role, do you feel expert in? Impress me with some insight. (This question can be tailored to any domain and role.)

9. In what discipline, relevant to this role, do you wish you were more adept? Why?

10. If you were the boss for a day and could tweak our organization's mission statement to suit you best, how would you change it? (This is a great framework for assessing alignment with your mission.)

11. How would you measure customer success in our domain?

12. What is the difference between customer success and customer satisfaction? (The former is a result you can quote forever. The latter is a transient opinion. It is amazing how much people in product businesses are overfocused on satisfaction and underfocused on success. In some service businesses, customer satisfaction is more meaningful, but customer success is still a crucial dimension.)

SOME IDEAS FOR INTERVIEWEES

Most interviewees, like most interviewers, arrive relatively unprepared for an effective interview. Before the internet, adequate preparation may have been difficult. Today there is no excuse: Almost everything you need to know is at your fingertips. Annual reports, corporate websites, and search engines all provide excellent mechanisms for you to prepare yourself. Understanding the context of the people and organization with which you are interviewing is an important prerequisite for creating a good impression.

Most candidates make an effort to find out something about the company. If a candidate came into an interview with me and asked for an overview of what we do, I would flush them right there. This person is not resourceful enough to be considered.

The biggest mistake made by interviewees is not checking out the roles and backgrounds of the specific people who are about to interview them. In a sequence of interviews, few things are more important. Today you can almost always find out the backgrounds of at least a few of the people who will be interviewing you.

About 10 years ago, I was interviewing an internal candidate for a new sales manager role. The hiring manager, one of my peers and close associates, asked me to interview his two leading candidates. He already preferred candidate A because he was the leading sales rep in a company we had just acquired. Candidate B was an old-timer with a solid reputation and track record. The other interviewers (four members of the sales team this person would manage and one peer sales manager) agreed that candidate A was preferable to candidate B. The hiring manager wanted me to be the final endorsement, because the person hired would have significant interactions with my own organization and because sales manager roles were crucial to our company's business.

My interview with candidate A went something like this:

Me: So what do you know about me and my organization?

Him: Hmmm. Nothing really. Can you summarize for me?

Me: Let's see. You are a professional sales guy, right?

Him: Yep. I was 450% of quota last year and 300% the year before.

Me: Today you're here to sell yourself, right? And I'm the customer.

Him: Uh, yes, I guess so.

Me: Do you always make cold calls on your customers without knowing who they are, what their role is, and what their challenges or values are?

Him: Uh, uh, no. That would be stupid.

Me: (Knowing that I now had my opening to stress this dude out and observe his true colors) Then why aren't you prepared for this interview?

Him: Well, I didn't have time. You know, quarter close and all the business demands. I just didn't have time to prepare because the needs of my current job are higher priority. (He said this smugly, trying to show he put the company first.)

Me: Really! Well, I can only conclude that this new role isn't as important to you as other things to which you assigned a higher priority.

Him: Can we start all over?

Me: Sure. Let's try another topic. Did you do the homework that I sent you about prioritizing our product lines in the context of achieving your sales targets in your territory?

Him: I looked at it, but I had already built a plan that shows how we can meet our targets without selling any of the legacy product line.

Me: Okay. But the skills that would be on your new team are mostly legacy product skills. How are you going to accomplish that skills transition?

Him: It's relatively easy. The products are similar.

Me: From your perspective, what is the primary difference between a sales manager role and a sales rep role?

Him: No big difference. Achieve quota.

Me: Well, there's a big difference. You are also responsible for growing the territory, and that requires selling across our diverse product line.

Him: I know that, but the main priority is meeting sales targets.

Me: Okay, Ralph. Thanks for your time.

Him: We're done? We've only spoken for 10 minutes.

Me: Well, I don't see a match here. You're obviously a good sales rep, but your preparation for a more responsible position as a manager is lacking. My opinion is that you feel entitled to this promotion because of your record as a rep, but that is not my view, or the company's view of what it takes.

Him: Sorry you feel that way.

This was a classic case of an interviewee not doing their homework, on two fronts. First, I was a well-known leader in the company, and this employee had access to tons of information and other employees who would have gladly prepared him for our interview. Second, to not understand the role and the measure we look for in sales managers was suicidal. I don't know how this person got through the other interviews, but he was undoubtedly good at dominating the conversations, and the other interviewers were just flat-out irresponsible. They had thought this guy was the slam-dunk candidate because of his performance record as a rep. My peer, the hiring manager, had a clear reputation for such promotions, and everyone knew it. My conversation with the hiring manager was a difficult one, but I told him that this candidate would only be endorsed over my dead body. My interview with candidate B went phenomenally well. He got the job.

Whatever your situation, you should do everything you can to understand who is interviewing you. Then research their biases, positions, history, resume, or anything else you can get you hands on. While this may seem difficult in some circumstances, you should still try. Here are a few suggestions.

- Research the company, the specific organization, and the role on the web. If you know people who work for the company, talk to them beforehand about culture, current circumstances, important lines of business, recent reorganizations, and whatever you can think of to demonstrate to your interviewers that you have done your homework and you are resourceful.
- If you are working through a recruiter or a corporate human resources rep, ask them who will be interviewing you and find out who the hiring manager is.
- Google the names you get both internally on the corporate website and externally. You may find biographies, papers they have written,

quotations in the media, or other material that gives you a perspective on their likes and dislikes.

- If you can't get much information before your interviews, feel free to ask each interviewer who else you are talking to, what their hot buttons are, and what role they have. Ask the interviewer's opinion on how to deal with the next person. Some people may not confide in you, but many will, and everyone will respect your desire to be prepared.

Be honest in your interview. Candy-coating your answers or avoiding sensitive topics is easy to see through. Just speak your mind, be yourself, act confident in what you are good at, and be humble in what you don't know or have no experience in. For me and most other interviewers, the difference between ignorance (answering "I don't know") and arrogance ("BS"ing your way through an answer because you don't want to appear unqualified) is a showstopper.

Based on the information you have about your interviewer and your observations as the interview unfolds, recognize what sort of personality you are talking to: analytic, driver, expressive, amiable. Embrace their style and communicate with them as discussed in Chapter 4. This will be noticed, and it will increase your comfort level as well as theirs.

If some jerk interviewer (like me) tries to stress you out and provoke you to get a reaction, embrace it. Do the best you can and play offense: Attack with your strengths and knowledge. Don't be defensive and don't make excuses. If the interviewer is adding stress for the reasons I do, they will not expect heroic responses. They will just want to gauge your reaction and natural tendencies. If they are adding stress because they are a jerk or because they already have a negative opinion of you, this position is probably not for you anyway.

CHAPTER 8

Is English a Romance Language?

Romance languages are the languages derived from Latin, such as French, Italian, Portuguese, and Spanish. The word *romance* has its origins in Latin. *Romanici Loqui* meant to speak in Roman, referring to the local dialect in Rome as opposed to the more formal dialect of Latin itself. Across Western Europe during medieval times, serious writing such as religious doctrine, scientific research, and nonfiction news accounts were usually written in Latin, while popular folklore was written in local dialects (vernacular). The folklore consisted of stories, plays, and writings that were often centered on love. Later, books of fiction came to be known as romance novels.

English is not a Romance language. It is the product of Anglo and Saxon dialects brought to Britain by Northern Germanic settlers in the 5th century. Nevertheless, English can be used romantically. This chapter is intended to prove this point (although it will not withstand the tough scrutiny that should be applied whenever the word *prove* is used). Humans spend much of their time pursuing love, and this pursuit clearly involves some crucial communications that can make or break a relationship.

If you find this subject to be an odd topic for this book, remember that this book is full of odd topics. Almost everyone would like to be more effective at communicating romantically, at least when the time is right and that is their intent. It is a topic worth covering.

Few people would call me romantic. But those few people who would—my spouse and a few close friends and family—know me intimately. Romance and intimate communications are best reserved for those people with whom you are close and intimate. There are precious few acquaintances with whom it makes sense to share such communications.

Communicating romantically can be done in any language. It is not the words, sounds, syntax, or semantics that make a communication romantic. It is the intent, the tone, the creativity, the imagery, and the personal expression of your intangible feelings. The two poems at the end of this chapter say essentially the same thing, but one uses the English language like a Don Juan and the other uses it like an automaton.

Most people are pretty uncomfortable with romantic communications. They become more comfortable when they feel deep love for someone. Then it is easier to communicate romantically, and your partner will feel loved and become more comfortable with reciprocating. In this cycle of loving communications (both words and actions), trust, intimacy, and safety become stronger and communicating safely and intimately becomes more comfortable. As most happily married couples can attest, this sort of interaction strengthens a relationship. Exchanging an occasional romantic communication is a healthy practice and is certainly a recurring theme of most relationship advice. Conversely, couples in rocky relationships or divorced couples will cite a lack of romance (that is, intimate communications of some sort) as a key reason for their unhappiness.

A few first-hand experiences have shaped my views on romantic communications. My wife Jennifer has opened my mind on this front, and I'm sure that is one of the main reasons we are so happily married. We lived 2700 miles apart for more than a year of our courtship, which contributed greatly to our appreciation of romantic communications. Emails and phone conversations represented most of our interaction during this phase of our relationship.

Jennifer and I decided that our marriage ceremony would include each of us reading a poem. We agreed that our poems would answer the question, "What does my partner mean to me?" We both worked through many versions to get these poems just right. In retrospect, I would recommend this exercise to anyone who is in a new relationship, getting married, or in a longstanding relationship. It will help you communicate with each other in a way that builds trust and intimacy. Sharing your communications with other people is not necessary, but when you do, it certainly raises the stakes and adds a new dimension of significance.

The catalyst of my attraction to my wife was a puzzle. Several years ago, I was obsessed with identifying English words that contained all five vowels. As I ran across them in newspapers, magazines, and books, I added them to a list. After the list reached 30 entries, I created a piece of prose that included all these a-e-i-o-u words structured into meaningful sentences. After a year or so, the list was up to more than 50 and my essay grew longer. Each time I added to it, I refactored the paragraphs to shorten the length. I tried to include all the a-e-i-o-u words with as few other words as possible to make a reasonably sane and literate storyline. It occurred to me that this essay would test observation skills by asking someone to determine the odd thing about this single paragraph. Here is the original version of this puzzle, circa 2002.

PUZZLE 6 REVISITED

Evaluation of Auditioned Dialogue Caught on Audiotape

I have a questionable reputation and inconsequential preoccupation with abstemiously outmaneuvering the word elitists so proud of their vocabularies. I offer this nefarious and unorganized paragraph as a poser to those tenacious puzzle solvers who consider themselves unequivocal authorities in such sacrilegious education. This poser is authorized by an unsanctioned, consultative group of unrecognizable experts with no boundaries and no regulation of the puzzle's equation. One of these experts is ambidextrous, the other mustachioed, but both are overanxious with speculation on the graciousness with which our discouraged readers will facetiously appreciate a tale that is as tall as a sequoia. The solution is not insurmountable, but any underestimation of the "strangeness" of this paragraph will result in an unavoidable anxiousness, mental exhaustion, and evacuation from one's subordinate sensibilities rather than the euphoria of an uncomplicated solution. The revolutionary title is simultaneously an ostentatious hint and a precarious permutation of encouraging words for those unaccomplished souls of the word-puzzle persuasion who need evolutionary rejuvenation and a perturbation of consciousness. The unprofessional words "menstruation" and "ejaculation" belong in this paragraph as well, but why? Any denunciation or repudiation of the gregarious sentence structure would be counter-productive and result in an attenuation of interest. One precaution: The word choices are not unintentional. No more recapitulation. Most solvers get it instantaneously without requiring a continuance.

The solution to this puzzle requires:

1. An appropriate number to describe the extent of strangeness of the paragraph.
2. Two additional words that the meet this strangeness standard.
3. Identification of the two most special words used in the paragraph in the context of this puzzle.

This version has 65 a-e-i-o-u words. The two special words are *abstemiously* and *facetiously*, which have the vowels in alphabetical order and even include the y, which is sometimes a vowel. Of the 228 words in the puzzle paragraph, more than 28% of them have all five vowels. That is strange! Puzzle 6 evolved this puzzle to 100 a-e-i-o-u words and a few additional paragraphs. Of the 252 words in the later version, almost 40% of the words have all five vowels. Not only is that even stranger, you are probably thinking that I am the king of strangeness for wasting so much time on such trivial diversions. No doubt you are correct. Nevertheless, I found that this exercise required creative writing and was a great mental exercise. It would work as a creative writing assignment in an English class, where the constraint need not be words with all five vowels but could be something just as strange, such as the following.

1. Words that are also common first names
2. Words that begin and end with the same letter
3. Words that are palindromes
4. Words that don't contain an E or an A

Back to romance. I offered the early version of the a-e-i-o-u puzzle to various friends and colleagues who are bright, educated professionals. Only my best friend of 30 years had the observation skills and insight into my odd brain function to solve the puzzle. But I hadn't yet tried it out on my future wife. She and I had worked closely for a few years at the same company. One day, she told me that some of her projects were like puzzles and she enjoyed solving them. With that cue, I sent her a few of the puzzles I had concocted over the years, fully expecting her to be flummoxed by my obtuse a-e-i-o-u puzzle. She solved it in less than one day.

That was a major wake-up call to me. Suddenly, I was acutely attracted to her and wanted to know her better. This was the first seed of our romantic relationship. We lived on opposite coasts, 2700 miles apart. After she solved the puzzle, our communications became friendlier and one thing led to another. We wrote poems, made up puzzles, recapped the highlights of the relatively rare times we were together, and simply learned to communicate intimately through writing.

I am not surprised that so many people start relationships now through internet interactions. Many people—myself included—used too think this was a strange way to court someone. Maybe it is, but it will teach you the power of words. There is nothing like a new relationship to motivate your romantic creativity and improve your communications skills. I imagine that most people consider these discussions high stakes and take great care in investing time to communicate with clarity and purpose.

That Jen and I connected through our love of puzzles may seem far-fetched, coincidental, or trivial. But it is the sort of seemingly insignificant shared interest that underlies many relationships. It is also the sort of sentimental memory that can be used effectively in subsequent romantic communications such as birthday cards, anniversary cards, valentines, and wedding ceremonies. Effective romantic impact stems from personalized communications. They need not be works of art, take extensive preparation time, or be mushy. They simply need to come from your heart and reveal some personal connection.

People with children can attest to the great joy of receiving a gift from them. With young kids, the gift is usually handmade and simple: a handprint in a plate of clay, a bunch of doilies glued randomly into a Valentine, a pipe-cleaner reindeer Christmas tree ornament with the child's name pasted over the reindeer's face. You save it for years or still remember it vividly because it made an indelible impression on you. Such personalized expressions of love, gratitude, or appreciation are very, very romantic in the truest sense.

The word *romantic* means characterized by a preoccupation with love; displaying or expressing love or strong affection. Parent-child love is perhaps the strongest kind of love we ever experience. Although this is not what most people think of as romance, the patterns of communication seem congruent to me. If the simplest, most personalized expressions between child and parent are perceived to be the most memorable and joy-producing, why wouldn't the same thing be true among adults?

I think simple communications and personalized expressions of love between adults are the mainstay of romantic communications. They add energy to a relationship; they are essentially free; and they are far more memorable than a big piece of jewelry, new lingerie, or high-tech golf clubs. I am not talking about mushy love letters, although they too may have their place. I am talking about making a personalized effort to communicate on special occasions like a birthday or anniversary, or even everyday occasions, leaving a note or a voicemail for the person you love.

What does it take to create romance? Some choice words and a little personalization. Here are a few ideas, ranging from trivial to more elaborate expressions.

1. Instead of just picking out and signing that Hallmark card, try changing the card just a little or adding a sentence to personalize it into something that will be more meaningful.

2. Send a personalized card for no reason other than to show gratitude or appreciation.

3. Buy a blank card and write a message appropriate for the occasion.

4. Leave a loving message or send a loving email for no particular reason. We all expect something on Valentine's Day, but unexpected loving communications have a very romantic impact.

5. Construct a word search puzzle where the words being searched are personally relevant to your recipient. For example, for your wife, it could be places where you have vacationed; for your child, it could be trophies or awards they have received; for your girlfriend, it could be places you have visited together on dates.

6. Construct a gift hunt with a sequence of clues that lead to successive clues, with each one personalized to some facet of your relationship. At the end of the clues can be the gift. This approach is great fun to create and very romantic to receive.

7. Take a photograph that is meaningful to you (a place, an event, another person, a thing) and write a personalized poem that expresses some aspect of your love, gratitude, or attraction to your partner. Frame the picture so that the poem and the photo are visible or, if the poem is private, so that it appears on the back.

It is folly for me to advise others about *how* to be romantic. There are so many dimensions and specific parameters to a loving relationship, and they are so widely varying and personal, it is impossible to give specifics that anyone would find useful. Examples from my own experience would not be meaningful—the word choices, the allusions, the symbolism.

The reasoning in the previous sentence strikes me as one of the best yardsticks for judging your success:

A romantic communication should have impact only on the one for whom it is intended.

If your communication would mean the same thing to anyone who read it, it is probably not that romantic.

Suppose you and your wife met at college, in Professor Plum's history class. You buy your wife an anniversary card that reads: The last 10 years have been the most wonderful years of my life. Now you tailor it by adding a note that says:

The Plum we shared 10 years ago changed my life. I love our history together.

Only you and your wife will understand the note which makes the card more romantic.

A Tale of Two Poems

Poetry offers almost complete creative freedom. You are less constrained by formal rules, and you can break the rules, exercising *poetic license*, to create artistic or romantic effects. You can twist words, arrange them any way you like, and add other stylistic elements such as tone, alliteration, and rhyme.

I wrote a poem to express my feelings about getting through my mid-life crisis. There is no need for detailed context. Suffice it to say that I was struggling with a lot of stress the year after 9/11, a time that caused many people to stop and reflect. As I look back, I have great appreciation for the three primary women in my life—my wife and two daughters—and for the love and companionship we gave to each other to move from a troubled state into a happy one. Here is the poem.

> Togetherness.
> Parenthood can change you like nothing else can.
> Bringing two daughters into the world turned me into a man.
> We got by together. They toddled and grew and became best friends.
> Their mom passed on too early and our memories of her have no ends.
> We got by together. We escaped to the Sierras each year.
> Backpacking with them was a special way of teaching them how to persevere.
> Those teenage years can break almost anyone.
> Sure there was stress, as well as fun.
> College struggles left us all looking in the mirror.
> Pursuing happiness elsewhere was distinctly clearer.
> When I struggled to dig myself out of a difficult ditch,
> They both moved east to help me make a switch.
> We all thrived in New England where Jen helped set us free.
> She is a giver, a lover, a friend, and an angel for us three.
> We got by together.
> We will get by together.

I expect most readers to feel blasé about this poem. Because it expresses my personal feelings and love for the people closest to me, it will feel romantic to those people, but not to others. That's what makes it romantic: It's personal.

In time, I decided that this simple poem was not personal enough. My wife and daughters know how I love mental torture, word fun, and subtle symbolism. So to make the poem even more personal—in other words, more romantic—I added some special effects that better reflected my personality but required additional mental gymnastics for me. I hope it provides a more loving memory for them.

I asked myself what I could add to the poem. Here's what I came up with.

1. Add some of my favorite words (torture, hairy, conifer).
2. Make the title a meaningful anagram. (I worked the title to be an anagram of my daughter's first names, Cameron and Emily.)
3. Shape the words into a visual. (With a few structural changes, poetic license regarding phrase length on each line, and more thoughtful word choices, the words could be reorganized to represent some memorable symbolism.)

The final poem, which concludes this chapter, took me another hour or so to specialize and customize. The outcome of that hour was a quantum leap in the way the poem expresses my feelings. I wanted these three special women to say, "That is so Walker-like," "That is so daddy-like." This is exactly the reaction you are looking for and the sort of romanticism that anyone can practice in their own personal way.

My purpose in this chapter was to expose readers to another form of acutely sensitive high-stakes communications. Most people feel uncomfortable in romantic communications and other emotional interactions such as anniversary celebrations, valentines, and expressions of sympathy. If they didn't, sales would be off at greeting card stores.

Writing this strange chapter was a useful mental exercise that forced me to get out of my normal default mindset and emote openly. I feel great when I can enter this other world and act like a romantic. It is freeing, and it feels good, especially when it makes someone else feel loved.

My
One
Miracle

Parenthood
can change you
like nothing else can.
Raising two daughters
transformed me into a man.
We got by together.
They toddled and grew
and became best of friends.
Their mom passed on too early
Our memories of her have no ends.
We got by together.
We escaped to the Sierras each year.
Backpacking with them was a special
way of teaching them how to persevere.
Those teenage years can be torture to everyone.
Sure there was stress, as well as fun.
College struggles left us all looking in the mirror.
Pursuing happiness elsewhere was distinctly clearer.
When I struggled to dig myself out of a big hairy ditch
they both moved east to help me make a remarkable switch.
We all thrived in New England where Jen helped set us free.
She is a giver, a lover, a friend, and a coniferous angel on our family tree.
We got by together.
We will get by
Together.

My one miracle is togetherness.

Conclusions

The ability to communicate well affects everyone's pursuit of happiness. My goal in this book was to expose some of the more interesting aspects of English, its diverse usage models, its humorous side, and a few of its perverse complexities. I hope this material stimulates readers to appreciate the language and increases their commitment to communicate more effectively. Writing and researching this material was certainly stimulating and educational for me. I was amazed at how many web sites, books, and references there are with interesting perspectives on the use of English. I just had to look for them.

In several places throughout this book, I have emphasized that *words count*. They define your writing style and your speaking style, and they are crucial to communicating clearly. Making lists of your favorite words and the words you loath the most is an enjoyable and enlightening exercise. Providing some brief rationale on why they make your lists will cause you to reflect on word selection.

Here are my 10 favorite and 10 un-favorite words, with short descriptions of why they make my top-10 lists.

My 10 Favorite Words

Hairy. I didn't know this was one of my favorite words until my kids informed me that I use it all the time to refer to something that is complicated. Luckily for me, *Dictionary.com* lists an informal definition as *full of hardship or difficulty.*

Circumlocution. A great word. It is hard to parse, fun to say, and self-defining. It requires no emoticon because it carries its derogatory tone right along with it. Circumlocution is my pet peeve. Rigmarole is a good synonym.

Conifer. This taxonomic order of beautiful living plants has a descriptive name that rolls off the tongue. It also represents a symbolic word for my wife, who shares my love of conifers. The symbolic connection struck me because when we met, her last name started with "con" and her first name ended in "ifer."

Torture. I love to torture people in a mentally stimulating way. I tend to use this word with a positive connotation when I direct it toward other people but infer a negative connotation when it is directed toward me.

Coprophagy. As a puppy, our dog had a bad habit of eating his poop. (I realized that *shit-eating grin* has a factual basis. He seemed to be smiling at us and enjoying our convulsions every time he wolfed down dog-doo.) Horrified, I researched this problem on the web. I discovered the word *coprophagy*, which means the consumption of feces by certain animal species. Unbelievable! There's a word for everything.

There is also a company that claims to have a cure. They produce For-Bid, a powder that you sprinkle on the dog's food. We ordered some. Here is a quote from the product literature:

> *"Simply sprinkle on dog food and after the food is consumed, this will impart a forbidden and unpalatable taste to the feces."*

When I read this, I went berserk. I had found one of those humorous nuggets you just can't make up. It has to be true to be so funny. My whole life, I thought that *tastes like crap* was the ultimate in bad taste. Someone invented a powder that would make crap taste *worse*? The people who conceived of, tested, and marketed this product are probably all dead now. They died laughing.

Knucklehead. This word makes my list because I use it often to describe myself, and because its true derivation is so different than one would expect. Most of us think this is a synonym for *ass, birdbrain, blockhead, bonehead, buffoon, dimwit, dolt, donkey, dope, dork, drip, dufus, dullard, dunderhead, fool, goof ball, ignoramus, imbecile, jerk, lame-brain, moron, nerd, nincompoop, nitwit, numskull, oaf, pinhead, scatterbrain, simpleton,* and *twit.* (Thank you, *Dictionary.com.*) But *Wikipedia* tells us that the *knucklehead* was a Harley-Davidson motorcycle engine that was so-named because of the distinct shape of the rocker boxes. As the design of Harley-Davidson engines has evolved through the years, the distinctive shape of the valve covers has allowed Harley enthusiasts to classify an engine simply by looking at the shape of the cover. A knucklehead engine has round knobs on the cover that resemble knuckles, giving the knucklehead its name.

Fido. Alas, this is not a recognized word that means dog, but it is a real word. *Dictionary.com* lists two meanings: (1) a system for evaporating the fog above airfield runways by the heat from burners (an acronym for <u>F</u>og <u>I</u>nvestigation <u>D</u>ispersal <u>O</u>peration), or (2) a defective coin (an acronym for <u>F</u>reaks, <u>I</u>rregulars, <u>D</u>efects, and <u>O</u>ddities). Nevertheless, I use it to show affection to any dog, especially mine, like most people use *honey* or *darling* or other terms of affection for their sweetheart.

Miaoued. The cat miaoued! It is allowable in Scrabble® and the only word I have found with all 5 vowels in a row.

Zarf. My only explanation for why I like this word is its beautiful sound. A zarf is an ornamental coffee cup holder with no handle, usually made of metal.

Whatchamacallit. This word is a classic placeholder for something you just can't define with a better word, either because there is no good descriptor or you can't remember the right word. It is a useful contraction of what-you-may-call-it. Other good words in this class include contraption, doohickey, gizmo, and thingamajig.

My 10 Un-Favorite Words

Actually. This is my favorite word to hate. It is the most annoying, overused, and misused word in our language, an empty placeholder used to fill space.

But. I was born a cynic, and this is a word that comes altogether too naturally for me. I need to cut back consciously on using the word *but*, but it still remains my top critique of my own communications style and word selection. (Rats! That resolution didn't get far.)

Very. This is another word that I, and most other people, overuse. As I edited an early manuscript of this book in preparation for my copy editor, I found that I had used the word 164 times. After assessing each usage, I ended up deleting 120 of these. Most of the instances were easily deleted and the sentences sounded better.

Cacophony. This word has its place, but I always misspell it and it just sounds too smarty-pants. I once sat in a lecture next to a mild-mannered mid-westerner with a dry wit. The speaker complained about "a cacophony of voices" rebelling against something. It was the first time I had heard that word and I turned to my neighbor and said, "What did that mean?" He just smiled and said, "I think it means shitload." In that context, he was right.

Do. This is another overused, redundant word. Do you ever hear people say, "I do think…" or "I do want…" or "I do (pick a verb)…"? Why add the *do* when the verb works fine without it? My guess is that this usage stems from a reverse double negative. Here is my amateur psychoanalysis. Many people who are born cynics have the word *don't* loaded and ready to shoot at all times. You need *don't* to negate many verbs (like, want, think, make), and negation is the natural default thought for pessimists and contrarians. So their brains naturally substitute the positive word *do* because they need to consciously negate their negative instincts. This is a pretty harsh judgment, but it might get these doers to observe their use of *do* a little more dutifully.

Precise. I dislike this word because I rarely see it used precisely. Most people use *precise* when they mean *accurate*, and too many disciplines use precise representations for things that are rough estimates. This misusage drives me nuts. I shouldn't blame the word, but I do.

IMHO. Okay, this is not a real word. It is an acronym or on-line shorthand for In My Humble Opinion. The people who use this acronym are rarely humble. Truly humble people feel no need to emphasize that they are humble.

Qi and Za. When these two-letter words were added to the *The Official Scrabble® Players Dictionary* it changed the strategy of the game in significant ways. In my opinion, this is comparable to shortening the distance between the bases in baseball by 10 feet, thereby exploding the offensive scoring statistics and changing some of the beautiful balance in the game.

Like. This is another overused word, especially in, *like, California where I, like, lived for most of my life*. It's, like, such a misused word that I don't like it. If you are, like, okay with this usage, then you should, like, move to California and work with, like, airheads.

Bad. Used as in "my bad," this is a cheap, abstract way to avoid saying, "Sorry, my fault." Where did this usage come from? It sure sounds lame. Saying "That's bad" when you mean "That's good" is another silly usage that seems to come from people who don't understand the difference between bad and good.

Analyzing your favorite and least favorite words is an exercise in observation. After you have done it, you will likely want to update it every now and then. I wanted to conclude with this simple exercise because it reinforces the main theme of this book: Observe the way you and others use our language to communicate. View it as an educational pastime and enjoy it.

I leave you with a final poem as my last puzzle in observation. Poetic license was needed for my final attempt at enjoying English. This poem has a few special attributes that should be easy to detect now that you've read this book and this paragraph. Eureka!

English shining linens in eggshell sheen.
"Negligees, leggings, high heels," he sings.
Giggling, she senses illness in his singleness.
Lessening his lies is senile.
Is she seeing his sinning signs?
She sighs. He is selling silliness.
His highness is senseless in English!

A Team Dynamics Workshop

n 2002, when I worked at a large software company, we were merging four different groups of highly experienced software consultants into a worldwide team. After reading *Personal Styles and Effective Performance* by David Merrill and Roger Reid, and *First Among Equals* by Patrick McKenna and David Maister, I developed a professional workshop to apply what I had learned to the challenge of integrating our team. This appendix provides the framework and results of that workshop as a detailed case study.

Our four groups of software consultants were managed separately in different regions of the United States and Europe. They generally knew each other, and many had worked with each other on occasion. Although the teams had somewhat different cultures, they shared the common mission of providing high-leverage consulting and selling services to large, industrial-strength software organizations.

This collection of some of our best and brightest employees included a mixture of high IQ and high emotional quotient (EQ) people. They had diverse styles— the usual mix of prima donnas, workhorses, and competing professionals—and, in some cases, dysfunctional relationships. We knew we had to establish at the outset a strong foundation of teamwork, open and honest communications, and participatory management culture, or this talent pool could run onto the rocks.

First Among Equals and *Personal Styles and Effective Performance* provided plenty of material to build a workshop for our management team. Our goal was to accelerate our transition from four separate teams into one team with shared objectives and a common culture. Our approach was to get everyone together, face to face, for 2 to 3 days to accomplish three things:

1. Build stronger interpersonal relationships and an appreciation for the strength inherent in the diversity of the team
2. Explore techniques for communicating better
3. Build the rules of membership for our team in dealing with our clients, our employees, one another, and ourselves. We, the management team, would own these rules and demand adherence to these standards as a community of peers.

If we were even mildly successful in meeting these goals, the impact, although hard to measure, would be well worth the time invested.

This workshop was the seed of our group's management culture, creating a team dynamic that stood the test of time and even survived an acquisition. Our team of managers worked together for more than a decade with low attrition while growing nearly fivefold. We maintained consistent performance measures, steady business results, and an esprit de corps that stood out in a company known for esprit de corps. As we grew, the workshop was repeated three times with different subsets of managers. Each time, the participants saw it as a watershed accelerator in teamwork and improved communications.

Although it would be difficult to quantify the value of such workshops objectively or in financial terms, here are some observed benefits.

1. The workshops provide a great starting point for any newly formed team, organization, or re-organization.
2. Their relatively small cost is easy to measure, although their immense return on investment is difficult to measure.
3. People *always* appreciate a concrete investment in improved teamwork, communications, coaching, openness, and trust, even if they are skeptical at the outset.

4. As the team leader, you will accelerate your knowledge of the team and your ability to communicate with them by preparing the prerequisite work, analyzing the inputs, tailoring the presentations, and facilitating the workshop.

Preparation

Each participant was asked to do homework to prepare for the workshop. This work involved two simple assignments. The first was to provide a few observations about themselves.

1. The proudest result (personal or professional) they had achieved
2. A significant shortcoming they wanted to work to overcome, to increase their contribution to the team
3. An embarrassing moment in their professional life

Participants provided this information to the facilitator. They were told that the information would be presented at the workshop to see how much group members already knew about each other. They were told to provide meaningful responses about themselves that were not well known by all the participants so that they could learn more about each another.

The second assignment was for each participant to review a two-page introduction on social styles, and then to assess their own social style and those of the other participants. If they did not know another participant well enough to have an opinion on their style, they were to leave that assessment blank.

Participants were told that we would compare everyone's views of themselves and others during the workshop, to see how well they aligned. There were no right or wrong answers. The purpose of the exercise was to learn and reflect on how they saw their own style and how others saw it. Assessing and discussing the diversity of styles and the perceptions of others helped us build stronger interpersonal relationships and therefore a stronger team.

It was surprising how many of the participants were uncomfortable with assessing themselves and others. Engineers are notoriously apprehensive about their soft skills, and this workshop had a touchy-feely quality that made many of them skeptical and defensive. It took a fair amount of discussion and cajoling to convince everyone that this would be a productive exercise.

This preparatory work was well worth the time it took. Many of the discussions prompted by the skeptics ended up being great coaching sessions, with honest self-reflection. Figure A-1 synthesizes the preparatory work and illustrates the range of social styles across the participants.

FIGURE A-1. *Results of Social Style Survey of Workshop Participants*

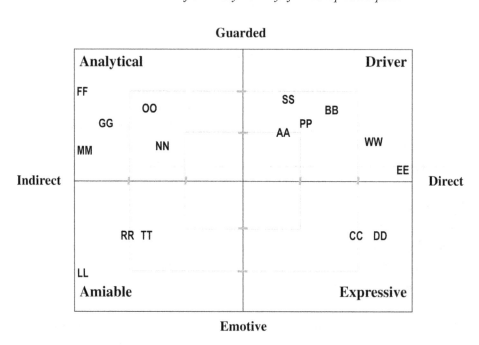

Because this workshop was for software engineering leaders and managers, it was not surprising that the team was composed of more driver styles and analytical styles. The data prompted some eye-opening discussions. Here are a few observations.

- Four of the 16 people were judged to be a different style than they judged themselves to be. These were pretty senior people, who should have been mature enough to self-assess accurately. They struggled with their identities in the team, and three of them were the most difficult people to manage and coach.
- On average, most people assessed about half of the individuals the same as the team consensus.
- The most capable managers assessed people more accurately.

WORKSHOP AGENDA, MATERIAL, AND RESULTS

The workshop was scheduled for a day and a half, with time to interact during breaks, lunch, and dinner. The agenda was roughly as follows.

Context	**Morning**	
Introductions and goals	Exercise/presentation	90 min.
Styles and coaching	Presentation/discussion	90 min.
Team Dynamics	**Afternoon**	
Leadership, trust, teamwork	Presentation/discussion	60 min.
Communications	Exercise	60 min.
Communicating better	Exercise results/discussion	60 min.
Future Actions	**Morning**	
Team principles	Discussion	30 min.
Team principles; breakout sessions	Exercise	60 min.
Consensus	Exercise results/discussion	90 min.

The sessions were light on presentations and rich with topics for discussions. An exercise where the teams would interact and construct material for discussion and team consensus was built into each morning and afternoon session.

Introductions and Goals

It was important for the introduction to set the right tone of openness and trust. Although many participants knew each other well, some knew each other only by reputation. The introduction emphasized that the workshop was experimental and would succeed or flop based on our ability to open up and establish trust as a team with a common purpose. Everyone knew that a big state change was in process—namely, a formal reorganization—so the stakes were high for everyone.

Practicing what you preach is a powerful motivator, especially for the leader and facilitator, so I began by demonstrating my own openness. I posed a question, and then answered it.

"Why am I subjecting us to this fiasco? It came from you."

We had recently completed a 360-degree performance assessment where 10 of my colleagues, subordinate managers, and technical leaders (all of them workshop participants) were asked to assess my skills and attributes. The most glaring need for improvement that the survey results highlighted was my mentoring of others; my own perception was similar. This is a common weakness of managers in high-tech fields. I told the team that I had read a couple of books on coaching and teamwork, and had built this workshop as a means of pushing myself into the "coaching pool." Not only did I need to become a better trusted advisor, I needed each of them to become one too.

I presented the following hypotheses as the needs for the workshop. The general consensus was that these rang true for all the participants.

1. High-performance individuals have many characteristics that are barriers to being even more successful as a team.
2. Our team dynamics and growth profile demanded a high level of trust to succeed.
3. We all had high IQs, but not many of us had a high EQ, especially as a team.

I presented the outcomes I expected from the workshop:

1. A better understanding of each other and our diverse strengths and weaknesses
2. Increased teamwork and trust among team members and shared leadership
3. Consensus on the "rules of membership" for our management team.

After this introduction, everyone was more comfortable. The air was only half as thick as when we started.

Exercise: Who are We?

As the facilitator, I had edited everyone's responses to their proudest moment, their significant shortcoming, and their most embarrassing moment into a handout. The exercise I used to start off the workshop was simple, and I posed it as a puzzle (of course!). Each participant tried to determine which row in the table corresponded to each of the participants. We gave everyone 20 minutes to make their speculative assessments. To provide some incentive for giving it their best effort and to stoke the competitive natures of the workshop participants, $50 was offered to the person (or people) who got the most right answers. The 20 minutes of intense thought was broken up by occasional snickers and sly comments by a few wise guys looking for some hint of who was who. A few good shushes kept the room focused.

We then began exposing identities. Each person was asked to identify their row in the table and to describe a little more of the context around their accomplishment, weakness, and embarrassing moment. Even the most introverted engineers in the room enjoyed sharing personal insights, and a few verbal jabs opened up the atmosphere surprisingly well. Two people tied for getting the most right (10) and shared the $50. This exercise proved to be a great ice breaker for the workshop because the participants learned a little more about each another.

In the discussion afterwards, we answered two questions:

1. Did we learn a little more about each other?
2. Did we take some personal risk?

Everyone felt they had gained some insight, although most thought it was trivial and of marginal value. Someone noted that they would have preferred performing this exercise before being assigned to assess social styles because they saw some things in people that they hadn't seen outside of work. This was a breakthrough insight, and a few people were anxious to change their assessments.

On the second question, about taking personal risk, there was a broad spectrum of responses. Most participants felt that they had responded to the questionnaire with substantial caution because they didn't know some of the other participants well enough. This led to a great discussion about trust. We observed that if you trust other people, you are much more willing to risk being more open with them. And if someone is open with you, you tend to trust them more.

We came to the conclusion that communicating openly builds trust, empathy, and intimacy.

- Trust: reliance on the integrity, ability, or character of other people
- Empathy: understanding of another's situation, feelings, and motives
- Intimacy: the quality of feeling comfortable, close, or familiar with another person

This discussion led to a need for everyone to understand better each other's strengths and weaknesses, successes and failures, and diverse motivations and styles.

The last discussion topic of this exercise was about establishing a "setbacks are OK" attitude that reduces individual vulnerability. Our high-technology world requires a tremendous amount of pioneering and trial-and-error discovery. (Although this is true of many endeavors, it is particularly true for software development.) If we are all going to feel safe with each other, we must know that mistakes are going to be made and the team must learn, forgive, and move on.

Styles and Coaching

Everyone was anxious for the next discussion topic: social styles. Having studied the social styles quite a bit, I could just imagine the four different questions that were going through everyone's mind:

The Drivers wanted to know: What were the results of the exercise?

The Analytics were pondering: Is there enough scientific data to support this model?

The Amiables wondered: Why can't we just accept people as they are, without labels?

The Expressives asked themselves: Who will see these results?

We discussed each style and unfolded the team's results (shown in Figure A-1) in front of everyone. It was incredible how much more comfortable the audience became. A few people genuinely could not believe the styles that others had judged them to be. But as they saw their own assessments and the team consensus, most moved to a perspective of, "Wow! There is something here that I could use."

The discussions resulted in some interesting outcomes and observations.

1. The main point was well understood: People have diverse styles, and when two people interact, they can be more comfortable (and less tense) if both people recognize and adjust to each other's style.
2. Although there are no prescriptions, there are many patterns for simple adjustments in style that can make a difference.
3. Everyone had a few anecdotes on why some past conversation or relationship was very tense or very comfortable.

4. People who judged their style differently than the team consensus had their eyes opened in a meaningful way. Each expressed and demonstrated a noticeable change in attitude and behavior in the days and weeks that followed.

5. Although the discussions bordered on being uncomfortable—everyone dislikes being pigeonholed—the participants had empathy for one another's discomfort. They were all experiencing roughly the same feelings. Consequently, it was easy for them to open up and discuss honestly how they felt.

As the leader of this team, I was overwhelmed by the positive results I saw. These capable individuals had opened up their communications channels and let trust grow. They already had competence and integrity going for them; their communications skills had been the weakest link.

As anecdotal evidence of the value of this workshop, two of the participants chose to run similar workshops a few years later as they inherited new, growing organizations. The outcomes were similar, and our three organizations have strong reputations for esprit de corps, trust, effective business results, and low attrition.

Leadership, Trust, and Teamwork

Our next discussion topics focused on establishing a common understanding of what we were all looking for in leaders and highly effective teams. These integrated topics provoked a lively discussion. The results follow.

What does a leader need to do?

- Motivate
  - Create energy and excitement
  - Encourage creativity as well as routine high performance
- Steer
  - Make things happen and break down barriers to progress
  - Set, adjust, and reinforce shared objectives
- Make quality judgments
  - Understand viable alternatives
  - Judge risks and opportunities objectively

- Coach people and facilitate teamwork
  - ○ Listen, speak, and care
  - ○ Set the bar, enforce the bar, and raise the bar for everyone
- Be trustworthy

As I facilitated this discussion and organized the words on the white board, I was manipulative and purposeful in ending up with the five top-level categories shown. The first four were intended to align well with each of the four social styles; the fifth was trust. It was eye-opening for most participants to realize that we are asking our leaders to excel in all four social styles. Perhaps some people in the world can do this, but everyone understood that such people are scarce. The key conclusion we reached was the need for shared leadership, diversity, and teamwork, especially among the leaders of any organization.

Our next discussion produced a description of what good teamwork looks like and what poor teamwork looks like. This discussion is summarized below.

Evidence of Good Teamwork

- Open information sharing
- Honest, objective assessments (including "I don't know")
- Following through on commitments
- Teammates doing what they say and saying what they cannot do
- Confronting and resolving issues firsthand
- Disagreeing without disrespect
- Minimal fear of error, failure, and mistakes
- Consensus risk taking
- Valuing each teammate's time as much as your time
- Developing a track record of timely and efficient accomplishments

Evidence of Poor Teamwork

- Searching for blame when things go wrong
- Protracting minor issues by excessive debate
- Misplaced or out-of-proportion recognition
- Post-decision sniping and second-guessing
- Closed doors or just-between-you-and-me discussions
- Multiple coalitions engaging in competing discussions

- Disagreement dressed up as "the devil's advocate"
- Unresolved issues, missed deadlines, vague agreements, and unfulfilled commitments

Establishing Trust

Discussions of teamwork and leadership can easily be brought back to one magic word: trust. Consequently, we concluded this section of the workshop with a deeper discussion of how we can all establish trust in other people. Here is the outcome.

- Honesty
  - The truth: keeping people informed
  - The whole truth: including everything relevant
  - Nothing but the truth: excluding everything irrelevant
- Dependability/reliability
  - Putting the team's win in front of your own
  - Achieving whatever you commit to do
  - Accurately assessing what you cannot achieve
- Competency
  - The capability to achieve results
- Open and honest communications

The first three bullets were pretty well understood and unambiguous for the workshop participants. The last and most important item was easy to write down but hard to elaborate, so we structured the next exercise to go deeper into a few critical dimensions of improved communications.

Exercise: Communicating Better

The workshop participants were members of a team distributed worldwide. We needed efficient communications among ourselves, with our sales teams, and with customers. The goal of this exercise was to establish more teamwork and trust, so we focused on improving communications among ourselves. Within our organization, we had to live within certain constraints.

- Most of our communications occurred when we were participating together in client engagements.

- We held face-to-face meetings for strategic planning and review twice a year.
- Weekly conference calls were our reliable periodic communications channel.
- We used Email, phone calls, and so forth for most of our communications.

Clearly, without much face-to-face contact, our written and verbal communications were the mainstay of team interactions and were vitally important to establishing trust and collaborative leadership. We challenged ourselves to improve in three critical areas. The first was general presentation skills. We all presented frequently, to each other and to our clients, and everyone's presentation skills can use critique and improvement.

The second was a challenge for our newly formed mix of distributed organizations and a leadership team full of respected and accomplished managers. How would we achieve consensus on decisions where there were competing views or positions? We had several strong leaders who were accustomed to running their teams with a fair amount of autonomy. They used different measures of performance, different hierarchies of values, and different methods of communicating status and plans. As one organization with a common purpose, we knew we would need to agree on measuring, valuing, and communicating more consistently.

Finally, there was the logical counterpart of the consensus challenge: How can we disagree without disrespect? There was a fair amount of friction in interactions among these highly accomplished and competent technical people when they had differences of opinion. These usually involved design concepts, planning approaches, or competing technical solutions, often in gray areas. Challenges, critiques, and exploration of alternatives were necessities in our organization. We needed to brainstorm openly around ambiguous and complex situations. There was rarely consensus on what was absolutely right or wrong. More often than not, a proposed solution was probably better or probably worse than the alternatives. Everyone knew that honorable people don't always agree, but our team was often unsuccessful at disagreeing without being disrespectful.

The exercise was structured so that three different groups attacked the three different topics.

1. Improving presentation effectiveness
2. Achieving consensus among competing alternatives
3. Challenging someone else's opinion, position, or proposal without creating discord

Participants were assigned to groups based on who would contribute the most to each topic and who would benefit the most by applying the results. Each group had a common goal: Come up with the most important ground rules for achieving the most substantial improvement.

After an hour, the groups presented their results to the whole team for discussion, critique, endorsement, and wordsmithing. The outcomes are listed below.

Improving Presentations

- Start by stating a singular purpose.
- Finish with a list of potential actions. Agree on at least one action, even if it is no action.
- Finish prepared remarks in two-thirds of the time slot. Reserve one-third for discussion.
- Table contentious stuff for discussion time and move on.
- Tolerate no distractions (PCs off, cell phones off). Insist on the audience's undivided attention.

Achieving Consensus

- Explore alternatives. Ensure that each alternative considers:
  - The expected, most likely, outcome
  - The worst that could happen
  - The best that could happen
- Use the democratic process where consensus is not obvious. For contentious cases that result in a "vote" among team members, defer the vote so that everyone has time to reconsider.
- Provide a rationale for overruling the consensus. The team leader can overrule a decision for other reasons, but these reasons must be communicated.
- Team consensus trumps individual preference.
  - Always state, "This is what we agreed…"
  - Never state, "I don't agree, but I am abiding…"

Challenging the Positions of Others

- Listen to the entire position. Interrupt only for clarification.
- Don't say "I agree, but…" This is patronizing; the *but* means "I don't agree."

- Seek first to understand. Don't offer a contrary view until you show clearly that you have listened to and understood the position being taken by others. For example, restate the view that is on the table.
- Disagree with the position or the facts, not the person stating them.

These outcomes are not earthshaking. But the process of dedicating time to defining a set of principles for improving communications among peers, writing them down, and agreeing on them as a team resulted in some breakthroughs in relationships and insight into the importance that communications play in teamwork, leadership, and trust. These outcomes set standards to which the team members all agreed. They also helped us segue into the final exercise, where the stakes were much higher.

Team Principles

The goal of this workshop was to create a common culture among a new leadership team. This is a mechanism for building an esprit de corps that promotes teamwork and high standards. Our diverse team of high-technology professionals distributed across the world needed a set of shared values and some bonds that would encourage mutual accountability. (This is how effective community watch programs work, for example.) We had just worked through most of the prerequisite building blocks with discussions on leadership, trust, teamwork, and communications. Now it was time to bring these together into a set of rules to live by.

Exercise: Defining our Rules of Membership

We organized our rules into four categories of commitments to our constituents:

1. Working with our company's other teams (sales, marketing, development)
2. Working with external customers
3. Working with ourselves
4. Working with each other in the services organization

Each breakout group's assignment was to propose five ground rules pertinent to their category stated as behaviors and activities, not attributes. They could come up with as many behaviors as they wanted to consider. The whole team would narrow them down to the three or four most important. Topics to consider ran the gamut of operational behaviors:

- Interpersonal interactions
- Decision making
- Conflict resolution
- Frequency and format of group meetings
- Attendance and punctuality
- Participation in business planning, execution, and assessment
- Project initiation, status, and completion
- Customer priorities, escalations, proposals, and results
- Reuse and knowledge sharing
- Supervision, training, delegating, performance assessment, and hiring
- Feedback and performance evaluations

Each breakout team was told to exclude the obvious stuff:

- Keeping issues within the team
- Considering trust, integrity, and ethics as paramount
- Everyone doing whatever it takes, independent of our charters
- Doing what you say you will do
- Communicating openly, honestly, and straightforwardly
- Giving team goals precedence over individual goals
- Not abusing power
- Not being disrespectful, backstabbing, gossiping, rumor-mongering, whining, or complaining

The creative ideas within the teams and the interactions among the teams were joys to behold. Each team quickly created about a dozen candidate ground rules. Then they spent most of their time culling, prioritizing, combining, and wordsmithing to gain consensus among the breakout team members.

Each team presented their session's top five ground rules to the entire group of participants. There was further discussion, further culling, some reprioritizing, and ultimately a vote on the top three or four ground rules in each area. The outcomes were synthesized onto a single sheet of paper, worded as if written by a single author, and circulated among the team for comments. With a few more additions and edits, and after just a week, we had a unanimously agreed-to set of standards that became the seeds of our organizational culture and identity.

Working with Yourself

Bend, but don't break. Your professional development and your work/life balance are your responsibility. Manage your time and commitments to fit within your professional and personal boundaries.

Increase your value over time. Your "supply" for our "demand" must be differentiated. We must each continually expand and exploit our skills by becoming *more of an expert* (depth) and/or *expert in more* (breadth).

Practice what you preach. Expertise and credibility grow primarily by performing directly with and for customers. 80% of what we learn is driven by first-hand participation on the front lines. The other 20% is synthesis: reflection, re-factoring, and reinforcement.

Working as an Extended Team with Sales and Development Teams

Be influential by being a trusted advisor. Live vicariously through your team members' goals. Keep their best interests at heart. Be smart in ways they are not. Be trustworthy and constructive at all times.

Leverage shared objectives. Bring best practices *to* sales teams and customers. Learn *from* sales teams and customers, and package lessons learned for reuse.

***Practice* leadership (doing it) trumps *thought* leadership (expounding on it).** Build your reputation on results, then leverage that reputation. Best thoughts (plans, models, and ideas) are easy and speculative; best practices (execution proven through results) are more powerful and tangible.

Working with Customers

Understand our role in the customer's context. Seek first to understand each important dimension of the customer's world: pains, improvements, priorities, and constraints. Then determine how you can add value.

Manage scope to drive results incrementally. Simplify and prioritize continuously. Attack important things first.

Expand and exploit results. Harvest and share reusable patterns of success, learn from customers, and increase the breadth of our product/services leverage by increasing customer capability incrementally.

Customer success is persistent; customer satisfaction is transient. Customer satisfaction is necessary, but not sufficient. A sequence of incremental results builds anchor points and enables continuous feedback.

Working with Others in the Services Organization

Accept that commitments are binding. Set expectations, checkpoint them en route and meet expectations.

Accept that honorable people can disagree. Diversity in exploring alternatives is crucial to consensus. Debate alternatives without disrespect and act on the decisions as though they were yours. Feel free to challenge the status quo.

Communicate honestly. Communicate straightforwardly, including what is relevant and excluding what is not. Celebrate successes and openly support learning from mistakes.

Raise the bar. We are mutually accountable for our culture, our performance, and our execution. Push yourself, your teammates, and your customers toward quality, growth, and business excellence. Expect change.

Workshop Summary

This case study has described a relatively broad set of topics and results from getting together some competent professionals who have a long track record of success together. This experience produced many highlights. These were the most important ones for me: Diversity can be channeled into team strength. Teamwork is impossible without trust. Trust demands effective communications among individuals with diverse styles. If everyone is willing to give generously, and to compromise their competitive tendencies, for the benefit of others, it is possible to communicate more effectively, establish more trust, and accomplish more as a team with higher levels of comfort and lower levels of tension. The result is the magic of teamwork.

Vision Document for Working-Out-Values Camp

I n 2005, I attended a year-end retreat in the foothills of the Sierra Nevada with my wife and close friends. The four-day retreat, which was packaged as a New Year's alternative, included yoga sessions and spiritual discussions. During a multi-day workshop, each of us reflected on the previous year and set goals for the coming year.

This experience proved to be a much healthier alternative to other forms of New Year's celebration, and it was a great forum for communicating with myself. I realized that, having spent 30 years in the high-pressure, high-travel, high-tech consulting field, I was ready to look at teaching others what I had learned. What came out of that workshop for me was the initial concept of an adolescent leadership camp where kids could learn some of the things that just can't be taught in school. My main idea was to provide a month-long experience where malleable adolescents could explore a pragmatic balance of values, exercise those values, and learn some of the benefits of value-based reasoning.

The idea of an adolescent leadership camp has stayed with me; it was the primary source of inspiration for this book. I think of this book as the homework I've done to prepare for the camp

GOALS

Today's youth are confronted with increasingly more complex situations and diverse sets of values. Our education systems, parenting trends, and information sources provide many diverse styles but our youth have fewer outlets in which they can apply their outdoor skills, stretch their minds, and solidify their value frameworks. Their one-month camp experience would include elements of military boot camp, leadership workshops, classroom exercises, and field exercises. Through a set of fun, challenging, and intense elements, this camp would have three distinct goals:

1. Appreciate balance in lifestyle and choices.
2. Build a deep connection to a healthy framework of values.
3. Develop self-awareness in the context of group awareness.

The curriculum would provide a framework of challenging, meaningful, and memorable opportunities for adolescents in their formative stages to choose productive paths.

MOTIVATION

The camp leaders will share simple motivations. They will be people who have been reasonably successful in a diverse set of professions. They will have made a commitment to a learning experience that can help young people from all walks of life. They will share a common goal of building the next generation of leaders with a stable foundation of core values.

The camp's core values are contained in 10 principles:

1. **Self-respect**. Personal health (mental, physical, spiritual) is a prerequisite to happiness.
2. **Sincerity**. Practice what you preach. Hypocrisy is always poisonous.
3. **Production**. Value what you produce more than what you consume.
4. **Teamwork**. Celebrate team results over individual accomplishments.
5. **Environmentalism.** Treat nature as a sanctuary of shared resources.
6. **Insight**. Diversity of thought, and critical thinking are crucial components of progress in any field.

7. **Sharing**. Communicate with purpose. Stress accuracy over precision.
8. **Priorities**. Do what you should before you do what you want.
9. **Integrity**. Build trust in all relationships. Always take the high road.
10. **Balance**. Build usable broad skills. Avoid obsessions.

These core values will be the basis of the camp's atmosphere and teachings. However, one of the main purposes of the camp experience will be for participants to realize that their values may vary. We will not try to endorse and instill these values narrowly. Rather, we will try to instill them as a good example of a place to start, emphasizing the importance of personalizing and tailoring this starting point to each participant's context, aspirations, and lifestyle.

Course Syllabus

The course of activities for this camp will span a broad range of activities and workshops spread over a few weeks.

Week 0: Pre-Work

Before attending the camp, students will be expected to complete preparatory surveys and assessments.

- Background, interests, and track record for the camp leaders to determine team assignments with diversity and balance
- Personality self-assessment, and assessments of peers, coaches, and parents
- An answer to "Who are you?" for a five-minute presentation as an introduction to the group

Daily Routine

6:00	Wake up
6:15	Morning exercise (yoga, hike, gym, mountain bike, jog), different each day
7:15	Showers
7:30	Breakfast, clean up. (Teams share cooking, cleaning, serving, and meal-planning duties.)

8:30	Daily puzzle description. (Teams work on solutions during the day, whenever they can.)
8:45	Morning instruction
11:45	Lunch, clean up
1:00	Afternoon instruction
5:00	Pre-dinner break
6:30	Dinner, clean up
8:00	Evening event: a lecture on a featured topic, skits, or reflections on the day
10:15	Puzzle solution
10:30	Personal time
11:00	Bunks

Week 1: Education

Introduction

The purpose, the principles, the students, and the coaches. Five-minute personal presentations by students. Team formation. Team workshop conducted around the principles. Presentation of the results.

Relationships/Teams/Trust

Understanding expressive-analytic-driver-amiable personality styles and how to communicate/motivate different styles. Discussion of trust as a combination of intent, competence, and capability. Establish trusted advisors.

Diversity of Thought

Multiple puzzle solving sessions to illustrate various skills of individuals and the need for multiple perspectives in solving most problems.

Communications (Listening-Speaking-Writing-Selling)

A set of four workshops focused on communicating with purpose, understanding your audience, proper preparation, and assessing the outcome.

1. Interviewing and being interviewed: Time management; differentiating others and yourself.
2. Performance assessments: Evaluating people, ranking performance, and allocating rewards.

3. Negotiating: Buyers and sellers negotiate a transaction based on a predefined situation. Assess the various outcomes.
4. Sales workshop: "Selling" your parents on bending a rule.

Estimation and Measurement

Basic statistics, differentiating accuracy from precision, estimating and measuring.

1. Statistical deception examples
2. Sampling and estimation
3. Measuring and estimating unknowns; dealing with uncertainty

Debates

Assess the U.S. Constitution and consider the differences between the late 1700s and early 2000s. What should be changed? Examine and appreciate both sides of societal issues.

1. Freedom of speech in today's world of the internet
2. Right to bear arms in today's world
3. Resource management (land/air/water/energy) in today's world
4. Taxes and welfare in today's world

Leadership

Five-person teams tackle five different outdoor tests. Each test uses a new person as the leader. Each test represents a relatively straightforward task that requires some analytic thinking or problem solving with limited tools, materials, or gear, and requires team effort. For example, crossing a river, climbing over a wall, getting to an out-of-reach food source, or saving a stranded colleague.

Communities/Government/Economics (Team Dynamics Exercise)

Participants will be grouped into teams and spend a full morning developing a set of membership rules for living together on a four-day trek, including organization and responsibilities, conflict resolution, governance, and values. The afternoon will be spent planning the trek, determining the gear, purchasing the supplies, and preparing for the adventure. Each team will have a budget and decide as a group how they can operate within its constraints.

Week 2: Team-Based Field Exercises

Day 1, Teamwork: Team obstacle course competition. Teams will practice as individuals in the morning on 10 events requiring diverse physical and mental skills. Based on preliminary trial runs, they will then allocate individuals across the events to maximize the team result. Constraints will be applied to assure that planning and execution require team-based decision-making and optimization across all team members.

Day 2, Applied Problem Solving: Model rocket targeting. Teams will build a simple model rocket in an evening workshop. In the morning, they will be given a simple math and physics lesson in trajectory analysis. They will get three practice shots to calibrate their rocket. In the afternoon, there will be a competition to see which team can shoot the rocket closest to a target.

Day 3, Paintball Economics: A paintball competition with predefined targets, values, costs, and consumption/production relationships. Teams will be given finite resources to purchase an initial set of different paint balls with variable purposes and values. Each paintball color will have a supply and demand profile, and the teams can trade with each other, with profit-oriented vendors, and with non-profit groups to achieve targets, compete with other teams, and win the contest by accumulating the most resources.

Days 4 and 5, Outdoor Living and Community: Introductory education on the basics of outdoor survival (water, shelter, food, fire, maps, physiology, terrain).

Cook breakfast, lunch, and dinner outdoors. Hike to different stations during the day with lessons on water, shelter, navigation, first aid, flora, and fauna. Sleep in tents. Night telescope viewing. Lectures on astronomy and infinity.

Rope course. With rappelling, knots, and climbing.

Days 6 and 7, Give-Back Project: Complete an approved construction/ improvement project at the camp. Each class will contribute something to the camp's betterment for future classes. Build a bridge, upgrade landscaping, refurbish the dorms. Students will manage the teams, work assignments, and project execution.

Week 3: Games, Applications, and Competitions

Days 1 through 4, Survival/Evasion Trek: Navigate as a team to food sources, water sources, and shelters. (A chaperone with each team remains uninvolved unless safety issues arise.) Compose a puzzle, rather than solving one.

Day 5, Rest.

Day 6, Final Field Competition: All-day event with push ball, tug-of-war, tag-team obstacle course, orienteering, log rolling, and other activities.

Day 7, Final All-Day Treasure Hunt: Collaborative puzzle solving as a team, navigating from clue to clue across the entire camp. Intermediate treasures will include lunch and snacks. 60 minutes of introduction, 60 minutes of team planning, and 6 hours to complete. Total scores based on number of targets found, value of targets found, and time.

Awards and Graduation: Awards will be determined by the staff and camper's peers.

1. Best teammates (top 5)
2. Most desirable person as a survival partner (trustworthiness)
3. Most likely to be a good boss (leadership)
4. The first person you would hire if you started a company (work ethic)

PREREQUISITES

Parents and campers must commit to participate and to abide by these basic rules:

1. No drinking, smoking, or drugs other than prescribed medications
2. Daily chores, schedule compliance (7 a.m. through 10 p.m.)
3. Discipline, respect for authority, and conformance to all policies
4. No TV, radio, video, cell phones, electronic or computer games except as integrated into the curriculum

Participants must be fluent in English.

Participants must be 13 to 15 years old, male or female, physically fit or not. Qualified attendees may be from all walks of life, cultures, and backgrounds.

Price is based on the ability to pay. Scholarships will be offered to schools that select low-income candidates based on our criteria and that participate in our sponsor program using the scholarship as an incentive award for the most balanced student.

CAMP INFRASTRUCTURE

Facilities

The camp would need to be in a wilderness, 200 acres or so with an integrated, self-contained set of facilities, including a dining hall, meeting hall with multiple breakout rooms, lab facilities, computer room, dormitories, outdoor lecture area, obstacle course, leadership course, rope course, paintball field, open athletic field, and access to a large area of backcountry. A typical class size would be 30 to 40 students.

Personnel

Camp staff will include 5 to 10 mentors (providing permanent camp leadership) and 5 to 10 interns (graduates who return to help run the program and continue their leadership learning experience). Camp staff will be unpaid volunteers, except for room and board. Interns will also receive room and board plus a small stipend payable on completion of a month or two of summer duty.

This appendix is a dream, but it is the dream that motivated me to write this book and start thinking about some of the material that would be the basis for some teaching workshops.

Exercising Observation Skills

Your brain needs exercise to improve your mental agility. An active mind is an observing mind, and a key attribute of mental health. *Wikipedia.org* defines *mental health* as either a level of cognitive or emotional well-being or an absence of a mental disorder. This book probably won't improve anyone's emotional well-being, and it probably won't help people avoid mental disorders. But it will certainly provide a workout for keeping your cognitive well-being in tip-top shape.

I initially constructed the puzzles in this appendix to torture (i.e., entertain) my family on holidays and other special occasions. Then I came up with an idea for an adolescent leadership camp. A key part of this vision was to demonstrate the power of group collaboration, brainstorming, and diversity of thought in general problem solving through team exercises. The puzzles have since evolved into foundations for those exercises.

In 2010, my wife and I started adapting many of these puzzles to the Geocaching community of southern New England by creating "mystery caches." Geocachers represent the perfect audience for such mental exercise because they love good treasure hunts, especially ones that require some mystery to be solved through intellectual breakthroughs, eureka moments, or analytical detective work.

For examples of how these puzzles can be adapted to Geocaching, go to *www.geocaching.com/seek/* and search for caches Hidden by: JWCOREY (our user name). These puzzles are the starting points for many of the puzzle cache descriptions. Feel free to reuse the puzzles in your local Geocaching hides. This community loves such fun.

Eureka Puzzles

These unique word search puzzles were crafted for teaching teamwork and diversity of thought. To solve them, you must deduce the *theme* by determining enough of the hidden elements that are disguised in a set of short sentences. The hidden elements could be words in the sentence, or words within words (as in the word searches presented in Chapter 2), or syllables, or letter sequences. The theme could be almost anything. There is something in each sentence that binds it to the other sentences as a set with a cohesive and well-defined identity.

The solution to each puzzle will usually be accompanied by an *Aha!* moment. You won't have to ask if you have it right. You will know because everything will fit together in a way that could not be a coincidence. *Eureka* means *I have found it*, and that will be your response when the solution unfolds in your mind. Each puzzle has a title, a set of objectives, and a list of discrete sentences. The title is usually a subtle puzzle in itself, sometimes an obscure hint, or perhaps an anagram of a hint, or an obvious synonym, or even a direct hint. It usually won't help you until you solve the theme. Once you know the theme, the title should make sense in some obscure way. Here is an example.

PUZZLE 13: SO, LARS IS TIM?

Consider the following list of grammatically correct short sentences. Each sentence contains a hidden element. Together, the elements form an obvious pattern or connection to a common theme. The title is a subtle hint, probably too subtle to understand the connection until you have discovered the common theme.

To solve this puzzle, you need to:

• Discover the hidden elements in the sentences and deduce the theme that binds those elements together as a set.

1. Some inept, uneducated people fell into the scam-artist's trap.
2. General Motors initiated the Saturn brand to compete with Japan.
3. There were only seven usable images in the whole batch of photos.
4. Nondescript, vague art hung in every room.
5. Opossums, koalas, and kangaroos are examples of marsupials.
6. Jupiter, Florida, is a popular retirement community.
7. If you concur, an usher will take you to your new seat.
8. The San Jose Mercury News is the primary newspaper in Silicon Valley.
9. Goofy and Pluto are the original Disney dogs.

Turn the page to see the answer.

Did you find it? Each sentence contains the name of one of the nine planets of our solar system. With that knowledge, the connection to the title should be possible to reason through. If you speak the title in a slurred way, you should come up with something close to "solar system."

1. Some i<u>nept, une</u>ducated people fell into the scam-artist's trap.
2. General Motors initiated the <u>Saturn</u> brand to compete with Japan.
3. There were only se<u>ven us</u>able images in the whole batch of photos.
4. Non-descript, vagu<u>e art h</u>ung in every room.
5. Opossums, koalas, and kangaroos are examples of <u>mars</u>upials.
6. <u>Jupiter</u>, Florida, is a popular retirement community.
7. If you conc<u>ur, an us</u>her will take you to your new seat.
8. The San Jose <u>Mercury</u> News is the primary newspaper in Silicon Valley.
9. Goofy and <u>Pluto</u> are the original Disney dogs.

That was easy enough. Here's a more obscure puzzle.

PUZZLE 14. IN THE NEWS

Consider the following list of grammatically correct short sentences. Each sentence contains two hidden elements. Together, the elements form an obvious pattern or connection to a common theme. The title is a subtle hint.

To solve this puzzle, you need to:

* Discover the two related hidden elements in each sentence and the theme that binds these sentences together as a set.

  1. If the Red Sox win or the Yankees lose, we move up in the standings.
  2. John's outhouse was thirty meters down past his garage.
  3. We left the brand-new establishment with a poor first impression.
  4. They were astounded by how right he had been all along.

Turn the page to see the answer.

In Puzzle 14, the theme is two words hidden in each sentence. Each sentence has a compass direction (north, south, east, west) embedded as a hidden string and the more common word (up, down, right, left) aligned with the compass direction. The connection to the title is that the first letters of the compass directions can be anagrammed into the word *news*.

1. If the Red Sox wi<u>n or the</u> Yankees lose, we move <u>up</u> in the standings.
2. John's <u>outh</u>ouse was thirty meters <u>down</u> past his garage.
3. They wer<u>e ast</u>ounded by how <u>right</u> he had been all along.
4. We <u>left</u> the brand ne<u>w est</u>ablishment with a poor first impression.

Here is a final example where the elements are less obvious.

PUZZLE 15. NOISEMAKERS

Consider the following list of grammatically correct short sentences. Each sentence contains two hidden elements. Together, the 24 hidden elements pertain to a common theme. The title is a subtle hint.

To solve this puzzle, you need to:

- Discover the two related hidden elements in each sentence and the theme that binds these sentences together as a set.

  1. The fishing ban jolted the ecology, and the amoebas soon overpopulated the pond.
  2. It was an odd story about three homeless hoboes involved in a love triangle.
  3. Ensnared in the trap was the young wolf that escaped from the Alaska zoo.
  4. The unorganized, impromptu barbecues were the highlight of the summer.
  5. To enhance their flavor, the ravioli needed some sharp Parmesan.
  6. No audit violations occurred in the transaxle assembly unit.
  7. Zigzagging among the rose's thorns, the bug left a distinct trail.
  8. The university chancellor stated that he too was a thespian once.
  9. After she turned the charm on, I carefully moved in to sit around the fire.
  10. Across a wide spectrum, Pete set the bar for blue ribbon gossip.
  11. The last topic Colonel Smith presented was the effectiveness of flu tests.
  12. The woman doling out the mixed rum drinks at the bar was quite efficient.

Turn the page for a hint to get you started.

In the noisemaker puzzle, the hidden elements are all musical instruments. See if you can now find all 24 of them.

These three examples of eureka puzzles should give you the general idea. The themes of the puzzles that follow are very diverse. Keep these observations in mind as you try to solve them:

- A funny sentence structure or odd word usage is usually a good place to start looking.
- These puzzles are exercising your observation skills. Look for word connections, words within words, patterns of sounds, or patterns of syllables or phrases.
- For many of the puzzles, you need to get outside your normal frame of reference and observe the words and structures from a different perspective.
- Read the instructions carefully. They sometimes contain other clues that will help you adjust your perspective and achieve a complete solution.
- There are some meager hints at the end of this Appendix, if you are looking for a nudge in the right direction.
- The best way to solve these puzzles is with a group of people. You should find that brainstorming leads to solutions more quickly, with multiple people barking out what they see. These puzzles were created to demonstrate that a group, with diverse perspectives, can reach a solution more rapidly than a single person.
- The puzzles start off requiring very basic knowledge. They are ordered so that they are successively more difficult (although my estimation of difficulty may not coincide with yours). Most can be understood and solved by children over 10 years old. A few of the later puzzles require high school knowledge, and a few may be biased toward baby boomer knowledge of popular culture.

PUZZLE 16. CREDIT, GREETING, ST. LOUIS, BUSINESS, UNION?

Consider the following list of grammatically correct short sentences. Each sentence contains a hidden element. Together, the elements form an obvious pattern or connection to a common theme. The title is a subtle hint.

To solve this puzzle, you need to:

- Discover the hidden elements and deduce the theme that binds those elements together as a set.

1. We sold an antique end table.
2. His kids begged for a clubhouse.
3. We need a person in each role.
4. Her face was scarred, but she was beautiful.
5. *Little deuce coupe* referred to a 1932 Ford model B coupe.
6. The dog could hear the high pitch, but not us.
7. Sneaking in stealthily, he tiptoed.
8. Sometimes an amusing joke reflects reality.
9. Some of our team left before the end.
10. The sixties were downright wild.
11. Christmas Eve never lasts long enough.
12. A diamond is a rhombus but not always square.
13. Freight trains carried hobos at night.
14. A mud wasp adeptly constructed a multi-hole nest.
15. If I veered right, I could avoid the wreck.
16. There is not enough time left.
17. In the theatre, you want to put your mobile phone on *vibrate*.
18. She hit the jackpot right after me.

PUZZLE 17. OLD AND NEW

Consider the following list of grammatically correct short sentences. Each sentence contains two hidden elements that are related. Together, the two elements from each sentence form an obvious pattern or connection to a common theme. The title is a subtle hint.

To solve this puzzle, you need to:

- Discover the two hidden elements and deduce the theme that binds those elements together as a set.

    1. Every mark on the map specified a new job site.
    2. None of the other radio acts was as good as Amos and Andy.
    3. Elected in 1856, James Buchanan was President at the genesis of the Civil War.
    4. Samuel Morse's revelation of the telegraph was a breakthrough.
    5. The celebrity judges included Dr. Ruth and Magic Johnson.
    6. A young Luke Skywalker joins the Jedi exodus from the rebel alliance.
    7. The musical numbers included one Peter Frampton song.
    8. Many old proverbs were first coined by the Romans.
    9. The song *Hey Jude* was about John Lennon's son.

PUZZLE 18. MINIMUM VOCATION

Consider the following list of grammatically correct short sentences. Each sentence contains a hidden element. Together, the elements form an obvious pattern or connection to a common theme. The title is a subtle hint.

To solve this puzzle, you need to:

- Discover the hidden elements and deduce the theme that binds those elements together as a set.

  1. The jury's decision was a foregone conclusion.
  2. Of all the roles in Winnie the Pooh, I opted to play Eeyore.
  3. In the mountains of Northern India, natural springs are plentiful.
  4. There was increased incidence of asthma in every age group.
  5. It took about a half an hour to reach the summit.
  6. She bought some very feminine bras, Kashmir sweaters, and sheer scarves.
  7. The radio was blaring.
  8. On the very first play of the game, my new jersey was covered in mud.
  9. Farmers were the primary landowners in colonial New England.
  10. Out on Boston common, tanagers were singing their dull songs.
  11. She needed the payments spread over months to afford the loan.
  12. She did a horrible job of vacuuming the floor.
  13. The coroner examined the cerebral cortex as the interns watched intently.
  14. The color *adobe* is a soft, red tone for southwestern décor.
  15. If you really want to know about Uncle Al, ask Aunt Edna.

PUZZLE 19. TEMPT US, FUDGE IT

Consider the following list of grammatically correct short sentences. Each sentence contains a hidden element. Together, the elements form an obvious pattern or connection to a common theme. The title is a subtle hint.

To solve this puzzle, you need to:

- Discover the hidden elements and deduce the theme that binds those elements together as a set.
- Construct a 19-letter anagram, relating to the theme, using the first letter of each sentence.

1. Each salmon thrashed upstream against the current.
2. Every weekend brought a new reason to binge.
3. Even sugary raisins tantalized the mice into the trap.
4. Earlier, she had promised to lease me stereo equipment.
5. For every action, there was an equal and opposite reaction.
6. I led a decadent life of excess and drugs.
7. Immediately after missionaries settled the coast, there was growth.
8. It was a minute lens scratch that marred the photo.
9. Mom entertained the kids while dad napped.
10. Next, he raised his arms over his head.
11. Nobody could teach our children better than Alice.
12. None of my early childhood friends were at the reunion.
13. Nora's horse placed second by a nose.
14. Outside, a bearded bum begged for a quarter.
15. She had to raise a son on her own.
16. The only way to go was up and to the left.
17. They put forth their best effort, night after night.
18. Tiger Woods drove up in a Buick Century.
19. Up until yesterday, the situation seemed to make sense.

PUZZLE 20. A HEFTY MONOLOG POEM

Across ten states, a few oceans and seas
this Eureka puzzle has strange properties
A thimble or a cannon can be forged from iron ore
as can railroads that travel from Ohio to Baltimore
Travel around and make twenty sawbucks each trip
in a wheelbarrow, a car or even a battleship
You might see a dog with a shoe or a hat
while you work hard to become a rich fat cat
This monolog poem is hefty with many a clue
so the puzzle below is simpler to do.

Consider the following list of grammatically correct short sentences. Each sentence contains multiple hidden elements that form an obvious pattern or connection to a common theme. To solve this puzzle, you need to:

- Discover the hidden elements in the sentences and deduce the theme that binds those elements together as a set.
- Determine the single missing element.
- Determine an anagram of the title that defines this puzzle's theme.

1. The General Electric Company sponsored deep-water workshops to research coastal wind energy.
2. From North Carolina to Pennsylvania, we drove through hundreds of miles of calm pacific wilderness.
3. We have cruised on the Baltic, the Adriatic, and the Mediterranean seas.
4. Good oriental cuisine was hard to find along Interstate 91 from Derby Line, Vermont to New Haven Connecticut.
5. It cost James only $10 to see Tennessee Williams' *The Glass Menagerie* in a New York theater in 1945.
6. The final four teams included Illinois, Duke, Indiana, and Kentucky.
7. I read in GQ magazine that Sal Bando's son was a surprisingly short linebacker who now lived in Scranton Pennsylvania.
8. The Titanic was designed and built to circumvent North Atlantic icebergs.
9. The planning board walked briskly to the parking lot when the meeting adjourned.
10. The newest Charles Schwab office opened in West Virginia and specialized in large estates.

PUZZLE 21. YULETIDE EUPHORIA

Consider the following list of grammatically correct short sentences. Each sentence contains a hidden element. Together, the elements form an obvious pattern or connection to a common theme. The title is a subtle hint.

To solve this puzzle, you need to:

* Discover the hidden elements in the sentences and deduce the theme that binds those elements together as a set.
* Determine the one missing element in the context of this theme, alluded to by the title.

1. Evading the wild animals was critical to survive.
2. Armed guards were needed to control the crowd in the bar.
3. Cubic zirconium is now a primary export of Iraq.
4. Wise men know how to avoid sounding silly.
5. You just can't ignore the specialties on this menu.
6. Delayed flights heading west had trouble making up time in the strong wind.
7. Effortlessly, the fleet deer evaded the wounded wolf.
8. HIV rates across the world have not reduced by that much.
9. Elbow grease was a necessity to break the lug nuts from the wheel.
10. Jade stones were used to line the entry to the Taj.
11. Empty pages made up over half the photo album.
12. Entire villages were wiped out by the tsunami that hit southern Japan.
13. Pizza kitchens flourished in the suburban buildup.
14. Vehicle sales skyrocketed after advertisements were seen on TV.
15. Zenith set television standards with a display refresh rate of 60 hertz.
16. Seeing her enjoy his gift made him feel even more romantic.
17. Estate sales have blossomed in these troubled times.
18. Before long, the baby would outgrow its crib.
19. Cane sugar is cheaper to refine and transport in bulk.
20. Exhausted, the marathon runner entered the arena for the final lap's climax.
21. Island natives were the best guides on the bus and boat tours of Hawaii.
22. Jeeps could not make it up the steep, rutty hill without slipping.
23. Oval shapes dominated the op art displayed above the piano.
24. Ace Ventura had never seen a pet ape from Africa.
25. Teaching hospitals provide the best experience for a medical student.

PUZZLE 22. THREE FOR A QUARTER

Consider the following list of grammatically correct short sentences. Each sentence contains a hidden element. Together, the elements form an obvious pattern or connection to a common theme. The title is a subtle hint, but probably too subtle to understand the connection until you have discovered the common theme.

To solve this puzzle, you need to:

- Discover the hidden elements in the sentences below and deduce the theme that binds those elements together as a set.
- Determine the one element that does not fit the theme perfectly.

1. After the markets close at 4 p.m., the local bars around Wall Street get very busy.
2. Husbands and wives were sleeping in separate beds until the late 1960s.
3. In the race for mayor, the independent candidate led the early polls by over 10 points.
4. Janitorial costs had risen 11% in the past year.
5. I think it was 1964 when Julie Andrews won the Oscar for best actress.
6. Mom wore an apron only once a year, when cooking Thanksgiving dinner.
7. Most of today's big action movies are augmented with computer-generated 3D imagery.
8. My prolific younger brother has just published his sixth romance novel.
9. Next February, the Super Bowl will be held in Dallas for the first time ever.
10. The ratio of frequencies of two musical notes one octave apart is 2:1.
11. We thoroughly assessed both of the options before we made our decision.
12. My son searched through four junk yards before he found a 1970 VW bus.

PUZZLE 23. ATLAS STARS

Consider the following list of grammatically correct short sentences. Each sentence contains a hidden element and a reference to a country. Together, the hidden elements and the countries mentioned in each sentence form an obvious pattern or connection to a common theme. The title is a subtle hint.

To solve this puzzle, you need to:

- Discover the hidden elements in the sentences and deduce the theme that binds those elements together as a set.
- Determine the connection between the hidden elements and the country references.

1. In ancient Greece, athletes competed in the decathlon donned in the colors of their flag.
2. Most of the Italian parishioners were appalled at the priest's non-traditional opinions.
3. Filipino casinos lost thousands of customers when Macao legalized gambling.
4. Grandfather's untimely death ensured a long, drawn-out legal battle for his German estate.
5. Number lines help Vietnamese students visualize the continuum of integers.
6. It is rare to find a Norwegian child that enjoys eating Brussels sprouts.
7. The French celebrate New Year's Eve with a noisy outburst at the stroke of midnight.
8. After listening to the wry wit of the Canadian funnyman, I laughed hysterically.
9. The Polish labor union decided to take a big risk and boycott a wage freeze.
10. Our Belgian tent provided a safe haven from the mosquitoes and the wind.
11. The girl from Ecuador was runner-up in the Miss World pageant.
12. Veterans of the Revolutionary War saw the English withdraw from the colonies with honor.

PUZZLE 24. AKA DR. BLACK

Consider the following list of grammatically correct short sentences. Each sentence contains a hidden element. Together, the elements form an obvious pattern or connection to a common theme. The title is a subtle hint.

To solve this puzzle, you need to:

- Discover the hidden elements in the sentences and deduce the theme that binds those elements together as a set.
- Once you know the theme, deduce the three missing elements.
- Determine how the title relates to the deceased subject of the theme.

1. A forensic CPA presented a community property balance sheet.
2. In our ballroom dance class we learned rumba, tango, waltz, and etiquette.
3. Most red-blooded Americans eat hot dogs with catsup, mustard, and relish.
4. Kent honed his bowie knife until it was razor-sharp.
5. Rose rented a studio with a small kitchenette and a Murphy bed.
6. Raytheon's executive dining room was reserved for the big-wigs.
7. A flywheel must revolve real fast without the slightest wobble.
8. The Red Sox held their team banquet at the JFK Library.
9. Let's avoid a formal presentation and do a whiteboard discussion.
10. Pine, spruce, and cedar are coniferous, aromatic evergreen trees.
11. Jane's bathroom was off-limits until the plumber showed up Monday.
12. I can still remember my father singing *We Shall Overcome*.
13. His anniversary gift included candles, tickets for Neil Diamond, flowers, and wine.
14. A great pub must have a billiard room, a dart board, and good draught beer.
15. She can even study in a noisy dormitory with her headphones on.
16. I wrenched my back on a trampoline at the local gymnasium.
17. After a good tongue-lashing, Oscar let the young punk go free.
18. We lounged around on the lanai for three hours doing crosswords.

PUZZLE 25. A THESPIAN'S PROMO

Consider the following list of grammatically correct short sentences. Each sentence contains multiple hidden elements. Together, the elements form an obvious pattern or connection to a common theme. The title is a subtle hint.

To solve this puzzle, you need to:

- Discover the 32 hidden elements in the sentences and deduce the theme that binds those elements together as a set.
- Anagram the title into a more appropriate three-word title.

    1. The chairman of the yearbook committee then looked into each estimate.
    2. I sent a warm telegram asking them to surface their issues by March.
    3. The artful whippet leapt high and pulled ahead with some flash in the last lap.
    4. Slipping horribly, the delivery truck needed four-wheel drive in the brown ice.
    5. Local frogs should eradicate the snails but they also lessen the flies.

PUZZLE 26. A PRIX FIXE MENU OF ZEROS

Consider the following list of grammatically correct short sentences. Each sentence contains three related hidden elements. Together, the 21 elements form an obvious pattern or connection to a common theme. The three elements in each sentence also form a triplet that is a distinct subtheme. The title is a subtle hint.

To solve this puzzle, you need to:

- Discover the hidden elements in the sentences and deduce the theme that binds those elements together.
- Discover three hidden elements in each sentence and the subtheme that binds each sentence's subtheme together.
- One of the three theme words in each sentence identifies a numeric position in each sentence. Extract the letter in the specified position from each sentence. Anagram the seven letters into a word that hints at the theme.

1. Twelve studies were published on the topic of adult literacy.
2. A gigantic production anomaly was due to an inexcusable human error.
3. Alex, the CTO, demanded the big incentives, but would he fund them?
4. Ski lodge three has serviced millions of customers since it opened in 1990.
5. Good cops weigh teenaged offenders, check them for gang tattoos, and examine their records.
6. Don decided to bake a low-calorie, homemade cake from scratch using honey instead of sugar.
7. We teamed with MIT to study some galaxies that emit six distinct bands of microwave radiation.

PUZZLE 27. SIGNATURES

Consider the following list of grammatically correct short sentences. Each sentence contains a hidden element. Together, the elements form an obvious pattern or connection to a common theme. The title is a subtle hint.

To solve this puzzle, you need to:

- Discover the hidden elements in the sentences and deduce the theme that binds those elements together as a set.

  1. The hurricane-force wind was unyielding for more than two hours.
  2. Two stopovers were needed to get home from Tokyo.
  3. Ice storms force us to drive with reduced speed, limited visibility, and caution on slick roads.
  4. The accident happened very fast, and none of the dead endured any pain.
  5. There was no park in Grenoble that would allow dogs.
  6. We do not entertain guests in our back patio very often.
  7. Pushing youngsters into the pool is the wrong way to teach them to swim.
  8. Many men work in garages without proper ventilation for painting or welding.
  9. The blue team emerged victorious after the hard-fought game.
  10. She has gone way past my threshold of tolerance for nosiness and gossip.

PUZZLE 28. IT IS QUANTITY, NOT QUALITY

Consider the following list of grammatically correct short sentences. Each sentence contains multiple hidden elements. Together, the elements form an obvious pattern and connection to a common subtheme. The subtheme of each sentence is different and, along with all the hidden elements, relates to a larger theme. The title is a subtle hint to the overall theme.

To solve this puzzle, you need to:

- Find the theme hidden in each sentence and the multiple hidden elements connected to that theme within each sentence. The number of hidden elements in each sentence is indicated by the italicized word in the sentence.

  1. Since I am on the second shift for *four* weeks in a row, my bedtime will be very early.
  2. After *five* p.m., I will slip into the bar, relax with some literature, turn the volume of the music up, and have a cordial.
  3. "Tonight's boxing program is a *five*-part slugfest," expounded the overweight announcer.
  4. "Oh, my!" I swatted *five* revolting termites laying eggs in the damp wood next to the electric panel.
  5. Beleaguered by a light year of rain in Darfur, long-distance racers ran *eight* miles in choking dust over some terrible military trails with bad footing.

PUZZLE 29. FREE BIRD

Consider the following list of grammatically correct short sentences. Each sentence contains two hidden elements that go together in a certain way. Combined, the pairs of elements form an obvious pattern or connection to a common theme. The title is a subtle hint.

To solve this puzzle, you need to:

- Discover the two hidden elements in each sentence and deduce the connection between those elements and the theme that binds together the 25 pairs of elements.

  1. Blindfolded and facing the piñata, the young boy raised his bat.
  2. Solidified magma becomes black and porous volcanic rock.
  3. Straight ahead, we could see the canyon narrow.
  4. Hardly anyone had dry eyes as Lou Gehrig walked off the diamond.
  5. Stiffness in her back caused her to be tentative on the diving board.
  6. White House officials had selected the wrong host.
  7. Neatly avoiding two defenders, Michael Jordan went up for a tap-in.
  8. Strong odors were coming from the old icebox.
  9. Wisecracks from a witty comedian can make an audience howl.
  10. Sickened by his friend's death, he went for a meditative walk with his dog.
  11. Slippery, icy roads need to be driven with both hands on the wheel.
  12. Tough acrylic polishes protected her fingernails.
  13. Tightly strung and close to losing his temper, he pondered his conundrum.
  14. Cleaning out his top drawer, he finally found his dog whistle.
  15. Thinking out loud, I talked to myself and walked on down the trail.
  16. Clearing my throat and prepared for rejection, I rang her doorbell.
  17. Highlighting the parade was a spectacular float with a young boy flying a kite.
  18. Sober alcoholics are easy to misjudge.
  19. *Simple Simon* is a nursery rhyme about a man obsessed with pie.
  20. Crazy outlaws and lawmen gathered at the town saloon.
  21. Pretty soon, his ex-wife would be completely out of the picture.
  22. Smarting from the insult, she snidely replied, "How hip."
  23. Cut each shirt collar so there is room for a button.
  24. Dry towels were used to shine up the old trombone.
  25. Lightning struck the mugger just before he threw a knife at her.

PUZZLE 30. MY ACORNS

Consider the following list of grammatically correct short sentences. Each sentence contains a hidden element. Together, the elements form an obvious pattern or connection to a common theme. The title is a subtle hint.

To solve this puzzle, you need to:

- Discover the hidden elements in the sentences and deduce the theme that binds those elements together as a set.
- Once you have uncovered the hidden element, put the phrases in the correct order.
- Determine the subtle connection to the title.

1. Email is getting harder to handle.
2. No one thinks Florida is red-state territory.
3. Boston educators firmly opposed reading essays that had included religious dogma.
4. Any fool that eats raw fish is fortunate to hurl.
5. Did Elvis always drink liquor after screen tests?
6. Senior engineers verified each new test harness.
7. Fortunately, our uncle remained totally healthy.
8. Shareholders elected company officers next door.
9. After failing to enjoy recreational therapy, he is remarkably dull.

PUZZLE 31. UNBIASED MEDIATOR'S PRONOUNCEMENTS

Consider the following list of grammatically correct short sentences. Each sentence contains a hidden element. Together, the elements form an obvious pattern or connection to a common theme. The title is a subtle hint.

To solve this puzzle, you need to:

- Discover the hidden elements in the sentences and deduce the theme that binds those elements together as a set.
- Construct a multi-word anagram using the last letter of each sentence and determine how it relates to the title and the theme.

1. The bank's safe was in a vault and protected by an alarm.
2. First, we went outside to breathe in Hawaii's beauty.
3. Wave interference occurs when two waves collide in a medium.
4. John Wooden hosted this year's charity ball for UCLA alumni.
5. Obstruction of justice is a common charge for a politician.
6. Leon was so high on heroin, he didn't recognize you.
7. Insider trading was under intense scrutiny at the SEC.
8. Red, yellow, and orange decorations were brought out in the Fall.
9. The Who would play their rock operas with a supporting orchestra.
10. The referee called a low blow on the boxer in red trunks.
11. The union decided to strike three weeks before the end of the year.
12. She was home, running on her treadmill, when she got the call.
13. Hunting is allowed if you are out of the game reserve.
14. This is the first time we got no hits searching on the web.
15. Police suspected foul play and cordoned off the area.
16. The ducks were over a pumpkin field flying east toward Maine.
17. We balked at their second offer, and they adjusted their price up.
18. With six strikes in seven frames, she was feeling energized.
19. Auburn hair and fair skin are common among people from Latvia.

PUZZLE 32. TOTALLY IRRATIONAL

Consider the following list of grammatically correct short sentences. Each sentence contains a hidden element. Together, the elements form an obvious pattern or connection to a common theme. The title is a subtle hint.

To solve this puzzle, you need to:

- Discover the hidden elements in the sentences and deduce the theme that binds those elements together as an almost complete set.
- Determine the one missing element. This will help you determine the connection with the title.

1. The stage hands were the first to find the emergency exit.
2. She talked and talked about nothing but mystery novels.
3. Every paraplegic aches to walk again under their own power.
4. Each missile was housed inside a deep silo north of Offutt AFB.
5. The talent show included several age-old dance acts.
6. Both ankles have to be taped before each game.
7. Democrats did not want to freeze tax rates in an election year.
8. Most authors are outwardly egocentric and proud of it.
9. Even with dry clothes on, we still felt chilled.
10. Her scalp has developed a dry, itchy rash.
11. Later, after 30 painful push-ups, I longed for a long nap.
12. His luck apparently ran out when he rolled that last seven.
13. Locals started to riot after the touchy incident at ground zero.
14. That USDA choice leg of lamb dangled from Fido's mouth.
15. The beast let out a deep sigh and vanished into the night.
16. The defendant replied, "I am innocent, Your Honor."
17. The lab tech measured the width to be exactly two microns.
18. An amalgam made of Ag and Hg is used in most dental fillings.
19. You must be a math whiz to solve that puzzle.
20. The third keynote address introduced the six-sigma quality model.
21. The weather prediction model takes two hours to compute.
22. Memphis is the home of traditional southern BBQ.
23. UCLA home games are played in the Rose Bowl.

PUZZLE 33. THIS HOUND AMUSED SICK PEOPLE

Consider the following list of grammatically correct short sentences. Each sentence contains a hidden element. Together, the elements form an obvious pattern or connection to a common theme. The title is a subtle hint.

To solve this puzzle, you need to:

- Discover the hidden elements in the sentences and deduce the theme that binds those elements together as a set.
- Construct an anagram using the first letter of each sentence and determine how it relates to the title and the theme.

1. Lunch consisted of salad and pizza made with garlicky dough.
2. Out beyond the reef was a stealthy manta ray.
3. Most of yesterday's mail was for me.
4. An obese comedian bellowed a huge guffaw.
5. Violet taught her children to sew.
6. I have never broken the law.
7. Four p.m. is the best time for afternoon tea.
8. Penny wanted a brand-new hair-do.
9. At night we sang around the campfire.
10. Predictably, the native New Yorkers preferred the lean pastrami.
11. Roaming the fields, the bison grazed on alfalfa.
12. The lightweight umbrella used for shade on sunny days is known as a parasol.
13. No event had generated so much hoopla.
14. Yesterday, we ate baked ziti.

PUZZLE 34. SNOOP DOG'S AMIGO

Consider the following list of grammatically correct short sentences. Each sentence contains a hidden element. Together, the elements form an obvious pattern or connection to a common theme. The title is a subtle hint.

To solve this puzzle, you need to:

• Discover the hidden elements in the sentences below and deduce the theme that binds those elements together as a set.

1. Joe Biden already owned a cocker spaniel and four basset hounds.
2. Country music with banjoes, jugs, and fiddles provided the ambiance for eating crawfish.
3. Ten years later, aftershocks of the market crash were still being felt.
4. Johnny Carson resided at 200 Amber Lane in Malibu during the wintertime.
5. We all sat quietly through the unpleasant analysis of business trends.
6. The recipe called for canned tomatoes and garlic simmered over low heat.
7. We were so grateful that the landlord had installed two new deadbolts.
8. Curiously, the accused and the victim's family came to court stoned.
9. The thousand people who signed the petition needed to be verified as voters.
10. The wedding band contained a two-carat emerald and four small diamonds.
11. Bing Crosby still seemed unashamed of himself and his spoiled youngsters.
12. Jefferson City airport's runways could not handle an airplane as big as a 747.
13. It is bad luck in Africa to squish a banana with your foot.
14. The blood oranges we ate made us sick, and we broke into tears.

PUZZLE 35. AARDVARKS DON'T BUZZ

Consider the following list of grammatically correct short sentences. Each sentence contains two hidden elements. Together, one of these elements forms an obvious pattern or connection to a common theme. The other hidden element forms a different pattern or connection to another theme. So you are looking for two strings of hidden elements relating to two different and somewhat opposite themes. The title is a subtle hint for both themes.

To solve this puzzle, you need to:

- Discover two different sets of the hidden elements in the sentences below and deduce the themes that bind those elements together.
- Determine the connection between the title and the hidden elements.

  1. Our foes were powerless as we smashed through their defenses.
  2. They stoned the prisoner before authorities could restore sanity.
  3. It was high time that we made a decision.
  4. The GIs were searching fearlessly, with their rifles loaded.
  5. Feeling no pain anymore, he was admitted to another hospital.
  6. The new walls were entirely ready to be plastered.
  7. We humbly asked to get paid under the table.
  8. I made a list and then hammered home the main point.
  9. If she amends the document, his effort will have been wasted.
  10. Our inventory was low as our business tanked.
  11. We turned to prayer and meditation as the planes bombed us.
  12. The flag was ripped but could still carry the message to our troops.

PUZZLE 36. LAND SHARK

Consider the following list of grammatically correct short sentences. Each sentence contains a hidden element. Together, the elements form an obvious pattern or connection to a common theme. The title is a subtle hint.

To solve this puzzle, you need to:

- Discover the hidden elements in the sentences and deduce the theme that binds those elements together as a set.
- Put the sentences in their proper order based on the hidden theme. One of the sentences has no defined position, so put it last.
- Once the sentences are in the proper order, the first letter of the first sentence, the second letter of the second sentence, and so on up to the sixteenth letter of the sixteenth sentence, will provide a clear explanation of the theme and help you make sense of the title.

1. We got soaked as I hailed one of the green-and-white checkered cabs.
2. After a serious brownout, energy supplies started to recover.
3. If he gets on the green in two, he will have a shot at an eagle.
4. Was it 1958 when the song *The Purple People Eater* hit the charts?
5. Many people drink orange juice only for breakfast.
6. Don't you think this puzzle is full of suspicious white noise?
7. A telephone book nowadays has more yellow pages than white pages.
8. Dawn played the Beatles' *White Album* over and over when she felt blue.
9. The waiter asked each guest if they preferred red or white wine.
10. Deep Purple concerts concluded with powerful white-light bursts.
11. There were twelve people named Bass in the Orange County white pages.
12. A total eclipse happens once in a blue moon.
13. My red, bloodshot eyes indicated just how exhausted I was.
14. Slow down when you see yellow lights.
15. Is it strange that the blacksmith is the only bachelor over 30 years old?
16. Charlie Brown and Lucy sang *White Christmas* with the carolers.

SEQUENCE PUZZLES

Sequence puzzles are one of the staples of IQ tests and brain-teaser books. The key is to identify some pattern that helps you deduce the next letter, number, symbol, or picture. These puzzles are great mental exercises, but many of them become rather one-dimensional. Here are some simple examples:

J, F, M, A, M, J, J, ? (A is next: the first letters of the months of the year)
1, 4, 9, 16, 25, 36, ? (49: the square of the sequence of counting numbers)
0, T, T, F, F, S, S, ?   (E: the first letter of the sequence of counting numbers)

There are jillions of sequence puzzles, and many of them are mind-benders. Here is my all-time favorite. This is either trivial or impossible for most people.

PUZZLE 37. WHAT'S NEXT? (PART 1)

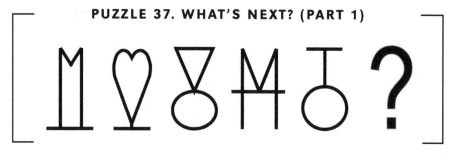

What is the next symbol in this sequence? When you deduce it, you will know it is correct. If you don't see the solution within 10 seconds, you probably won't see it in 10 hours. Most of the people who have struggled with this puzzle were bamboozled until I gave them a hint. The only hint I will offer is that its solution takes perception, not reason; an elementary school student is as likely to solve it as an adult.

Here is a sequence that is a little tougher because it takes both perception *and* reasoning.

PUZZLE 38. WHAT'S NEXT? (PART 2)

Here is a relatively challenging sequence that requires only a high school education to solve but demands some pretty abstract reasoning. This one is not easy.

PUZZLE 39. WHAT'S NEXT? (PART 3)

10, 11, 12, 13, 14, 15, 16, 17, 20, 22, 24, 31, 100, ?

Here is a more traditional sequence. Although this one is a little more indirect than usual, it should be solvable by anyone versed in American history.

PUZZLE 40. FROM MARTHA TO MICHELLE

23, 1, 10, 13, 13, 1, 10, 22, 8, 20, 16, 20, 6, 16, 2, ?

PUZZLE 41. INITIAL ORDERS

Use the appropriate letter to complete the following sequences. When you have solved them all, each letter of the alphabet will have been used once. The *who would know* column provides a hint for each sequence.

Example: S-M-T-?-T-F-S   answer: W for Wednesday (Days of the week)

If a sequence ends in an ellipsis (…) that means that there are many more elements of the sequence. If a sequence does not end in an ellipsis that means it is a complete set. The number of elements in a complete set sequence is also a good hint in some cases.

Sequence	**Who would know?**
1. R-O-Y-G-B-?-V	Leprechaun
2. O-T-T-F-F-S-S-?-N-T-…	Countess
3. ?-S-D-F-G-H-J-K	Secretary
4. T-Q-P-?-H-O-…	Shaper
5. D-?-N-G-C-M-M-S-N-V-N-N-R	History major
6. A-D-T-F-F-S-S-E-N-T-J-?-K	The Joker
7. I-V-?-L-C-D-M	Caesar
8. ?-R-M-F-S-L-T	Maria
9. M-V-E-M-J-S-?-N-P	Your son
10. C-A-P-A-T-G-C-L-V-L-?-S	Movie star
11. A-B-G-D-E-?-E-T-I-K-…	Olympian
12. K-F-S-T-F-F-S-S-E-F-S-?-S	Student
13. W-A-J-M-M-A-J-?-…	Mint worker
14. G-E-L-?-D-J-J-R-…	Rabbi
15. S-F-C-M-L-C-B-M-?-G	War protester
16. P-C-L-F-W-C-W-?-…	Bride
17. O-T-H-?-T-H-M-…	Numeroligist
18. S-M-H-D-?-M-Y-D-C-M	White rabbit
19. H-H-L-B-B-C-N-?-F-N-…	Mr. Wizard
20. H-P-T-T-S-?-F-F-S-R	Hoyle
21. K-Q-R-B-?-P	Russian
22. C-C-D-B-D-D-P-V-?	Elf
23. K-P-C-O-F-?-S	Biology major
24. P-?-F-S-T-S-L-C-R	Casey
25. O-S-C-?-S-B-T-D-…	Ballgame singer
26. P-T-F-C-G-G-S-?-L-L-P-D	Caroler

RELATIVE-ANTONYM-SYNONYM-HOMOPHONE (RASH) PUZZLES

When my kids were young, I spent a lot of time driving them to and from school and commuting to work on Los Angeles freeways. I listened to music on the car radio and enjoyed teaching my children the songs and artists that I liked. After a few years, they were familiar with many classic rock and roll artists, and they became interested in indentifying songs and artists. As grade school students, they would constantly ask, "Daddy, who does this song?" Always looking for ways to teach them while having fun, I would give them a hint in the form of a simple puzzle. My hints were often in the form of synonyms, antonyms, and such.

Example:

"This is the stinkbugs" (a beetle relative and a homophone for Beatle)
or
"This is the ant-listens" (a combination of syllables that includes an ant relative, *bee*, and an antonym of listens, *tells*)

My girls would try to decipher my hint to determine the correct artist. Because this was a verbal game, homophones, homographs, and homonyms became part of the code. They loved this game, and when they were older, I formalized the puzzle rules and handed out a written version at our holiday gatherings. I call them RASH puzzles.

Rash Puzzle Rules

The clues are mixtures of components (usually syllables) that, when verbally replaced with appropriate counterparts, will integrate into answers that correspond to the puzzle's theme.

1. **Relatives** are "like" things. Apples and oranges are relatives in the fruit family; Elly Mae and Jethro are relatives in the Beverly Hillbilly family; Mars and Jupiter are relatives in the family of planets.
2. **Antonyms** are opposites: black and white, will and won't, now and then.
3. **Synonyms** are different words with similar meanings: yellow and amber, cold and brisk, trash and rubbish, near and close.

4. **Homophones/homonyms.** Homophones are pronounced the same, have different meanings, and may or may not have the same spelling: merry, marry, and Mary. Homonyms have the same spelling and pronunciation but different meanings: bank (edge of a river, carom, or depository).

5. Some of the clues are a stretch. Get over it! I have poetic license. If you try to make up one of these puzzles on your own, you will understand the need to provide a clue that is as close as you can get and plenty good enough to help solve the puzzle.

6. If you can get a part of a clue, you can usually reason through the twisted combination of "nyms" to get the whole answer.

7. Some of the homonyms are not exact. For example, *day* may be as close as I could get to *Dave*. Such rough homonyms are denoted in italics to alert the solver to beware.

8. Hyphens separate single-syllable clues. For example, *Gas-yuk* could translate to *air* (synonym for *gas*)—*ick* (synonym for *yuk*). This results in *Eric* (translating the appropriate homophones).

9. Multiple words with no space constitute a single syllable or word. (For example, *foursidedfigure* could be replaced by square, rhombus, rectangle, etc.)

10. Underlined words or letters are not replaced; they are left as-is. (For example, <u>the</u> stays as *the*.)

PUZZLE 42: RASH MUSICAL ARTISTS

Example: Stoop Old → Neil Young

Neil (a homonym of k*neel*, a synonym for *stoop*) and *Young* (an antonym of *old*)

1. *Beers* Fall-*mug*
2. Me Also
3. Lupine-thugs Castletrenches-craft
4. <u>The</u> Criminals
5. Mute Tails
6. Congestion
7. Dog <u>St</u>-odds
8. Genuflect Emerald
9. Float Ocean-anxious
10. <u>The</u> *Cashew* Sisters
11. Hot-work
12. EllieMay *Tax*
13. Ominous Curves
14. Pal *Sacred*
15. Evil Guests
16. *Blackbirds*-ant, Photos <u>and</u> Grind
17. Magenta *Deluge*
18. Humor-ankle Dallas
19. *Shirtarm* Lose-lumber
20. Trailed Blimp
21. Shorthaircut *Sellingdrugs*
22. Auto-*win* Kriskringle-nope
23. Coldblooded *Dike*
24. Temperamental Pinks
25. Pumpkineater Angelofmary
26. Head-patella Dinero
27. *Chasm* Bald-daughter
28. Swift-iron PC
29. Belief Muddy-H2O Renaissance
30. Maleturkey Trivial or <u>the</u> Liver-waves
31. <u>The</u> Virtuous Siblings
32. *Look*-lowinfat Belowaveragegrade-off
33. Spade
34. <u>The</u> Against Bottoms
35. <u>The</u> Joint Fraternity
36. Oilrig ampersand <u>the</u> Bones
37. *Hipbone* Iron-meadow
38. UKwatercloset-isn't Leg-weak
39. Pub-bikinitop *Gait*-beach
40. Regal Sadmood Rant-street
41. Handtruck Excuse
42. Awesome-empty Alive
43. Regular-hobo
44. Utilityvehicle Less-daughter
45. Stylish-past
46. Toastmaster Mallet
47. Pointer-jones
48. Soil, Zephyr <u>and</u> Terminate
49. Pryopen Egglayer-*bores*
50. Bison Coil-pasture

PUZZLE 43: RASH CAPITALS

Example: Happy-isn't-ourstar → Madison

Mad (Antonym of happy) + is (antonym of isn't) + son (homynym of sun, synonym of ourstar)

1. Frenchman'sname
2. Autos-off burg
3. Pieceofchain-off
4. Heathen Ringo
5. Happy-isn't-ourstar
6. *Mt.*-rind-*nose*
7. Summermonth-ofcourse
8. *Hooter*-sheepnoise-shin
9. *Candlewax-inconvenience*-hear
10. Wizardcity-alloy
11. Chriskringle *price*
12. Sweetie-yes-doozie
13. Spinnaker-en
14. *Buck-under*
15. Row-wasp-a̲
16. Timid-*also*
17. Heaven-*road*-surprise
18. *Grease*-lamewalk-Zadora
19. *Ants*-grade
20. Poor-*smallhill*
21. *Termite*-orange-isn't
22. *Yaw*-field
23. Takeoff-hum
24. UnivTeacher-ego-smart
25. Coil-meadow

26. July-yes
27. Girl-sleepletter
28. Malecard-daughter
29. Honest-cavalryshelter
30. From-sneakalook-a̲
31. *Cook-against*-daughter Stand-coffee
32. Familyroom-*minkcoat*
33. Pepper Pond Town
34. Bag-stuff-women-piggy
35. *Snack-empty*
36. Fold-er-van
37. Redskin-orange-isn't
38. Relaystick Facemakeup
39. Night *Lawncuttings*
40. Pro-rope
41. *Choochoo*–2000pounds
42. Ticker-chevy
43. *Mt.*-Wrigleys-*wed*
44. *@-campinglight*
45. Maple-fa-abode-pa Stand-golfstart
46. Payment-nullify
47. Blacken-otherwise-zap
48. Huge pebble
49. Worker-heavyweight
50. Follicle-isn't-icechunk

PUZZLE 44: RASH CLASSIC TV SHOWS

Example: *Hades* Road Sadness = Hill Street Blues

Hades (synonym for Hell which is a rough Homonym of Hill) Road (synonym or relative of Street) Sadness (synonym of Blues)

1. The Sweetie-bumexposers
2. Ear Tennisnil Free-look
3. *Paddling* also *Venetian's* Chuckle-tavern
4. Mrs. *Noggin*
5. The Roll-cross Dossiers
6. Unknown Hike
7. The Detective SUV Dam Exposition
8. Put Stupid
9. Windfall
10. Bray
11. The Lady to Malekin
12. The *Front Inane*-movingtruck place
13. Every B&B the Genus
14. Poppy Avenue
15. The Dusk Area
16. The Few Adores *of* Bread-ant Cheek-*be*
17. Alphabet's *Banal* Paladin Hand-dance
18. Rod-vapor
19. Basic's Narrow Spun of Games
20. Eve Dozen
21. The Firestarter-jewels
22. The Divorce *Customize* Less Movie
23. The *Slant*-meadow Mountain-goats
24. Stay Addamsfamilycousin to Castor
25. The *Ricefield* Fist Exhibit

26. Muscle the Iron
27. Evade Bricklayer
28. The Tangible *PC*-bashfuls
29. Harbinger-axed
30. The Tame Crazy North
31. Hurrahs
32. *Pointat * Straw * Fool * Dullpain*
33. Peril
34. *Woodenrod*-missy
35. Live-*prudish*
36. Frank *Went-hooray*
37. Navajohome's Goats
38. Friday Morning Dead
39. Assignment Cinchy
40. PhD Murder-challenge
41. Tow-mesh
42. Espy Search
43. Em-Who-Legume-Lowgrade Aqua
44. Pinballgizmo
45. Ogle Wonder of Denimjoint
46. 118.3ml-i-rev's Nose-takeoff
47. Eleven-eleven Dusk Disrobe
48. Sandwichislands Fin-Alas
49. The Solo Vagabond
50. *Grit*-chevy or Ourstar

PUZZLE 45: RASH GAMES

Example: Mandarin-*praguenative*-his → Chinese checkers

Chinese (relative of Mandarin) check (a homonym for Czech, which is a synonym of praguenative) hers (antonym of his)

1. Agreement Riverspan
2. Scramble-plank
3. Commotion-benefit
4. Minutia Chase
5. *Hush*-plunders
6. *Ort*-malemoose
7. Eightfoottwobyfour Prod-him
8. Original-marbles
9. Stereo-*parrotname*
10. Stone, Shears, Essay
11. Vodka Drippy
12. Exponent-orb
13. Carpet-wasp
14. Neckpain-*dined*
15. Rat-snare
16. Select-tibia-gassy
17. Skip-whiskey
18. Evil-*glove*
19. Regular *Wed*-X Fraternity
20 *Peepers* Hambone-lock
21. Blink-ask-mail
22. *Sylvester'sbird* answers
23. Berserk Octets
24. Swagger-self
25. Legume-yield

26. Sonarecho *Patsy*
27. Teensy *Chasm*
28. Front-*wildlife*-off
29. Leather <u>and</u> Pursue
30. Garble-golfprop *Hog*
31. Invoice-lawns
32. Goodfortune-intersect
33. Sweets-acreage
34. Gosh-alas-depositing
35. Jackass *Bigcymbal*
36. Breathmint-digit
37. Twist <u>the</u> Glass
38. Label
39. Crimson Fido
40. Yank <u>of</u> Conflict
41. *Jesters*-orb
42. Seashore *nonconsonant*-pasture-cry
43. *Liquid-rabbit*
44. Uncertainty
45. Needle-dance
46. Suspend-mister
47. Average-curd-look
48. Raspy Dashing
49. Belt-him
50. *Uppertorso*

PUZZLE 46: RASH BRANDS

Example: Ear Ant *Seam* = IBM

Ear (relative of eye, homophone for I) Ant (relative of bee, homophone for B) seam (synonym for hem, which is a rough homophone for em, which is a homophone for M)

1. Legjoint-guy Patsy-swear
2. Head-daughter <u>and</u> Throne-boy
3. *Forgiveness-nights Straightens*
4. Fire-admonish
5. Trinket-Starwarssage
6. Vector-*archaicyou*-forward
7. Gunk-*tern*
8. Agent <u>and</u> Venture
9. *Pitch*-when
10. *Speak-cheer* Pasture
11. Maiden Pacific
12. Stitch-ankle
13. Formerwife-loaded Anchored
14. *Seamammals* Distant-halt
15. Envious Pygmy
16. *Murder*-journals
17. *Snub*-patella
18. Private Acoustic
19. Berkeley-caridentifier *Descend*
20. *Winner's* Classified
21. *Heaven. Heck.* Noggin
22. Comeoutwinners
23. Nile.*Serene*
24. New Fleet
25. Curly-rat *Gender*

26. *Gist-soup-stop*
27. Engine-*hiinspanish*
28. Wedded Broadcast-queues
29. Tony Muck
30. *Jeering*
31. Specific Dynamos
32. Barbarian-croak
33. *Glacialsound* Castleprotector-and
34. *Me-Drunk—Load-soft*
35. Lead-does
36. *Nuts Proceed*-fa
37. Bond'sboss Wow *BottomSeam*
38. Bro-*bull*
39. *Alaskanbear*
40. Asian Articulate
41. Ambiguous-pester
42. Sage Alarmer
43. Troika Dorothy'saunt
44. *Notquite* Evening-*gman*-ourstar
45. Bullseye
46. Precision
47. Lookout Spices
48. *Peterbilt*-Sunrise-*chevy*
49. Mystics Column-stag
50. *Termite*-stoned-ma'am Shrub

PUZZLE 47: RASH ANIMATED CHARACTERS

Example: *Max-ankle Rodent* = Min (antonym of max) Knee (relative of ankle, homonym of "nie") Mouse (synonym of rodent)

1. Greenshade Lubricant
2. Haze-antler Segment-noisemaker
3. Oak-him *Brownie*
4. Who-meadow *Sly*-hay-polo
5. Silo-joint Massage-steer
6. *Darling* Fowl
7. Glitch-*tern*-kisser
8. Child'swound
9. *Snorkle*–Paid
10. Turkey-meadow Coif-left
11. Could-golfprop *Estuary*
12. Dinger *Prawn*-star
13. Free-look SUV–Fur
14. *Scream*
15. Brutal-*re* Dopeslap *Chateau*
16. *She*-either
17. *Money*-via the Aloof Spirit
18. *Canyon of* a Forest
19. *Guzzle*-tail Smith
20. Howitzer Coffee
21. Color-you, Coif-us or John-I
22. Seethrough Felon
23. Touch-*formerspouse* the Kitty
24. *Auto*-pasture
25. Over-rover

26. Ms. Pa-gunk
27. Rare Pot-*here*
28. Yellowstone *Congruent*
29. Hitchhike-each
30. *Energetic* Re-bench
31. Annoy or Hyde
32. *Badger*-digout Mutt
33. Lumber-bond
34. Bothers Roll-previouslyknownas
35. Kentucky Formalwear
36. Stupid-boyfriend
37. *Chasm* Prop-daughter
38. Maid-the-duchess
39. *Scuttlebutt* Dark-annum
40. A Dog out the Chapeau
41. Wondering *Canyon*
42. Foolish Avoid
43. Hooter-Ethel *She*. Understood-*max*
44. *Parsley-ernie*
45. Dinero-podmember
46. Interference Black
47. Enormous *All* Derriere
48. Cow-*sparkle*
49. Fiddle-chime
50. Venus

GAMES AND OTHER MENTAL EXERCISES

The remainder of this appendix introduces some other stimulating mental exercise for improving your observation skills and enjoying the English language.

Crossword Puzzles

Boredom brought me to crossword puzzles. In the 1980s, I traveled more and more on business, enduring long and longer flights. Before laptop computers, a 5-hour coast-to-coast or 10- hour international flight was lots of time to kill. After I read the newspaper cover to cover, all that was left to consume time was that crossword puzzle, begging to be tested. I must have tried 20 puzzles before I finally finished one. It seemed quite difficult, but I did persevere. I learned that if I'd put a puzzle down for a while; when I picked it up again later, I'd inevitably make more progress. I just had to clear my mind and see it from a fresh perspective.

Although there are numerous crossword puzzle authors, Will Shortz of *The New York Times* is my favorite crossword editor. His puzzles are not the hardest, the funniest, the most error-free, the cheapest, or the most available. But for my taste, he's the best, simply because his style seems incredibly fair, entertaining, and consistent. *The Times* puzzles progress in difficulty as the week progresses, easiest on Mondays and most difficult on Saturday. On Sundays there is a larger special themed puzzle that is usually Thursday-ish in difficulty.

Over three decades and 4 million air miles, I have become good at crosswords. Not great, but good enough. I can almost always solve *The Times* puzzles completely, although sometimes it takes me a few hours and an occasional search on the internet for that one critical answer, usually some entertainment-oriented question (my weakness). Saturday and Sunday puzzles are the ones I look forward to enjoying with my wife.

Although doing a crossword puzzle alone is fun, doing one with a friend or spouse can be even more rewarding. Puzzles offer great mental exercise, and reasoning out loud with someone else can be a real eye-opener. There is no better example of the power of diverse thinking than working through a puzzle together and observing how your thought patterns differ. My wife and I have learned an immense amount about each other by reasoning through crossword puzzles on long drives, airplane flights, and snowy Sunday afternoons. These incredibly rich communications sessions have helped us understand each other's perspectives, outlooks, reasoning patterns, and priorities. No kidding. Try it.

SCRABBLE®

Scrabble® provides some of the best mental exercise there is. Although many online sites offer Scrabble®, the board game between two people is still the best way to play. Scrabble® is up there with chess and bridge as one of the three classic games of skill. I played Scrabble® extensively when I was younger; I have probably played monthly for the past 20 years as an entertaining diversion. Scrabble® experts, the world-class tournament players, are nuts. Some of them spend almost every waking hour categorizing words and organizing Scrabble® inventories in their memories. They study dictionaries and word forms. They exercise their mental abilities by anagramming words endlessly.

A Scrabble® expert will outscore an amateur every time, regardless of the lousy tiles he picks out of the bag. Several good books provide important word lists, basic strategies, and more complete advice. Here are a few pointers for the average person who is just starting to play Scrabble®. This advice will probably improve your average score by 50 to 100 points per game.

1. Two-letter words are the primary connectors for high-scoring words. Memorize all 101 of the two-letter words in *The Official SCRABBLE® Players Dictionary.*

aa	ab	ad	ae	ag	ah	ai	al	am	an
ar	as	at	aw	ax	ay	ba	be	bi	bo
by	de	do	ed	ef	eh	el	em	en	er
es	et	ex	fa	fe	go	ha	he	hi	hm
ho	id	if	in	is	it	jo	ka	ki	la
li	lo	ma	me	mi	mm	mo	mu	my	na
ne	no	nu	od	oe	of	oh	oi	om	on
op	or	os	ow	ox	oy	pa	pe	pi	qi
re	sh	si	so	ta	ti	to	uh	um	un
up	us	ut	we	wo	xi	xu	ya	ye	yo
za									

1. Never use a blank tile unless you are making a high-scoring play (50 points or more). Blanks are the most flexible tiles in the bag. They significantly improve your chances of making high-scoring plays, especially plays using all seven letters in your rack (called a *bingo*).

2. Never use an *S* tile unless you are making a high-scoring play (30 points or more). *S* tiles give you tremendous flexibility to add to an existing word and use all seven letters in your rack. If you can't score 30 points, make a play worth less and save the *S* tile for your next play.

3. If making the highest scoring play in your hand leaves you with tiles that are difficult to use in forming new words (for example, five vowels, or 3 *G*s, or 4 *T*s), consider making a lower scoring play that leaves you with a more flexible rack of tiles for your next turn.

4. *H* is one of the most valuable scoring tiles. It is a very common letter in the English language, and there are 10 two-letter words with *H* that make it easy to use. Note that *H* is worth four points, but it occurs just as frequently as many of the one-point letters (see Figure 1-1).

5. *U* is one of the least valuable tiles unless you also have a *Q*, in which case it becomes invaluable. The *U* is difficult to play and score well. Although *U* is worth only one point, it occurs as infrequently as many of the higher count letters. (Again, see Figure 1-1.)

6. Learn the obscure but important three-letter and four-letter words that use the high-scoring tiles: *J, K, Q, X,* and *Z*. These are some good ones to remember:

   J: raj, taj, jeu
   K: auk, koi, khi, kay, kex
   Q: qua, quay, qaid, qat
   X: cox, dex, lux, oxo, oxy, pyx, xis
   Z: adz, adze, biz, coz, fez, wiz, zoa, zoon, zee, zed, zax, zek

With just these tips, you will be amazed at how much more fun you will have and how much more competitive you will be playing Scrabble®. You must work on three other things to become an advanced player: anagramming, reading the board for scoring opportunities and placement, and vocabulary and word knowledge. Most of these skills come from playing and practicing and from daily mental exercise, not from studying.

Capable Scrabble® players should have fun solving the next puzzle. See if you can determine the significance of the following short paragraph.

PUZZLE 48. SCRABBLE® PERTINENCE

This "joked hoax" paragraph is crazy. A young informed novice will be able to determine a unique virtue of its elegant words.

Once you solve this puzzle, try to create your version. I predict you will find this task challenging. I did.

Word Mastermind

When I was in high school, my best friend and I played a one-on-one thinking game that was simple to explain but required tremendous skills in deduction and word forming. It provided great mental exercise and could be played anywhere with just a pencil and paper. Here are the rules.

Object: Guess the opponent's five-letter word in the fewest number of turns.

Setup: Each player thinks of a five-letter word and writes it at the top of a piece of paper, folding the top of the page down to conceal it.

Play:

1. Player 1 states any five-letter word as a guess at Player 2's hidden word.
2. Player 2 determines the hits and announces a two-digit assessment. The first digit corresponds to the total number of shared letters. The second digit identifies how many of those letters are in the right place. For example: if Player 1's word is *crypt* and Player 2 guessed *party*, the hit assessment would be 4-0 (4 shared letters and none of them in the right spot).
3. Player 2 then makes a guess at Player 1's word, and Player 1 determines the hits and announces the two-digit assessment.
4. Players must make accurate assessments. A player who makes an inaccurate assessment forfeits the game.
5. Play alternates back and forth until one player guesses the exact word (a hit assessment of 5-5). The player who guesses the opponent's word in the fewest turns wins.

An example game is shown at the top of the next page.

Player 1's hidden word: SISSY   Player 2's hidden word: BLAST

Player 1 Guesses	Player 2 Assessment	Player 2 Guesses	Player 1 Assessment
CRAFT	2-2	MONEY	1-1
CRUMB	1-0	DOCKS	1-0
EXALT	3-2	BAKER	0-0
YEAST	3-3	RINGS	2-1
MEANT	2-2	SILLY	3-3
BOAST	4-4	SISSY	5-5

Player 2 wins.

This game is addicting and much more a battle of wits than it seems at first glance. The English language has jillions of five-letter words, so the possibilities are endless. Logical thinking plays an important role in this game. Good players can almost always guess the word in seven or fewer turns. It sometimes helps to write out the alphabet at the top of your paper so that you can visualize the letters, cross out the ones you have eliminated, and reason through the remaining possibilities.

Dictionary

My parents taught us a great game when I was young that has been morphed into the popular commercial board game Balderdash. The original version that I learned is equally fun and requires no equipment other than a dictionary and some paper and pencils. It provides excellent mental exercise, and it builds communications skills in some interesting ways.

Rules: The game Dictionary can be played with 4 to 10 people. The object is to achieve a certain number of points. With 4 to 7 people, the first player who scores 10 points wins. With 8 to 10 people, the first one player who scores 5 points wins. You can define the threshold for winning at any level, or confine the game to two or three rounds for each player based on the time available.

A game consists of multiple rounds. In each round, one player acts in the role of dictionary master. The dictionary master rotates clockwise among the players from round to round. Each player is given a pad of paper to write down definitions. It is important that each player's pad of paper look exactly the same so that when multiple definitions are read from these papers, no one can tell who the author was.

The dictionary master looks through the dictionary, selects an obscure word, and announces that word to the other players. The master writes down the word and its primary definition in a concise form on a piece of paper. The definition can be paraphrased, as long as the essence of the definition is conserved. Each of the other players writes down the word and their proposed definition, and gives their pad to the dictionary master. It is important to write legibly.

The dictionary master puts the definitions in random order and reads them all aloud. The dictionary master then asks each player, starting with the player to the left, which definition is correct. Each player must commit to one definition. Once every player has committed, the dictionary master announces the correct definition and tabulates player's scores as follows:

1. A player earns 1 point for selecting the correct definition.
2. Players earn 1 point for every player who selects their proposed definition. (Exception: A player can select their own definition to bluff or influence others, but cannot earn a point for selecting it.)
3. The dictionary master earns 2 points if no player selects the correct definition.

Strategy: For the dictionary master, the key is to find a word that is counter-intuitive to its word formation, sound, or structure (prefix, suffix, root, and so on). For the players, the key is to create a credible definition based on their knowledge of roots, prefixes, suffixes, sounds, syllables, and the general feel of the word provided.

It is critical for players to get outside their realm of comfort. A known sports expert is likely to be associated with having created sports-oriented definitions, a science teacher with science-oriented definitions, and a professional nurse with medical terms. So this game is inherently a game of competing communications. A lot of bluffing and a lot of reasoning are involved. It is a great group game that allows people to open up in exercising their communications skills.

Fun Thought Problems and Brain Teasers

Some problems are best solved with a paper and pencil, some with a computer, some with a long analysis. There are also great problems that are more fun to solve in your head. These are appropriate for playing while driving, running, or camping, where you have no facilities but the use of your brain. A key aspect of these problems is that they must have a simple perspective that makes the problem solvable without any tools. Here is a good one that came from a timed Mathematics Association of America test that we took in high school.

PUZZLE 49. SUM FUN

What is the sum of the numbers from 1 to 1000?

If you look at this the right way, the solution is easy to reason through in your head.

Here is a more complex puzzle to noodle over. It forces you to reason about an infinite sequence. This is hard for most people, but the answer is easy to see if you look at it from the right perspective.

PUZZLE 50. PERCENTAGE POSER

What percentage of positive integers is represented with at least one 7? See if you can come within 5% just by reasoning in your head. Then work the solution out on paper.

The next brain teaser will not be solvable in your head unless you are truly a genius. Feel free to use paper and pencil. This one is a classic.

PUZZLE 51. THE GENIUS

Ralph meets his old high school classmate Norton at a Mensa party. Norton greets Ralph: "I didn't know you were a genius. See if you can pass my genius test."

Norton: "I am going to tell you some facts about my three sons. As soon as you know their ages, stop me. The sum of their ages is 13. The product of their ages is your age. My eldest son weighs 81 pounds."

Ralph: "Stop. I know their ages."

Norton: "You must be a genius. You stopped me at exactly the right time."

Can you determine the ages of Norton's sons from the information given? There is a unique answer of three integers. No fractions are involved.

Puzzle Hints

The hints that follow should help you get started with many of the puzzles. For additional puzzle-solving hints, go to *walkerroyce.com*. Search for *Puzzle 52* somewhere on that site.

Puzzle 1: Observations of an orthopedic surgeon

Count the number of words (hyphenated words count as only 1) and ask yourself how that could relate to the text.

Puzzle 2: Vowel blends

Try to think through 3- and 4-letter words that could begin or end with the digraphs. AA and UU require 6-letter words, II requires 5 letters, and the rest can be done in 4 letters or less. There are better answers, but the words are pretty obscure.

Puzzle 3: Consonant blends

My solution required one 8-letter word (HH), four 6-letter words (DF, GP, KK, WW), seven 5-letter words, five 4-letter words, and eight 3-letter words.

Puzzle 4: Letter sequences

No hint.

Puzzle 5: First impressions

Same hint as Puzzle 1.

Puzzle 6: A questionable preoccupation with vocabularies

As you read the text, notice how much your glottis is used in an unpressured way. If that doesn't help, read the chapter on English as a Romance language.

Puzzle 7: Word safari

Most of the animals in this puzzle are well known, but there are several obscure 3-letter words that are animals. A web-search for 3-letter Scrabble® words should help you identify many of the lesser known animals.

Puzzle 8: Word geography

This puzzle is challenging, but searching for the most populous cities in some of the less populated states is a good way to uncover a few of the obscure city names.

Puzzle 9: Symbol hunt

A web-based search of keyboard symbols may help. Also, realize that many of the letter keys and number keys can be represented by words (e.g., be, bee, see, won, etc.)

Puzzle 10: Anagram trivia

Part 1: No additional hints.

Part 2: There are two vowels and one consonant.

Part 3: There are two consonants and one vowel.

Puzzle 11: Postal abbreviation words

Start by finding SD, MT, NH, MD, NM, and TN. Once you have marked off those words (and there is only one possibility for each), the rest should be straightforward.

Puzzle 12: Could Jefferson write?

I am a 'FIERCE PUNSTER' and you can anagram those letters into two of the words in the preamble that are the instances of abuse.

Eureka Puzzle Hints

Puzzle 13: So Lars is Tim?

Plan it!

Puzzle 14: In the news

Read the directions!

Puzzle 15: Noisemakers

Read the directions!

Puzzle 16: Credit, greeting, St. Louis, business, union?

The element in sentence 12 is in plain sight.

Puzzle 17: Old and new

The first letters of each sentence can be anagrammed into a hint that goes with the title.

Puzzle 18: Minimum vocation

The title is an anagram of the first letters of the 15 hidden elements, and only 1 element is in plain sight.

Puzzle 19: Tempt us, fudge it

Sentences 8, 13, and 18 have elements in plain sight.

Puzzle 20: A hefty monolog poem

The opposite of monopsony.

Puzzle 21: Yuletide euphoria

Note the total number of elements and add 1 for the missing element. The theme of this puzzle is similar to the theme of Puzzle 2.

Puzzle 22: Three for a quarter

Think about how many total elements there are and the sorts of sets that have that many elements. Word placement in the sentences is important in determining the element that does not fit perfectly.

Puzzle 23: Atlas stars

Look for capital letters.

Puzzle 24: Aka Dr. Black

This is one of my favorite puzzles. You shouldn't need another clue, but I just gave you one anyway.

Puzzle 25: A thespian's promo

One of the words of the anagrammed title is *parts*.

Puzzle 26: A prix fixe menu of zeros

One of the hidden elements in each sentence is a number. Use that number to solve the anagram.

Puzzle 27: Signatures

Sentence 7 is the only sentence with an element in plain sight.

Puzzle 28: It is quantity, not quality

The subthemes in each sentence are hidden in plain sight.

Puzzle 29: Free bird

This puzzle is easy as pie.

Puzzle 30: My acorns

Anagram the title.

Puzzle 31: Unbiased mediator's pronouncements

Starting from a sports perspective will help you solve this one.

Puzzle 32: Totally irrational

This one is hard to see, especially since most of the hidden elements are small.

Puzzle 33: This hound amused sick people

The ends justify the means. The title is a beauty. Slur it together a little.

Puzzle 34: Snoop Dogg's amigo

Add up all the numbers in the sentences. The resulting calendar year is good context for solving this puzzle.

Puzzle 35: Aardvarks don't buzz

If you only get half of the elements, you probably need to do some research into the other half.

Puzzle 36: Land shark

Yes, it is about colors, but where would you find this color scheme?

Puzzle 37: What's next? (part 1)

Symmetry is beautiful.

Puzzle 38: What's next? (part 2)

Symmetry is key, and there is only one remaining symbol.

Puzzle 39: What's next? (part 3)

Only one of the numbers is in base 10.

Puzzle 40: From Martha to Michelle

The title names are the wives of this sequence.

Puzzle 41: Initial orders

The white rabbit in Alice in Wonderland was always worried about time.

Puzzle 42: RASH musical artists

Beers Fall-mug is Brews Spring-Stein or Bruce Springsteen.

Me also is You too or U2.

Puzzle 43: RASH capitals

Frenchman's name is Pierre. Autos-off Burg is Carson City.

Puzzle 44: RASH classic TV shows

The Sweetie-bumexposers is The Honeymooners. Ear Tennisnil Free-look is Eye love loose-see or I Love Lucy.

Puzzle 45: RASH games

Riverspan is Bridge.

Puzzle 46: RASH brands

These brands are well-known corporate names, not individual products.

Fire-admonish (axe-censure) is Accenture.

Puzzle 47: RASH animated characters

Animated characters include characters from cartoons, movies, comic books, and comic strips.

Seethrough Felon is Shere Kahn (Sheer Con) from Disney's *The Jungle Book*.

Puzzle 48: SCRABBLE® pertinence

Get out a Scrabble® bag of tiles.

Puzzle 49: Sum fun

Pair up the numbers that add up to 1000 (1 and 999, 2 and 998…etc.).

Puzzle 50: Percentage poser

Don't look at this problem from zero to infinity. Think about it from infinity to zero.

Puzzle 51: The genius

Start by writing down all the possibilities. Then remember that even though you don't know the genius's age, the genius does know his own age.

BIBLIOGRAPHY

drew on many books and websites in the preparation of this book and the various lists of pleonasms, oxymorons, heteronyms, and so forth. I also used some other sites for puzzle generation and reference. Here are the main sources that contributed to my compilations.

1. http://a2zwordfinder.com

2. http://askoxford.com

3. http://cooper.com

4. http://dictionary.com

5. http://enchantedlearning.com

6. http://fun-with-words.com

7. http://oxfordonline.com

8. http://pleonasms.com

9. http://refdesk.com

10. http://wikipedia.org

11. http://wordle.net

12. http://wordsmith.org

13. http://www.geocaching.com

14. Burke, David, *Biz Talk 1: American Business Slang & Jargon*, Optima Books, 1998.

15. Burke, David, *Street Talk 1: How to Speak and Understand American Slang*, Optima Books, 1991.

16. Burke, David, *Street Talk 2: Slang Used by Teens, Rappers, Surfers, & Popular American Television Shows*, Optima Books, 1992.

17. Butterfield, Jeremy, *Damp Squid: The English Language Laid Bare*, Oxford University Press, 2009.

18. *The Chicago Manual of Style*, University of Chicago Press, 2003.

19. Covey, Stephen R., *The 7 Habits of Highly Effective People: Powerful Lessons in Personal Change*, Free Press, 1990.

20. Covey, Stephen M. R., *The Speed of Trust: The One Thing that Changes Everything*, Free Press, 2006.

21. Fiske, Robert Hartwell, *The Dimwit's Dictionary: 5,000 Overused Words and Phrases and Alternatives to Them*, Marion Street Press, 2002.

22. Gray, John, *Men are from Mars, Women are from Venus*, HarperCollins, 1993.

23. Grothe, Mardy, *Oxymoronica: Paradoxical Wit & Wisdom from History's Greatest Wordsmiths*, HarperCollins Publishers, 2004.

24. Hitchings, Henry, *The Secret Life of Words: How English Became English*, Picador, 2009.

25. Hubbard, Douglas W., *How to Measure Anything: Finding the Value of Intangibles in Business*, John Wiley and Sons, 2007.

26. Khalsa, Mahan, *Let's Get Real or Let's Not Play: The Demise of 20th Century Selling and the Advent of Helping Clients Succeed*, Franklin Covey, 1999.

27. McKenna, Patrick J., and David H. Maister, *First Among Equals: How to Manage a Group of Professionals*, The Free Press, 2002.

28. Merrill, David W., and Roger H. Reid, *Personal Styles & Effective Performance*, CRC Press, 1983.

29. *The Official Players Dictionary*, Fourth Edition, Merriam-Webster, 2005.

30. Owen, James P., and David R. Stoecklein, *Cowboy Ethics: What Wall Street Can Learn from the Code of the West*, Stoecklein Publishing and Photography, 2006.

31. *The Oxford English Dictionary*, Second Edition, Oxford University Press, 1989.

32. Patterson, Kerry, Joseph Greney, Ron McMillan, and Al Switzler, *Crucial Conversations: Tools for Talking When Stakes are High*, McGraw Hill, 2002.

33. *Roget's Thesaurus*, 6th Edition, Harper, 2003.

34. Roam, Dan, *The Back of the Napkin (Expanded Edition): Solving Problems and Selling Ideas with Pictures*, Portfolio, 2009.

35. Royce, Walker E., *Software Project Management*, Addison-Wesley, 1998.

36. Ruiz, Don Miguel, *The Four Agreements: A Practical Guide to Personal Freedom, A Toltec Wisdom Book*, Amber-Allen Publishing, 2001.

37. Saffire, William, *The Right Word in the Right Place at the Right Time*, Simon Schuster, 2004.

38. Shapiro, Fred R., editor, *The Yale Book of Quotations*, Yale University Press, 2006.

39. Strunk, William, and E. B. White, *The Elements of Style: 50th Anniversary Edition*, Pearson Longman, 2009.

40. Tolle, Eckhart, *A New Earth: Awakening to Your Life's Purpose*, Penguin, 2005.

41. Truss, Lynne, *Eats, Shoots & Leaves*, Profile Books, 2003.

42. Venolia, Jan, *Write Right! A Desktop Digest of Punctuation, Grammar, and Style*, Ten Speed Press, 2001.

43. Wallraff, Barbara, *Word Court: Wherein Verbal Virtue is Rewarded, Crimes Against the Language are Punished, and Poetic Justice is Done*, Harcourt, 2000.

44. Will, George F., *Men At Work: The Craft of Baseball*, Harper Perennial, 1990.

45. Zinsser, William, *On Writing Well, 30th Anniversary Edition*, Harper Collins, 2006.

BUY A SHARE OF THE FUTURE IN YOUR COMMUNITY

These certificates make great holiday, graduation and birthday gifts that can be personalized with the recipient's name. The cost of one S.H.A.R.E. or one square foot is $54.17. The personalized certificate is suitable for framing and will state the number of shares purchased and the amount of each share, as well as the recipient's name. The home that you participate in "building" will last for many years and will continue to grow in value.

Here is a sample SHARE certificate:

HABITAT FOR HUMANITY

THIS CERTIFIES THAT

__YOUR NAME HERE__

HAS INVESTED IN A HOME FOR A DESERVING FAMILY

1985-2005

TWENTY YEARS OF BUILDING FUTURES IN OUR COMMUNITY ONE HOME AT A TIME

1200 SQUARE FOOT HOUSE @ $65,000 = $54.17 PER SQUARE FOOT
This certificate represents a tax deductible donation. It has no cash value.

YES, I WOULD LIKE TO HELP!

I support the work that Habitat for Humanity does and I want to be part of the excitement! As a donor, I will receive periodic updates on your construction activities but, more importantly, I know my gift will help a family in our community realize the dream of homeownership. **I would like to SHARE in your efforts against substandard housing in my community!** *(Please print below)*

PLEASE SEND ME _____ SHARES at $54.17 EACH = $ $_____

In Honor Of: _____

Occasion: (Circle One)   HOLIDAY   BIRTHDAY   ANNIVERSARY

　　　　OTHER: _____

Address of Recipient: _____

Gift From: _____ *Donor Address:* _____

Donor Email: _____

I AM ENCLOSING A CHECK FOR $ $_____ PAYABLE TO HABITAT FOR HUMANITY OR PLEASE CHARGE MY VISA OR MASTERCARD *(CIRCLE ONE)*

Card Number _____ Expiration Date: _____

Name as it appears on Credit Card _____ Charge Amount $ _____

Signature _____

Billing Address _____

Telephone # Day _____ Eve _____

PLEASE NOTE: Your contribution is tax-deductible to the fullest extent allowed by law.
Habitat for Humanity • P.O. Box 1443 • Newport News, VA 23601 • 757-596-5553
www.HelpHabitatforHumanity.org

Printed in the USA
CPSIA information can be obtained
at www.ICGtesting.com
JSHW012014140824
68134JS00025B/2414